MIND OVER MATTER

Mind over Matter

*Memory Fiction from
Daniel Defoe to Jane Austen*

SARAH ERON

UNIVERSITY OF VIRGINIA PRESS
Charlottesville and London

University of Virginia Press
© 2021 by the Rector and Visitors of the University of Virginia
All rights reserved
Printed in the United States of America on acid-free paper

First published 2021

9 8 7 6 5 4 3 2 1

Library of Congress Cataloging-in-Publication Data
Names: Eron, Sarah, author.
Title: Mind over matter : memory fiction from Daniel Defoe to Jane Austen / Sarah Eron.
Description: Charlottesville : University of Virginia Press, 2021. | Includes bibliographical references and index.
Identifiers: LCCN 2020039063 (print) | LCCN 2020039064 (ebook)
  | ISBN 9780813945668 (hardcover ; acid free paper)
  | ISBN 9780813945675 (paperback ; acid free paper)
  | ISBN 9780813945682 (ebook)
Subjects: LCSH: English fiction—18th century—History and criticism.
  | Memory in literature.
Classification: LCC PR858.M44 E76 2021 (print) | LCC PR858.M44 (ebook) | DDC 823/.509—dc23
LC record available at https://lccn.loc.gov/2020039063
LC ebook record available at https://lccn.loc.gov/2020039064

Cover art: MF3d/iStock

In memory of Selma and Theodore Eron

❖ CONTENTS ❖

Acknowledgments ix

Introduction: Memory Fictions 1

1 Accounting for Crusoe's Survival: How Memory Matters 33

2 Re-membering the Real: Uncle Toby's Maps and Models 67

3 Evelina and the Virtues of Memory 109

4 Strange Concussions of Nature: Celestina's Mindscapes 142

5 Wistful Thinking: Fanny's Absent Forms 176

Afterthoughts: Remembering the Archive 209

Notes 217
Bibliography 243
Index 259

❖ ACKNOWLEDGMENTS ❖

The first image of a brain I ever saw was in the film-viewing room of my stepmother's radiology office. Illumined from behind by bright light, the photograph, like all MRI technology in the 1980s, seemed to tell the whole story of a person, from his past history to his future fate. For me, that dark room was a source of knowledge and comfort. And yet brains would become objects of constant debate in my household in the years to come. My father, a psychologist, would spend a lifetime analyzing clinical narratives while extolling the virtues of William James; for him, family bonding consisted of quibbling with his stepson (the neurologist), his wife (the radiologist), and his daughter (the doctor of philosophy) about the mysteries of the conscious mind. In many ways, this book is a tribute to him.

You might say I was destined to write a book about literature and philosophy of the mind. But it was not until 2015 that my faith in that photograph of the brain was truly shaken. This is when I first became acquainted with Dr. Carolyn Bernstein and her work. For many reasons, Dr. Bernstein has made this book possible. But what I have learned from her about neurology sparked an insatiable interest to read more widely in the field of cognitive science: brains are fluid networks of information that change in time. In no way can we ever capture the working brain with a single, static picture.

Ideas emerge and change through the conversations we have with other people. In addition to those named above, other forums for intellectual exchange, such as the Harvard Humanities Center, the American Society for Eighteenth-Century Studies, and the North American Society for the Study of Romanticism, have been instrumental in shaping the course of this book. Thanks are especially owed to the following people who organized some of those events and panels: Sue Lanser, Ruth Perry, Deidre Lynch, Yoon Sun Lee, Jacques Khalip, Mark Vareschi, Lisa Zunshine, Margaret Doody (respondent), and William Warner.

This book has seen many iterations. I especially want to extend my gratitude to friends and scholars who generously donated their time to reading draft portions of the original manuscript: Melinda Rabb, Sarah Ellenzweig, Deidre Lynch, Audrey Wasser, Rob Lehman, David Alvarez, and Laura Brown. I was fortunate to write this book while living in Cambridge, Massachusetts, where there remains a vibrant community of scholars. Among those are Jess Keiser and Andrew Warren. While each writing monographs, we coalesced to form a writing group that managed to survive over several years. A special thanks to Jess and Andrew for reading so much of this manuscript and offering so many important revisions and suggestions. Finally, I must thank my incredible readers at the University of Virginia Press for their gracious, meticulous, and intelligent feedback. You have truly made this a better book.

Research for *Mind over Matter* has been substantially funded by the University of Rhode Island's Division of Research and Economic Development. This grant made travel to the British and Chawton House Libraries in England possible. Many thanks to all the staff at Chawton House for their assistance and hospitality in the summer of 2017. I am also grateful to the University of Rhode Island's Department of English for a subvention grant that has assisted with the publication costs of this book.

An earlier, shortened version of chapter 3 appeared as "More Than a Conscious Feeling: Reading Evelina's Mind in Time," in *Studies in the Novel* 50, no. 2 (2018): 171–96. Additionally, a paragraph from chapter 1 appeared as a brief example in an essay titled "Why Memory Matters: Surviving Intentions," in *Studies in Eighteenth-Century Culture* 47 (2018): 239–44. A portion of chapter 5 is also set to appear in the spring 2021 issue of *Studies in Romanticism* as "Jane Austen's Allegories of Mind: Memory Fiction in Mansfield Park." I am grateful to Johns Hopkins University Press for permission to use that material here.

Mind over Matter is evidence of what literature can teach us about the healing powers of the mind and brain when our bodies are in a state of crisis. A wise friend and mentor once told me, "We are always only ever writing about ourselves." In truth, survival is more than a state of mind; it is a community state. Thanks, then, to the hardworking and caring few who were physically there so that this book could make into the world: Dr. Kip Mackenzie, Dr. Carolyn Bernstein, Lee Orsky, Jackie and Jonas Havens, Joseph Eron, Ruth Tilley, and Kathia Havens. Above all, I want to extend my love and gratitude to Caleb Goodhouse, my partner in all things difficult, joyful, and adventurous, for his amazing patience in learning to live with this inveterate writer.

MIND OVER MATTER

❖ INTRODUCTION ❖

Memory Fictions

In the gallery there were many family portraits, but they could have little to fix the attention of a stranger. Elizabeth walked on in quest of the only face whose features would be known to her. At last it arrested her—and she beheld a striking resemblance of Mr. Darcy, with such a smile over the face, as she remembered to have sometimes seen, when he looked at her. She stood several minutes before the picture in earnest contemplation, and returned to it again before they quitted the gallery. Mrs. Reynolds informed them, that it had been taken in his father's life time.

There was certainly at this moment, in Elizabeth's mind, a more gentle sensation towards the original, than she had ever felt in the height of their acquaintance.
—JANE AUSTEN, *Pride and Prejudice*

In one of the most famous scenes in English literature, Elizabeth Bennet enters a family picture gallery only to emerge with a mind and a life forever changed. The gallery is housed on the Pemberley estate, where she has just arrived with mixed feelings. The grandeur of Pemberley impresses her almost enough to regret refusing Mr. Darcy's marriage proposal, but her worldly ambitions dissipate when she is reminded of her suitor's pride, which might forever divide her from her beloved family. Elizabeth describes this self-rebuke as a "lucky recollection" that "saved her from something like regret" (159). This seemingly pristine and moralizing memory comes under scrutiny, however, once the reader travels inside to hear the housekeeper's glowing account of Mr. Darcy. Just after hearing this praise, Elizabeth walks into the exhibit.

From the start of *Pride and Prejudice*, Austen parodies a model of retentive memory that first represents information only to form the basis of moral judgment. Her use of the gallery draws on an eighteenth-century philosophical archetype for a kind of memory that operates as a collection. Elizabeth enters the gallery like the ideal empiricist, searching the collection (her mind) for what she already knows. But the picture gallery is an aesthetic assemblage that also reveals the powers of art to alter our "original" impressions. Artistry here is less about the portrait's painterly realism than it is about the literary context in which the portrait is hung. Finally "arrested" by the "striking resemblance of Mr. Darcy," Elizabeth claims that the picture jogs a memory of what she *actually* has never before observed in the novel. Where does this memory come from?

The account slyly indicates that Mrs. Reynolds's flattering reflections of the young Fitzwilliam may be the source of Elizabeth's newfound memory. The transacted remembrance causes a new and "gentle" sensation, one that supplants Elizabeth's previous anxieties to keep Darcy at bay. The novel intimates that this new "recollection" may be what truly saves Elizabeth "from something like regret" (159). As though the happy feeling produced by the altered memory is not enough, Darcy himself (rendered in a new light) magically appears at Pemberley's threshold immediately upon Elizabeth's change of mind.

The passage is a literary trompe l'oeil that uses free indirect style as a vehicle for satirizing empirical assumptions about memory. For a moment, we may conflate our narrative memories with Elizabeth's, failing to see the true source of the heroine's impressions. Austen presents us with a gallery of curated memories that evolve through social networks; they are fictionalized as easily as they are penetrated by the remembrances and impressions of other persons. Most significantly, these memories have a powerful ability to soothe distress as they conjure up new feelings, circumstances, and events.

Mind over Matter changes how we think about "personal" memory within, and as the defining structure of, the early novel. Specifically, it revises our current understanding of memory in eighteenth-century novels, which have traditionally been associated with mimetic accounts of mental imprinting in philosophical empiricism.[1] Instead, I reveal a social model of memory in Enlightenment fiction that is fluid and evolving, one that has the capacity to alter personal histories. This book shows how memory shapes the process and outcome of the novel's imaginative world-making. Through a close engagement with representative eighteenth-century texts, I track the force of memory's transpositions and alterations. Persistently, I find that memory enables the creation of worlds that make it possible to endure and work through situations of crisis. Through new readings of works by Daniel Defoe, Frances Burney, Laurence Sterne, Jane Austen, and others, I revise our notions about early novelistic consciousness and how memories become socially integrated. This proto-Romantic history of the novel reveals the unexpected origins of William Wordsworth's "emotion recollected in tranquillity" in fictional biographies of distress. Crusoe's island (Daniel Defoe, *Robinson Crusoe*), Toby's bowling green (Laurence Sterne, *Tristram Shandy*), Evelina's garden (Frances Burney, *Evelina*), and Fanny's East room (Jane Austen, *Mansfield Park*) are all realms in which I investigate memory's empowering and healing way of reconstituting worlds.

My readings expose the fictional qualities of memory as a *force*, much like that of the Romantic imagination, that transposes time and alters forms and places. For eighteenth-century novelists, memory embellishes more than it records, creating just as it retains and recalls. *Mind over Matter* is about how memory's creative force empowers both characters and readers, how that force alters, reconstitutes, and even overcomes the conditions of our physical environment. Memory does not merely "store up"; it makes up.

I want to begin by elaborating on my claim that memory can operate as a force, a term derived more from theories of the imagination in phenomenological Romanticism than from eighteenth-century epistemic accounts of recollection. Imagination has long been heralded as that mystical quality of Romanticism and the eighteenth-century mind; it is transformational, metaphysical, and immaterial. "The imagination offers the dynamic and active," James Engell writes. "It is a force, an energy, not a state of being. It more easily explains the interchange of state and the transforming, organic qualities of psyche and nature."[2] Engell's definition of the creative imagination as a force of mind stems from Coleridge's use of the term to describe our mental faculties in his *Biographia Literaria*:

> DES CARTES . . . said, give me matter and motion and I will construct you the universe. We must of course understand him to have meant; I will render the construction of the universe intelligible. In the same sense the transcendental philosopher says; grant me a nature having

two contrary forces, the one of which tends to expand infinitely, while the other strives to apprehend or *find* itself in this infinity, . . . Every other science pre-supposes intelligence as already existing and complete: the philosopher contemplates it in its growth, and as it were represents its history to the mind from its birth to its maturity."[3]

For Coleridge, intelligence "finds" itself within "infinite" nature, and, like nature's own organic force, it grows. As Engell captures in his account of the Romantic imagination, forces are dynamic, active, and transpositional. By definition, they move, transform, interchange, and mature, both within themselves and in their relationship to other things.

If imagination is a force, then Enlightenment philosophy generally treats memory as a thing. In one of the most seminal works on consciousness, *An Essay Concerning Human Understanding,* John Locke's famous aggregating mind presumes that knowledge and memory are part of the same process by which sensation becomes fact, and what was once subjective renders itself into an objective idea. For philosophers of the Enlightenment, memory is imagination's shadowy counterweight. Samuel Johnson describes memory as a stronghold of the past, cast against the brighter light of imagination: "It is . . . much more common for the solitary and thoughtful to amuse themselves with schemes of the future, than reviews of the past," Johnson writes. "For the future is pliant and ductile, and will be easily moulded by a strong fancy into any form. But the images which memory presents are of a stubborn and untractable nature, the objects of remembrance have already existed, and left their signature behind them impressed upon the mind, so as to defy all attempts of erasure or of change."[4] For Johnson, mimetic memory leaves inert and indelible traces of objects that will always remain, in some vague sense, as they originally appear. In other words, Johnson argues, *fancy alters form; memory copies it.*

The purpose of this book is to expose memory's capacity to fictionalize (or alter) experience as a *power.* In demonstrating the elusive nature of memory as something that evolves in slippery ways through the linguistic medium of fiction, I contend that for early novelists, it is this fictional quality of memory that allows us to adapt to and, more important, alter our environment. We survive sensation *because* we are apt to remember and fictionalize it, accepting always that feelings have the power to change.

In the introductory sections that follow, I situate this book in relation to other literary historical discussions of memory and imagination before tracing assumptions about the "memory storehouse" to its roots in empiricist philosophy. This book disrupts our categorical distinctions about these supposedly antithetical mental faculties in the fiction of the Enlightenment and proto-Romantic periods, arguing that for early novelists they work in tandem and often as the very same mental force. I depart from a logic of memory as mental repository to a more temporal theory of mind. To use Robinson Crusoe's phrase, memory is a "World of Time" that takes us away from the realm of the present only to "bestir" the creative faculties. For Jane Austen or Laurence Sterne, memory perforates the boundaries between fact and fiction; it is a healing force that recreates and alters forms in the world. Memory is not a container of sensation but an electrical converter, as it were: the agent that seeks to fictionalize and transform human experiences and environments. There is a limit to how much bodies can feel. On that sublime edge of human feeling is where memory resides, teasing out the possibilities of a past remembered and realized into new and pleasing forms.

What Is a Real Memory?

Early novel studies has long been invested in the constructs of autobiographical thinking, so much so that for literary historians, the novel has practically become synonymous with cognition itself. Whereas older accounts of the novel's origins heralded the genre as a representation of personal history and psychology, newer accounts consider how novels as mediating forms interact with readers in the real world.[5] Nevertheless, literary scholars of the novel's origins continue to treat memory as the great reservoir of human consciousness. Novel and memory studies have long been linked because of their historical interest in consciousness and fictional autobiography. According to Douwe Draaisma, psychologists began using the term "autobiographical memory" only in the 1980s. Suzanne Nalbantian traces the term's equivalent in neuropsychology, "episodic memory," to 1972.[6] This term for the long-term memories of personal experience entered the canon of novel criticism at a much earlier date.[7] Given that we typically locate the novel's genesis in the same literary historical period (1700s) as the rise of philosophical empiricism (the epistemic belief in the efficacy of subjective, sensory experience) this comes as no surprise. Every student of the early novel knows of Ian Watt's and Michael McKeon's "realist" accounts of the genre of individual, autonomous minds.[8] In *The Rise of the Novel*, Watt reads the literary realism of the eighteenth-century novel as associated with the empiricism of John Locke and René Descartes because of its emphasis on individual sense experience.[9]

Later readings of early novels are equally preoccupied with "how novels think."[10] But these more recent studies entertain the mediating roles that novels play for readers in social networks. No longer do we simply consider the novel as the great imitator of consciousness. Rather, it is understood to be part of a larger web of cognitive interplay.[11] However, early novel studies has not considered what such mediational accounts of novel reading might mean for memory. This oversight has much to do with the long-standing assumption in eighteenth-century studies that memory is a record of experiences written on the mind. But what happens to modernity when we discover that the stories we tell ourselves about ourselves are not our own? That they change through processes of reading, writing, and retelling, or that they defy notions of memory as empiricism's great storehouse? My readings of early novels in this book reveal how memories become socially integrated, thereby prompting us to revise how we think about "personal" memory within, and as the defining structure of, the early novel.

To situate my work in the context of fictionality studies, I want briefly to invoke a more recent definition of memory. Contemporary science regards memories as neural associations that change and interact with histories, environments, and *fictions*. In other words, "real" memories do not represent our reality but rather mediate it and are in turn mediated by it. Such a limning of memory is reminiscent of recent shifts in the way reality has come to be parsed in Enlightenment studies of the novel. William Warner and Clifford Siskin's notion of the Enlightenment as "an event in the history of mediation" disrupts the association of the Enlightenment with epistemic ideas and asks scholars to consider how knowledge is mediated in the eighteenth century. For Warner and Siskin, "mediation" is broadly defined as "the work done by tools." This new theoretical history has essentially changed the way we view modernity's treatment of the real in this period.[12]

Catherine Gallagher's work on fictionality, which redefines the genre of the early novel as a paradox that simultaneously engages readerly speculation and disbelief, has had a similar effect.[13] Gallagher's conceptualization of the novel as a "free space in which to temporarily indulge imaginative play" but also as a "protective enclosure that would cordon off imaginary yielding from any dangerous consequences" assumes that novels have a mediational power to alter their readers' mental states.[14] Although Gallagher's theory of fictionality in the Enlightenment implicates the reader's use of judgment and imagination, it never explicitly tackles the novel's capacity to mediate readers' memories. Most likely this is due to her understanding of the novel as a "temporary" system of cognitive play, as a definitively circumscribed space of "free" thinking. Such a conception of the novel does not dovetail with what memory means in philosophical empiricism; the fact that memories cannot transpose or transform but only decay excludes them from any world, however tenuous, of mediational free play. In short, by implicitly continuing to think about memory through the frame of empirical discourse, eighteenth-century fictionality studies still depends to some extent on Watt's early concept of realism in the novel insofar as it derives from eighteenth-century philosophies of mind. This book's mediational approach to memory in the eighteenth-century novel thereby makes an important contribution to recent work in fictionality theory.[15]

I want to turn now to some of the ways in which scholars have accounted for memory in and around the eighteenth century. Literary scholars, scientists, and philosophers perpetually evoke bodily, spatial, and architectural metaphors as explanatory devices for memory. Enlightenment literary scholarship is no exception to this rule. In fact, the rising interest in metaphor in eighteenth-century studies practically constitutes our work on memory in the period.[16] Brad Pasanek's *Metaphors of Mind* reads the mind as a compendium of metaphors and thereby makes a capacious argument for seeing memory as a mere metaphor during this time period. My objective here is to disrupt categorical distinctions in the Enlightenment between the supposedly antithetical mental faculties of imagination and memory, arguing that they work in tandem and sometimes as the very same mental force.[17] One avenue is to think about how we have historically leaned on metaphor as a way of understanding the abstract nature of the mind.[18] Metaphor has been defined as a form constitutive of both memory and imagination.[19] Our critical conception of Enlightenment memory as a *thing* most likely stems from its entanglement with the language of metaphor across eighteenth-century disciplines. Taking Pasanek's notion of the mind as a vast "conger[y] of metaphors" to heart,[20] but likewise wishing to dispense with the notion of memory as mere matter, *Mind over Matter* considers the *active* nature of trope.

The close readings presented in this book suggest that literary devices like metaphor often provide an indexical map of memory's own creative history, a way of tracking an otherwise elusive force of the mind. When it comes to memory in fiction, metaphor is the stuff of transformation—the linguistic thing that allows the mind to enact formal and emotional change. Gesturing toward the etymological root of metaphor as a "crossing over,"[21] I consider it a mode through which memory works and identifies itself. Metaphor is an external sign that evinces memory's power to alter form and environment. Toby's bowling green and Fanny's East room are the places wherein things index memory's creative powers; they allow the reader to see memory's tangible effects. In this sense, memory is made legible not merely in the way that the faithful Jane Austen student might assume—from, say, free indirect style, or what cognitive studies call "mind reading"[22]—but through new semiotic systems.[23] In the world of objects, we are apt to find evidence of memory's greatest mental powers.

Traditional approaches to memory and metaphor in literary studies, however, function rather differently from this book's method. In her account of memory in the literature of the medieval period, Mary Carruthers compares memory to a book.[24] This is her dominant metaphor for the mind, and one that asks us to imagine the activity of remembrance as organized through cognitive systems of booklike collation, rereading, and recall: "The 'art of memory' is actually the 'art of recollection.' . . . The crucial task of recollection is *investigatio*, 'tracking-down,' a word related to *vestigia*, 'tracks' or 'footprints.' All mnemonic organizational schemes are heuristic in nature. They are retrieval schemes, for the purpose of *inventio* or 'finding.'"[25] This rhetorical art of memory, its commensurate status with knowledge, if striking to the modern reader, is rather familiar to the student of modernity. Eighteenth-century scholars typically consider memory in the tradition of empiricism—as a type of knowledge born out of sensation and recall; memory is a textual site within the mind that houses collected impressions, or inscriptions. As Margaret Doody has noted, "It is a truth universally acknowledged that the Enlightenment depends upon memory. Indeed, the Enlightenment in a sense—in its very sensations of thought—loves memory. Memory in the Lockean world is the foundation of consciousness."[26] For the student of Enlightenment, remembrance savors of the same kinds of activities that Carruthers describes in her depiction of medieval memory: it is an act of seeking or "finding" out—*inventio*—that bears on the eighteenth-century notion of genius as invention or discovery.

To remember, for empiricists, is to revisit the mind's long-established "tracks" and "trains."[27] In his recent work, *The Mind Is a Collection,* Sean Silver likens eighteenth-century "memory storage" in John Locke's tradition to a "museum, cabinet, library, [or a] . . . heap of particulars."[28] In Enlightenment and medieval philosophy, memory and books were similar things. Imprinted, collated, circulated, searched, and read, they dominated the purview of knowledge systems much as the computer or internet has come to represent minds as networks of information today. (Take, for example, the word that neuroscience uses for memory formation: the "encoding" of information in the brain's nervous system.)

Although Carruthers longs for a reprivileging of memory's status in intellectual fields of inquiry, she maintains notions of imagination and memory as discrete mental faculties. Her book begins by underscoring the postmodern tendency to privilege imagination over memory: "At best, for us, memory is a kind of photographic film, exposed . . . by an amateur and developed by a duffer, and so marred by scratches and inaccurate light-values. We make such judgments (even those of us who are hard scientists) because we have been formed in a post-Romantic, post-Freudian world, in which imagination has been identified with a mental unconscious of great, even dangerous, creative power."[29] Carruthers bemoans memory's bad reputation, only to reclaim it in a history that seeks to identify memory with the institutional processes of learning. Memory, like imagination, has its own form of genius. For the modern reader, Carruthers's account is surprising and instrumental. In essence, it provides us with a road map for how to preserve memory records and how to prevent memory errors. This too is thus far true for our studies of the Enlightenment period. Literary critical attempts to overturn memory's place in theories of the early novel and empiricism never question its foundational efficacy as that great recordkeeper of thoughts, sensations, and things. Rather, like Hobbes, many critics turn to memory's decay, its lapses and absences.

Forgetting has taken on a new cachet in literary studies of the mind, posing a threat to what Margaret Doody depicts as the Enlightenment's long-term love affair with memory. Perhaps this is because, as Carruthers points out, we live in a post-Romantic, posttraumatic age, wherein remembering too much or too acutely can be a painful event. (I address some of these more troubling accounts of memory, such as trauma and the nostalgia disease, in chapters 2 and 5.) In this manner, forgetfulness overshadows our previous historical interests in empiricist recollection. Nicholas Dames's work on nostalgia in the nineteenth century glorifies the concept of forgetting by turning our attention to the "death of memory within": pleasure arises from memory's "absence," "erasure," and "eradication."[30] Pitting Victorian forgetfulness against the later modernist interest in the "everydayness" of remembrance, encapsulated in "a madeleine, a bar of soap," Dames turns away from what he describes as modernism's "capacity for [the] unlimited exfoliation" of memory by calling attention to what is *not* or *no longer* there.[31] Similarly, Margaret Doody intimates that forgetting may be the true power of empirical accounts of mind in the Enlightenment age when she writes, "Incidentally, what beautiful images Locke chooses for insubstantial wavering of personality, for *forgetting*—the flickering lights in a mirror, the waving shadows flying over a wheat-field. There is a sense of the beautiful—even of pleasure, though an unwilling pleasure—intruding into Locke's vision of forgetting, even as there are strong marks of pain associated with Lockean memory."[32] For Doody, forgetting speaks to a powerful human capacity for change. Still, memory is either mundane or a real pain; its oblivion is where these readers find bliss.

What these literary studies of forgetfulness do speak to is the pliable, flexible nature of mentality. For even in the Enlightenment novel, memory's art is best described as *no thing*: it is not like the pages of a book that collect images and inscriptions. In attempting to disentangle memory from epistemology, the philosopher Annette Baier homes in on memory gaps as a site of distinction: "The gaps in my memory are not like the gaps in my knowledge of things I am and was ignorant of. The gaps constitute *lapses* of memory, whereas the gaps in my knowledge . . . can be, or be due to, mere absence of conviction."[33] In other words, forgetting itself is proof enough that a memory is not knowledge, for the latter depends not on recall but on a sense of certainty, a conviction. Curiously, it is through this pathway of distinguishing memory from knowledge, or fact, that Baier arrives at a picture of the conscious memory, one that finds a kinship between the structures of intending and remembering: "It is memory with its distinctive failings, loss, and lapse, which shows the continuity and narcissism which parallels, in the past, that of the intended future."[34]

I will not herald the memory lapse as the singular (albeit absent) aspect of remembrance that paves the way for obtaining our greatest fantasies and desires (or of revising our most difficult experiences). My readings of memory in the eighteenth-century novel underscore its reconstructive and transformative capabilities. However, studies of forgotten memories are the closest we get to that force of mind that has delighted Romantics across the ages: the imagination. Defining Enlightenment memory as a collection, Sean Silver posits it as imagination's opposite: "This is of course radically different from what the imagination has come to mean. The imagination in its Romantic form—the active, energetic faculty called in the late eighteenth century 'the god within'—was largely fashioned through an extended episode of forgetting, slowly disentangling the productive work of creativity from the collecting and collating processes which, in the eighteenth century, were thought to make it work."[35] Only by way of forgetting, Silver suggests, does the Romantic imagination come to be. If we follow these snapshots in literary histories of the mind, they tell the following story of the late eighteenth century: memory, once the genius faculty of mind, was erased, forgotten. In its shadow, imagination provided a light for darker times. Only in the total absence of the past does fiction become a viable escape route. Imagination is the architect that benefits from a memory catastrophe. In other words, critics have argued that literary memory in the late eighteenth century transcribes or dissolves; it never transforms and reconstructs existent forms in the world.

But what memory or novel really works this way? To be sure, Enlightenment readers and characters may shed memories, or "prune" them, to use a neuroscientific term. Throughout the history of novelistic fiction, memories are associated, dropped, recalled, and revitalized—but they also create, and not just out of what is no longer there but out of what is readily at hand. Toby Shandy's tobacco pipe, Leopold Bloom's lemon soap, Marcel Proust's shell-shaped cookie: these "everyday" things of endless "exfoliation" are the stuff of memory *and* imagination.[36] In them, we encounter the pleasures of then and now collapsed into a single moment. A casual thing sensualized out of thin air is remembered as it never was before.

When Molly Bloom sends James Joyce's modern epic into a flourishing close, we are left with a resounding affirmation that weds past tense with future. The text is a comma-less hybrid that entangles historical feeling with present desire: "and then he asked me would I yes to say yes my mountain flower and first I put my arms around him yes and drew him down to me so he could feel my breasts all perfume yes and his heart was going like mad and yes I said yes I will Yes."[37] What lies within grasp here is a memory "drawn down" to the touches of the imagination—an exquisite entangling of mental faculties that perfumes forms with sensory phenomenalism. This may smack of nostalgia (in the present sense of the term as rosy-colored remembrance born of forgetting). But form is not *forgotten* here. It is simply just not *punctuated*. No limits lie between memory and desire, as the feelings of a past are remade into a future. Molly's affirmation is an intention, a desire, *and* a memory. It is not a known fact, a belief, or a "conviction," to use Annette Baier's term—either for the character or for the reader. Molly's memory is experience subjected to the fictionalizing networks of the mind—a voice that cries out so as to reorganize, and rewire, felt moments in time. The "yes" sends the past into new networks and pathways of pleasure.

Molly's "yes," I would argue, is the inspired legacy of the novel's eighteenth-century origins. Long before Molly Bloom's orgasmic memory fantasy, novels were a testament to memory's fictions, its creative power to reconstitute worlds so as to seek out pleasure and soothe distress. Enlightenment scholarship memorializes memory into some *thing* like a book, a page, a personal library, or nothing at all—evanescent, erased, a forgotten thing in imagination's wake. This study brings memory and books into a new relationship, one previously elided from empiricist studies of the novel's origins. In doing so, it is inspired by those novel theorists of late who envision the mediating capacities of fiction to transform readers, persons, and events. To use John Bender's phrase, to read fiction is to put the "unreality within the real" into motion.[38] When we read, we fictionalize our memories, but in a way that can positively reshape the worlds we inhabit. Dropping the strict division between memory and imagination that has so long persisted in Enlightenment studies allows us to consider memory's creative capacity as a vitalizing and healing power. Evolving with the organic folds of time, memory remembers through novel networks, finding new hope in what (perhaps) before never really was. Unpunctuated, the mind at work with and within fiction looks more like a sentence from *Ulysses*: it blooms.

Descartes' Wax

Descartes' wax is cool to the touch and still tastes of honeycomb. On its hard surface, he can smell the fragrance of flower petals that once brushed the bee's wings. He is sitting by the fire, curious and meditative. He raps on the wax; it emits a solid sound. As he draws closer to the fireplace, he carries the wax with him. The sweet smell vanishes; it no longer tastes of honey. Changing shape, the wax becomes so hot he can hardly hold it in his hands. Taste, smell, sight, sound, touch: they are as fleeting as the bee and the flower whence the nectar came. Skeptic that he is, Descartes questions everything that once lay in his grasp. It has all changed, and yet "the wax remains."[39]

Contemplating change, Descartes asks his reader to meditate on what remains when everything we once knew is now altered: "But what is it to be flexible and mutable? Is it what my imagination shows it to be: namely, that this piece of wax can change. . . . Not at all. . . . I would not judge correctly what the wax is if I did not believe that it takes on an even greater variety of dimensions than I could ever grasp with the imagination. . . . I do not grasp what this wax is through the imagination; rather, I perceive it through the mind alone."[40] What Descartes does here (aside from play with a bit of wax) is begin to challenge the very tenets of empiricism. If everything we know comes from sensation—touch, sound, color, taste, smell—then how do we account for the fact that those very forms in the world that make us feel, change? Although everything he was once sure of lies in question, Descartes does not come up empty-handed. The wax, in some sense or shape, is still there. Discovering that sensation can mutate rapidly, Descartes comes to distrust the sensory organs of the body as the faculties that allow him to know and perceive the world.

Moving from the eye to the mind, he tries to account for where knowledge comes from in new territories of human perception. His first instinct is to follow the tracks of the imagination. What else might be responsible for this sublime transmutability? This, however, he immediately rejects. The dizzying dimensions of the wax, once solid, now fluid, must be so infinitely numerous that they tax even the imagination, and so all falls to the "mind." But what does Descartes really mean by "mind" in this moment? His use of the word "judge" is telling of his rationalism. Some mental faculty must distinguish between the once fragrant block of yellow and its newly outfitted shape. This is what "judgment" meant in early modernity: a faculty of distinction, the mind's measuring tool for difference.[41] Later, Descartes' famous distrust of the body would leave him to defer to God and soul as the great knower of all things. Housed within the story of the wax, however, is a secret history of mind that Descartes never names.

My interest in Descartes is to underscore what is *not there* in his story of the wax, or rather that powerful force that is there all along but that goes unnamed. In an attempt to understand and accept mutability, Descartes gives the wax a story. The wax is no mere thing but a narrative of how the mind tracks and perceives the mutations of form over time. Although he rests on "mind" as the unifying principle of perception, something else lurks between these mental categories of "judgment" and "imagination." What Descartes attributes to mind or reason is what later writers would call "memory." Short term as it is, the memory of the wax brings to mind judgment and imagination too. It spurs them to action. Memory is the force that accounts for the mutations of Descartes' wax as it transforms from flower to bee to honeycomb to a solid form that melts in the palm of his hand.

Why does Descartes never use the term memory (reflection, or recollection) to describe his experience? The answer lies in the fact that what we today call memory operates in a way that would have been rejected by the famous cognitivist. For Descartes, memory was a corporeal thing written (or "traced") on the pineal gland—a material definition he elaborates more fully in his *Treatise on Man*.[42] As his language intimates, reason, for Descartes, is the organizing structure of thought; it is what carries the wax from one form to another. In this sense, I am guilty of reading Descartes against his own terms. Yet the story of the wax serves as both a foundation and a metaphor for how philosophers and writers would wrestle with memory over the course of the next two centuries:

> But I need to realize that the perception of the wax is neither a seeing, nor a touching, nor an imagining. Nor has it ever been, even though it previously seemed so; rather it is an inspection on the part of the mind alone. This inspection can be imperfect and confused, as it was before, or clear and distinct, as it is now, depending on how closely I pay attention to the things in which the piece of wax consists.
>
> But meanwhile I marvel at how prone my mind is to errors.[43]

Not only does the wax change, Descartes' perception of it also changes. What he "inspects" now, he did not perceive then. Descartes' skepticism arises from the natural properties of mutation. New experiences, revelations, discoveries have the capacity to alter our *memories* of a thing. Descartes' account of what the wax really *is* and *was* takes a slippery course. Memories shift with the fluidity of our sensations, changes in our environment, and the flexibility of the forms that surround us. They scale and rescale perception with the forms the senses follow. Descartes' meditation on mutability caused him for a moment to leave the world aside, to feel a little insecure about the senses, about bodies and the objects they encounter.

Although we often think of the Enlightenment as the age of truth, it is as easily characterized as an era of doubt. Many classify it as something beyond even historical periodization—that sneaking suspicion that causes us to look again at what we know.[44] Descartes' uncertainties would give rise to myriad questions that marked European thought in the long eighteenth century: Are minds and bodies really so different?[45] How, then, do they interact? Maybe everything changes because matter is not so inert after all? What if all *things* (not just minds) are in motion?[46] Perhaps objects are not even there, and everything is mind.[47] Or they are there, but things are only as they appear.[48] At the bottom of these Enlightenment inquiries lies an overwhelming interest in what we call epistemology—how we come to know what we know—and, added to this, the distinction between what is known and what is unknown, what lies in the mind's grasp and what perpetually eludes it. Among all the philosophies of the Enlightenment, empiricism has dominated our critical conceptions about memory in eighteenth-century studies, and it has resolutely pervaded our understanding of the novel form. However, I suggest that for early novelists, there was a difference between memory and knowledge (less so than we have assumed between memory and imagination).

René Descartes published his *Meditations* in 1641. Forty-eight years later, Locke's sensationalism would respond to the doubts raised in Descartes' work. For John Locke, everything we think and know takes its absolute foundation in sensory experience. Locke viewed the mind as that vast container of previously felt things, and in this vein, he would make up for Descartes' missing word.[49] Locke practically equates the mind itself with memory: "If *it* be not *in* the memory, *it* is not *in* the mind."[50] Things characterize the basic infrastructure of memory for Locke, and "memory" is itself a thing that contains many representations of objects that reflect our material existence. Memory is less sublime in Locke than that absent force that goes unnamed in Descartes' story of the wax. It is "*oftentimes more than barely passive*"; it depends on "the Constitution of the Body"; it may be "rouzed and tumbled" out of darkness. Most memorable for students of mind, Locke's memory "retrieves."[51] The psychologist Douwe Draaisma begins his recent book, *Why Life Speeds Up as You Get Older*, by avowing that "memory is a dog; it retrieves what we have just thrown away, wagging its tail."[52] Thanks to the powerful rhetoric of Locke's *Essay*, ideas about memory's unruliness color our cultural sentiments and assumptions to this day.

Locke's mind is distinctively of the world. As such, it is subject to the vicissitudes of bodily waste and pain: "Thus the *Ideas* . . . often die before us: And our Minds represent to us those Tombs, to which we are approaching; where though the Brass and Marble remain, yet the Inscriptions are effaced by time, and the Imagery moulders away." In Locke's book of memory, "the Print wears out."[53] This book's history of the novel delivers a picture of memory that travels far beyond the objects of John Locke's favorite storehouse. Still, Locke's picture of forgetting is most instrumental for my study of memory fiction and not simply for its use of trope. We are apt to read this sentence as metaphor. Lost in the gorgeous sublime of moldering images, brass tombs, and allegories of time that erase and efface, it is easy for us to fall in love with Locke's system of limits, the weaknesses of the mind. But the sentence's active verb, its syntax and structure, should not be overlooked. When Locke writes that our minds "represent to us those Tombs," is this a simile? Or is he deferring here to imagination? If we take the indirect object "us" to heart, then the mind shows us what lies beyond the power of memory (past feeling) via the imagination, its image-producing faculty. In this sense, there is something troubling about Locke's symbolic picture of forgetting as a mental death. The formidable future, cast as a moldy "image," is no more than an image unseen, never before experienced by the living human senses. It transgresses the very boundaries of empiricism. We can never remember, but can only imagine, death. Locke faults memory for what imagination can do.

John Locke's powerful description of wasted memories resurfaces in new ways in Thomas Hobbes's *Leviathan*, published ten years later. Unlike other empirical philosophers of his time, Hobbes equates imagination and memory, and for this reason cognitive literary theorists often identify Hobbes in the tradition of contemporary psychology and neuroscience.[54] However, Hobbes's theory of memory deprives it of any power to recombine or reconstruct experience. Rather, his interest is in how mental faculties (as amalgams of copied, sensory data) *decay*:

> And any object being removed from our eyes, though the impression it made in us remain; yet other objects more present succeeding, and

> working on us, the Imagination of the past is obscured, and made weak; . . . For the continuall change of mans body, destroyes in time the parts which in sense were moved: So that distance of time, and of place, hath one and the same effect in us. . . . This *decaying sense*, when wee would express the thing it self, (I mean *fancy* it selfe,) wee call *Imagination*, as I said before: But when we would express the *decay*, and signifie that the Sense is fading, old, and past, it is called *Memory*. So that *Imagination* and *Memory*, are but one thing, which for divers considerations hath divers names.[55]

Here, imagination and memory are distinguished merely by their degrees of decomposition. Although Hobbes defines memory as material waste, it is important to remember that he is still very much an empiricist. Accordingly, impressions are derived from sensory experience: "Imagination being only of those things which have been formerly perceived by Sense. . . ." Hobbes's material imagination is a moving foundation. As the mind encounters new objects, old impressions are laid to waste. Even though Hobbes writes that imagination and memory "are but one thing," his attempt to link these categories is not about their operational resemblance. Like his fellow empiricists, Hobbes attributes the creative and combining faculties of the mind to imagination only. What Hobbes calls a "compound imagination" splices together two sensory impressions so as to "conceive" of images that do not exist in the real world. (His example for this is a centaur.)[56] The Hobbesian mind of moving images bears a striking resemblance to Locke's "mouldering . . . Inscriptions" of forgetfulness. However, Hobbes posits a more extreme definition of material memory than his predecessor. For Hobbes, memory *is* sensory decay itself. As it were, memory describes imagination's death. The two faculties of mind are one "thing" only insofar as they track two stages in the material life of an impression. (Impressions, for Hobbes, like all material things, are finite.) Imagination defines the infancy of our impressions, when they still have life enough to transpose themselves, whereas memory is experience in its most aged sense, the near dead matter of a decomposing mind.

In a quest to define the truth of experience, empiricism places pressure on remembrance. With the later emergence of David Hume's radical skepticism, we might entertain a hope for the powers of memory and fiction, for Hume questions even experience itself. To some extent, Hume's entire system of philosophy is founded on "error." Investigating cause-and-effect relations, he locates everything in the way that the mind perceives things in and through time. In discovering that the future is nothing more than our expectation that tomorrow will look like our past, Hume delights in mental trickery and laughs at our assumptions. Like Locke's, however, Hume's entire system of thought is erected on memory and sensation, and this causes him to have absolute faith in one thing at least: that we "can never go beyond . . . [our] original perceptions."[57] This is true too for Hume's idea of imagination.

Therefore, when he comes to distinguish these two mental faculties in part 3 of the *Treatise*, he insists that both "borrow" from our sensory "impressions." We never arrive at something from nothing in empiricism. There remains always a certain trust in feeling. According to Hume, it is "a peculiar property of the memory to preserve the original order and position of its ideas, while the imagination transposes and changes them, as it pleases." Insisting that memory is the great "preserver" of experience, Hume gives memory the power to "repeat our impressions" with stunning "vivacity."[58] Memory grafts form and feeling onto the mind exactly in the same pattern or "position" as it was originally experienced. Memory inscribes; it encodes. Hume lends only to the imagination the power to transpose and change feelings, time, events, and things. In short, he does not believe, as this book does, in the creative, evolutionary qualities of memory, its capacity for changing and fictionalizing experience.

Things get interesting, however, when Hume insists that though the imagination and memory have antithetical powers and properties (the first alters or moves; the second preserves or records), in life, often we cannot tell the difference between the two. It is very hard to know when we are remembering something and when we are imagining it. His example is an "action" scene. Hume's story is vague, so I will fill in the details. Two acquaintances meet up, and one starts reminiscing about something that happened in their past. But his friend cannot remember a thing. Let's imagine how the conversation might go: "You know, that time, several years ago, we went to that bar in Cambridge, after dinner?" Nothing. "That song was playing on the radio. I spilled a drink on you." Nothing. "The place was dimly lit. There were plush velvet couches, and gold-embossed wall paper." Glittering in all its initial glory, wallpaper strikes a chord. "Ah, yes! It all comes back to me now." Up until the sublime "Aha!" moment, when the forgetful companion remembers gold, he receives all the particulars of his friend's story as ideas of the imagination—or, as Hume calls them, "fictions." According to Hume, "as soon as" the memory is "touch[ed]," it breaks wide open.[59] In that very moment, all the ideas that the man has just experienced as imaginations, as fictions, die away, and memories, triumphant, take their place.

With what we know about memory in cognitive science today, this seems a little suspicious. Can it be that the story is a mere trigger, a stand-in? That it does nothing to the original experience or record? But for Hume, it always comes back to our feelings. The same ideas, now received in the light of memory, are felt differently from how they were felt by the imagination just a few moments ago. Feeling makes all the difference. We can always determine whether something is a memory or an imagination by scanning our senses. The feeling we receive from a memory differs from the feeling that transpires with imagination: "The imagination can represent all the same objects that the memory can offer to us ... those faculties are only distinguish'd by the different *feeling* of the ideas they present. ... And here I believe every one will readily agree with me, that the ideas of the memory are more *strong* and *lively* than those of the fancy."[60] For Hume, the feeling we get from remembering is always more forceful than that of the imagination. The "true" thing is the thing most felt.

This book does not readily agree with David Hume. It argues that memory has the capacity to transpose and alter form. It believes that imagination and memory are entangled in ways that go beyond even the shades of feeling. Still, there is something striking about Hume's philosophy, especially compared to his predecessors'. Like Hume, this book considers what it means for mental faculties to operate as forces. Like Locke, it will find imagination and memory entangled and hiding behind beautiful metaphors. Like Descartes, it will marvel at the wonders of error and change. This book's approach to memory will resemble some of the ways that memory was talked about in Enlightenment theories of mind in even more ways than this. For the novels analyzed in this study were written and read in the period of 1719–1814, and they absorbed some metaphors and ideas from their culture. Minds and authors never exist in total isolation. But these works depart from philosophical empiricism in their thoughts about memory. Their stories uniquely expose memory's capacity for *making* and *making up*—its fictions, its errors, its fantastical way of allowing us to survive sensation when feelings become prickly or unpleasant.

Without leaving the body behind, this book argues for a new relationship between mind and matter in the eighteenth-century novel. Instead of viewing memory as an imprint, a container, or a representation of forms in the world, I contend that eighteenth-century novels envisage memory as a force with a distinctive ability to craft (and be crafted by) other persons and forms. For the Enlightenment novelist, memory has the power to alter environments and things in the world; it can change our stories of the past, and it can use stories to change present circumstances. In this manner, memory can free novelistic subjects from distressing situations or feelings. Memory may be the bedrock of the novel form, as it was of empiricism, but eighteenth-century fictions may be plumbed for ways that enlighten us to memory's creative and healing powers.

If the "mind is prone to errors," what errant pathways might we follow to change the status quo of feeling? Descartes changes his mind. The wax is still there. But it smells, it looks, it tastes, it feels—so different to the touch.

The Force of Habit: Associationism

I want to pause for a moment to consider Hume's use of the word "force" throughout *A Treatise of Human Nature* because it provides us with a point of departure for thinking about how memory actually operates in eighteenth-century novelistic fiction. By attributing the dynamics of force to imagination, Hume departs from Locke's empiricism. The word "force" first appears at the very opening of book 1 of Hume's *Treatise* as a way of categorizing ideas and impressions, the empirical building blocks of cognition. The philosopher Barry Stroud describes Locke's "ideas" as "the *materials* of thinking, as the things that the mind, so to speak, 'operates' within thinking."[61] In other words, for Locke, ideas are *objects* of thought. For Hume, ideas are better defined as "perceptions." Hume divides perceptions into "ideas" and "impressions," which can be distinguished, once again, by the forces of feeling. Impressions strike us most *forcefully*. Ideas are "faint images" in the mind.[62]

For many readers, Hume's use of the word "force" feels rather ambiguous; to some extent, it scales perceptions by degrees without ever really defining them. Stroud extrapolates further: "We know there is a difference between actually perceiving something and just thinking about that thing in its absence, and that, Hume says, is the difference between having an impression of something and having an idea of it."⁶³ Stroud's clarification is important for this book, since it essentially describes Hume's "idea" as what today we might call a "memory." Nevertheless, for both Locke and Hume, memory, like imagination, is a faculty that describes what *happens to ideas* in the mind. Locke defines memory as that faculty of retention that allows the mind to "revive again" our former perceptions, to activate ideas that have been "laid aside out of Sight." In this, memory is not simply a site like a "repository" or a "storehouse" but an activity of seeing "again."⁶⁴

The same reiterative nature of memory undergirds Locke's theory of the association of ideas:

> Some of our *Ideas* have a natural Correspondence and Connexion one with another: It is the Office and Excellency of our Reason to trace these, and hold them together in that Union and Correspondence which is founded in their peculiar Beings. Besides this there is another Connexion of *Ideas* wholly owing to Chance or Custom; *Ideas* that in themselves are not at all of kin, come to be so united in some Mens Minds, that 'tis very hard to separate them, they always keep in company, and the one no sooner at any time comes into the Understanding but its Associate appears with it; and if they are more than two which are thus united, the whole gang always inseparable shew themselves together.⁶⁵

Locke separates association into two categories. The first type can be found in nature. Since the mind houses replicas of nature, these ideas must likewise have natural connections between them. It is the job of our "reason" then to "trace" these natural connections in the mind. (Notably, "trace" connotes two types of mental activity, following and representing.) The second class of associations are created either by accident or more often by "custom." The mind habitually creates its own connections between ideas, and these associations are also habitually repeated. Locke argues that "Custom settles habits of Thinking in the Understanding . . . all which seems to be but Trains of Motion in the Animal Spirits, which once set a going continue on in the same steps they have been used to, which by often treading are worn into a smooth path."⁶⁶ This image of a train of animal spirits, famously satirized in Laurence Sterne's *Tristram Shandy*, exposes the mechanistic tendencies behind Lockean cognition. Thoughts start out on a path and have no choice but to retrace their steps. Here, Locke echoes

Descartes' *Treatise on Man* wherein "traces" from the animal spirits, moving through the channels of the brain, carve out pathways that are "imprinted" on the pineal gland, or the "seat of memory."[67] In this, memory replicates, preserves, and repeats.

Locke's first metaphor for associationism is the rote practice of a musician's performance; "the *Ideas* of the several Notes of it will follow one another orderly in his Understanding without any care or attention, as regularly as his Fingers move orderly over the Keys of the Organ."[68] If Locke's memory machine does not foreshadow Freud's later work on the subconscious for the postmodern reader, then perhaps it at least intimates what would later become the foundation of psychoanalytic trauma theory. All of Locke's examples of habitual association in chapter 33 of the *Essay* impress us with *pain*: a mother mourning the death of her child, a patient reliving the agonies of a medical operation, a child's first punishments. For Locke, a mind that represents natural connections is safe, but a mind that is prone to accident or habitual thinking risks pain.

As we have seen, Hume's empiricism invests memory with more positive connotations. Similarly, his new theory of the association of ideas consciously departs from Locke. Numerous literary critics have discussed the novel by way of Hume's tripartite classification of the principles of association: contiguity, resemblance, and causation.[69] But what interests me most for the purposes of this book is Hume's decision to move away from Locke's memory as the foundational faculty for the association of ideas. Rather, it is the imagination that separates and unites ideas in the mind "in what form it pleases."[70] The imagination for Hume is a free agent. Before Hume discusses complex ideas or the properties of causation, he heralds imagination as a space of associational free play that may "supply the place of that inseparable connexion, by which they [ideas] are united in our memory."[71] Again, Hume cannot fully dispose of Lockean memory as that space of "inseparable connexion[s]," that archive of the mind that permanently preserves the connective ribbons between ideas.

But Hume's idea of the imagination leaves us with a powerful impression of the social and transformative implications of his theory of associationism. As Wendy Lee writes, "In Humean terms we now see how my nearness of relation to you (by resemblance, contiguity, and causation) means not just that you make an impression on me, but that I share the impressions made upon you by other objects. . . . I can commit all these feelings . . . to memory.... But my imagination takes them farther. I do not just reproduce these ideas, but I can separate and recombine them."[72] Lee's summation of Hume's theory of the imagination might aptly serve as a vehicle for thinking about how I will describe memory in the eighteenth-century novel. But there's a catch to Hume's theory of association that puts the free agency of the imagination at risk. Early on in book 1 (1.1.4), Hume describes the imagination much as his Romantic successor Coleridge would: "We are only to regard it as a gentle force, which commonly prevails." Force here connotes physical "magnetism."[73] By the end of the *Treatise*, however, when Hume has fully addressed the tricky implications of causation, the word "force" takes on different connotations. The famous example of the billiard balls, which reveals the powers of our expectations to anticipate one object colliding with another, asks us to forget about physics, nature, or the mind in its environment. Our instinctive knowledge of what the billiard balls will do is, for Hume, evidence that the connection between things is nothing more than a thought process. We expect that things will happen because we have seen them happen before. In this, imagination's "gentle force" must somehow "prevail" against an altogether different dynamic, the force of "habit."[74]

Hume leaves behind physics and matter for a hegemonic mind. Yet what is intended as a radical departure from Locke shares with Locke's associationism a strange structural similarity. Even as imagination reigns, habit exerts a subtle pressure on cognition: "Our imagination has a great authority over our ideas; and there are no ideas that are different from each other, which it cannot separate, and join, and compose into all the varieties of fiction. But notwithstanding the empire of the imagination, there is a secret tie or union among particular ideas, which causes the mind to conjoin them more frequently together, and makes the one, upon its appearance, introduce the other."[75] Hume's discussion of imagination and habit, as two forces that govern the association of ideas, shares an uncanny similarity to Locke's classification of natural versus customary "connexions." If for Lock ideas flow together naturally or habitually, then for Hume they relate imaginatively or habitually. Neither philosopher can get beyond the force of habit. For Locke, this fits with his desire to organize the world according to what lies inside (habits) and outside (nature) the mind. But for Hume, since everything is triumphantly connected in and by the mind, his system reveals a paradox: associations are both free and stuck, infinitely changing and forever rotating on the same path.

For Locke, habitual associations are pathways to pain. By acknowledging the force of habit, could Hume's system be tainted by association? Can habitual associations be overturned? The novels that appear in this book envision a world in which this is possible. They posit a kind of memory that operates more like what Hume describes as imagination's "gentle force." By the *Treatise*'s end, however, Hume leaves us with no context to imagine the work of imagination and memory. In closing, he only enforces the power of association as those ties "that bind." As thought connects to thought, it becomes the thread that links ourselves to others, stirring "passions" of all kinds.[76]

Philosophers like Locke, and to some extent Hume, belong to what Jonathan Kramnick has called the eighteenth century's "dominant theory of perception." Kramnick's description of the representational model of consciousness in the eighteenth century provides us with a basic definition of "ideas or impressions" as "an internal picture of an external object or event or state of affairs."[77] It is clear that Locke fits squarely into this tradition because of his materialism; Lockean "ideas" are objects that "contain" and represent information from the outside world.[78] Whether or not Hume belongs to this tradition is more difficult to determine. Philosophers and literary critics generally agree that Hume's "ideas" are still representational, especially insofar as the degrees of feelings and the passions are concerned.[79] However, Don Garrett has argued that some of Hume's "impressions" and "ideas" are extended; they follow a mind-into-world trajectory.[80]

If we think of ideas as sensory impressions once removed, then the empirical mind exists, as literary critics Helen Thompson, Amit Yahav, and Kevis Goodman have argued, in a site of mediation.[81] This is mostly the case for these critical perspectives that focus on Locke's concept of memory. Since for Locke there are no innate ideas, he positions the perceptual mind at the margin of the internal and external world. For critics such as Kevis Goodman and Jonathan Kramnick, this means that the Lockean mind mediates our ability to directly and actively interact with our material environment; it cannot not be said to have the powers of extension.[82] Sean Silver's notion of the Lockean mind as an ecology that "locates the haptic ground of conceptual metaphor in the mind's elaborated and entangled relationship with its working environments" seeks to solve this problem when it lends embodied qualities to these mental activities themselves.[83] Silver develops this idea through Locke's metaphor of the mind as a library, which is an enclosed system that can shelve and rearrange information.[84] My reading of Locke in this introduction takes a more representational view of Lockean mentality: the mind is always at a remove from the world; ideas follow the same pathways; memory represents and preserves. If Locke's memory "mediates," it does so by acting more as a thin material barrier than a transformative agent. Moreover, this book takes a different approach when it considers not simply how memory mediates experience in eighteenth-century literature but also how early novels depict memories as mediated by new experiences. In this, memories do not represent material things (Locke), nor do they get stuck in a habitual rut or become preserved somewhere in a catalogue of perceptions (Hume). Rather, eighteenth-century novels approach memory much like Hume's imagination, as a free-floating "force" that transforms and transposes ideas. By extension, these memories can even alter things in the world.

This book's aim is to reveal a new account of the early novel that departs from a contemporaneous movement in philosophical empiricism when it envisions a constructive, instead of a retentive, model of memory. By divesting memory of Locke's painful associations, eighteenth-century literature considers the healing, pleasing potential of memory's creative force. This new way of looking at the early history of the novel affects more than just our sense of philosophy's relationship to literature in the Enlightenment period, however. For one, it gestures toward a prehistory of Romantic-era memory.[85] But most important, it alters our sense of memory studies in the history of ideas. *Mind over Matter* offers an alternative history of the novel that runs counter to a narrative trend best described as early trauma theory; it looks beyond one genre of eighteenth-century storytelling, akin to that enacted in Samuel Richardson's tragic *Clarissa,* to discover an equally powerful approach to memory in the novel's origins. Before turning to a brief review of the chapters that follow, I want to take a moment to account for the work that has shaped our idea of memory to date. At the risk of some anachronisms, I situate my study alongside these later historical accounts to expose the important impact that revising our assumptions about novelistic memory in eighteenth-century studies can have on intellectual history.

Neuropsychological Memory and Cognitive Literary Studies

What Samuel Johnson called the "untractable" markings of empirical memory did not, as it turns out, hold up for long. By the end of the nineteenth century, characterizations of memory had already begun to take on some of the "pliant" and "ductile" features that Johnson associated with fancy. For this reason, my work on the "forces" of memory in the eighteenth-century novel bears a relationship to various fields that arose in the wake of the Enlightenment, including psychoanalysis, contemporary neuroscience, and cognitive literary studies. In psychology, the entanglement of memory and imagination goes as far back as Sigmund Freud, who found in his analysis of patients' memories that they often borrowed from fiction, books, and the stories of others: "scenes from early infancy . . . are not reproductions of real occurrences . . . [but are] products of the imagination . . . which are intended to serve as some kind of symbolic representation of real wishes and interests."[86] In his constructivist model of memory, Freud demonstrates how memories are *made* by way of the mind's projected figments, or "phantasies." Freud's foundational concept of the "screen memory" posits that people "often construct . . . [memories] unconsciously—almost like works of *fiction.*"[87] For Freud, memories are propellers of wish fulfillment that aim to satisfy, as Wordsworth would have it, the "heart's demands."[88] To this end, my study of the eighteenth-century novel resembles Freud's constructivist account of memory as fiction-making. But of course, Freud often couches memory in a language of pathology. Works such as "A Child Is Being Beaten" and "An Infantile Neurosis" see imagined memories as the source, not the cure, of pathological pain. Freud's examples derive from his neurotic patients. His method is to excavate the "concealed . . . meaning" of memory constructs through symbolic analysis, and then cure his patients of them by bringing their unconscious fantasies into conscious view.[89] On the other hand, *Mind over Matter* locates a curative power *within* memory's ability to remake and fictionalize otherwise painful realities. In this sense, it shares more in common with adaptive accounts of memory in contemporary cognitive science.

Trailblazers in the field of neuroscience such as Erik Kandel saw its initial emergence as material proof of Freud's theory and method.[90] Neuropsychology today continues to explore the phenomenon of memory fiction at the level of the most mundane human behaviors.[91] The everydayness of memory error is the basic tenet of Daniel Schacter's recent work, *The Seven Sins of Memory*. Because it describes memory's susceptibility to imaginative constructivism as an "adaptive strength,"[92] current brain science bears a striking resemblance to the way I address memory in my study of the novel. In their groundbreaking research on the habits of bees, Kathyrn Chittka and Lars Hunt posit, "It is possible that memory errors are an inevitable by-product of our adaptive memories. . . . False memories, to some extent, might be a by-product of our ability to learn rules, categories and concepts."[93] The basic insight that neuronal plasticity brings to accounts of memory is that memories change with our experiences; since experiences are fluid, so are memories. Neuroplasticity opposes the Johnsonian ideal of memory as an enduring etching that mimics our experience of reality. In this manner, memory becomes an adaptive technology that systematically relates to and revises the world it lives in.

Now, memory science looks more like Coleridge's philosophical take on the forceful faculties of the imagination. Imagine nerves that erase old pathways and connections even as they form new ones, a material-transcendental intelligence that reshapes itself with the flow of haptic experience. Most striking is the role that language plays in directing memory's associative pathways. Another important neuropsychologist who is rarely cited in literary studies is Jonathan Schooler, who posits that verbal reports can "overshadow" ("not eradicate") our visual and sensory memories. Schooler writes that "verbalization impairs memory for stimuli" and that this effect is not "temporary" but "indicates relatively long-lasting memory interference."[94] As a testament to the powers of language and storytelling, this perhaps is one of the most significant scientific discoveries about memory for scholars of literature. In a similar study on social media's impact on the brain, Daniel Wegner describes what he calls "transactive memory." According to Wegner, as memory borrows ideas from the news, twitter, Instagram, and Facebook, it rewires and transforms its own history.[95] Such theories on memory's susceptibility to mediation have also affected the way clinical psychology approaches trauma studies. In the 1990s, cognitive psychologists like Elizabeth Loftus began to challenge age-old practices of trauma therapy by claiming that clinicians were unwittingly reconstructing the memories of their patients, implanting inklings of trauma where no such sentiments had been before. Loftus's methods led to a new field in the study of mind and brain called memory science. In an attempt to discover the plastic nature of neural associations, these researchers play with the minds of their subjects, wiring fictional memories into the brain's unsuspecting networks.[96] My readings throughout this book argue that early novelistic language infiltrates and alters readers' memories. Often, this effect of novel reading arises in surreptitious ways, as it parallels narratives of mediational memory that simultaneously occur at the level of character consciousness. My focus on the fictionalizing forces of language in the novel, however, underscores their capacity to heal (not create) existing traumas by reconstructing histories and circumstances. For eighteenth-century novelists, memory's transactive properties provide a solution to the seemingly unresolvable pains of physical and emotional crisis.

In light of the literary implications of such advances in brain science, the burgeoning field of cognitive literary studies should come as no surprise to scholars of memory and narrative. Insights into neurological phenomena such as "confabulation"[97] (false memories) or "source misattribution"[98] (memories derived from unclear sources) have a particular bearing on narratological approaches to consciousness in fiction. Cognitive literary critics in the fields of Romanticism, Victorian studies, and modernism, such as Alan Richardson, Beth Lau, Suzanne Nalbantian, Wendy Jones, and Kate Singer, to name a few, have capitalized on neuroscientific discoveries that cognition is both fluid and susceptible to the influence of imagination.[99] Especially significant for this book is the sea change that cognitive studies has wrought in Jane Austen criticism.[100] In his essay "Jane Austen and the Perils of Mental Time Travel," Alan Richardson defers to recent advances in neuropsychology on the plasticity of memory to demonstrate how Austen's novels exhibit an uncanny overlap between the apparently distinct mental faculties of memory and imagination. Like Richardson, I explore various scenes in which memory becomes infiltrated by imaginative desire in my chapter on Jane Austen's *Mansfield Park*. However, my mediational account of social memory in Austen's novel draws a conclusion inverse to Richardson's. Whereas Richardson reads Fanny's imaginative memories as productive of pain or "peril," I show how they reconstruct reality so as to produce healing pleasures.[101] To use Kay Young's term for Austenian neuroplasticity, I read *Mansfield Park* as a crowning moment in an eighteenth-century novelistic tradition of "resilience."[102]

Most important, cognitive literary theorists such as Alan Richardson read eighteenth-century empiricism as a direct precursor to neuroscientific models of memory, indicating that brain science today reifies epistemological theories of recollection in the Enlightenment.[103] My readings of Enlightenment philosophies of mind in this introduction has aimed to undo this threaded history by taking a nuanced look at how eighteenth-century empiricists categorize memory and imagination as discrete mental functions.[104]

When it comes to memory, I find that historical epistemology and contemporary brain science are at odds. Nevertheless, Richardson's neuroscientific readings of imagination and recollection in nineteenth-century literature set a precedent for reconsidering memory in the origins of the English novel, which was a major inspiration and foundation for Jane Austen's work.

All these diverse disciplinary approaches attempt to characterize memory's malleable and creative nature, but early novelistic mindscapes best capture memory's curative powers. Many of history's earliest novelists found pleasure in the possibilities of what memory could do to change our account of things. Most strikingly, they did so at a time when empiricism, the great investment in the truth of remembered sensation, pervaded philosophy, science, and culture. Even as they register somatic and emotional pain, the eighteenth-century novels I consider in this book seek to override the materialism that the Enlightenment has become famous for. They traverse unique territories beyond the nervous matter of the brain and body and in this way foreshadow the imaginative spirit of Romantic poesy. Eighteenth-century novels evoke qualities reminiscent of Hume's or Coleridge's imagination; as an intelligent faculty and a fictionalizing force, memory in the early novel alters (among other things) the memories of its characters and readers. These novels deliver an unexpected historical approach to memory, one that reveals the enticing and transformational powers of minds willfully to change their circumstances and their stories so as to survive sensation and render it pleasing.

Memory Fictions

This book is organized around four descriptive terms for recollection that early novel studies has long adopted so as to convey memory's epistemological and mimetic qualities. Trauma, *Bildung*, quotation, and nostalgia are memory structures that traditionally depend on cyclical patterns of repetition. (This is true, I would argue, even of the *Bildungsroman* novel, which is traditionally known for mapping individual growth only by *repeating* social norms through processes of assimilation.)[105] However, by turning to early novels as my case studies for what I call "memory fiction," I challenge our structural assumptions and discover that such novelistic memories do not merely repeat or return (as we might expect from trauma and quotation or Enlightenment associationism more generally). My readings of *Tristram*

Shandy, Evelina, Celestina, and *Mansfield Park* all overturn notions of memory as a traumatic, chronological, or mimetic faculty that assimilates, preserves, and repeats information from the outside world. By departing from some of the conventional ways we have talked about empirical memory in Enlightenment novels, I set aside the idea of memory as a rote process of learned cognitive patterns that habitually imitates what has come before. Narratological studies of structures like trauma, *Bildung*, quotation, and nostalgia have reinforced this empirical idea of memory without accounting for the ways that the early novel frees itself from these strict ideational patterns.

The authors featured in this book consciously adopt seminal memory structures in their narratives only to overturn them: a soldier who alters his personal war history so as to fortify his dismembered body, a young woman who enters society only to dismantle patriarchy and its history of rape, a young writer who quotes her male predecessors only to challenge their traditions of poetic remembrance, and two castaways whose fanciful memories cause them to shape and territorialize strange, new homelands. Added to these is the story of modernity's readers, whose own imagined memories are mediated by these novels' social networks while sharing their Enlightenment projects of world-making.

My history begins with Daniel Defoe's *Robinson Crusoe*, wherein memory still savors of empirical theories of recollection. Defoe's novel envisions memory as a Lockean process of retention and recall. However, Crusoe's deferral to memory as a tool for making the necessary things he lacks on his island sets us up for a different kind of memory that evolves throughout history's first novels. From even this early moment in the novel's origins, making and memory are miraculously aligned. Thus memory begins to exceed Locke's account as it extends into the world through activities of formal craftwork,[106] becoming a tool of survival that allows Crusoe to reshape his environment.

Chapter 2 counters traumatic readings of war injury in Laurence Sterne's *Tristram Shandy*. In turning to Uncle Toby's obsession with creating military maps and models, I argue that Toby's "trauma" is not in fact a trauma at all but something like its antithesis: a conscious remembrance that allays distress—a sealing, not a "speaking," of his wound that converts pain into pleasure and transforms his personal history.[107] Chapter 3 revises ideological notions of the *Bildungsroman* by recasting it as a story of memory growth. Frances Burney's *Evelina* invokes archetypes of the "she-tragedy" to posit a feminist message that reveals how memory mediates and overturns historical outcomes. As Evelina's thinking becomes less reactive and automatic, she gains an ability to survive and overcome situations that pose unremitting threats to her female virtue. Evelina's mind evolves according to its environment so that she can consciously avoid personal harm (rape) and change the reader's social expectations.

Chapter 4 challenges literary understandings of quotation as evidence of memory's mimetic nature. In Charlotte Smith's *Celestina,* quotation changes literary form and the status quo of feeling, taking minds, through memory, into new and healing contexts. In addition to inciting activities of production (for citing other authors inspires Celestina to write sonnets of her own), quotation invites the reader to participate in heuristic processes of remembrance and rearrangement. Chapter 5 builds on the work of Nicholas Dames to further reclaim the role of nostalgia in Jane Austen's *Mansfield Park*. Drawing on theories of transacted remembrance, this chapter demonstrates how memories borrow from acts of reading and the thoughts of others to heal psychic distress and create pleasing fantasies. Austen sees the enticing power of fiction writing as a practice of wish fulfillment, and yet wishes come true by way of their entanglement with memory. Memory is what makes illusion possible, what renders fiction real. However, the way that memories and desires are acquired in *Mansfield Park* can be as elusive as Austen's allegory of the ever-evolving hedgerow.

On the one hand, I am interested in where memories come from (if they can be said to have an origin at all). In the novels examined in chapters 2 through 5, memories are not simply derived from individual sense experience as per empirical models of cognition. Rather, they are easily transacted through dialogue and reading. These novelistic memories are never strictly personal; at no point do they become cordoned off from the world. For this reason, they continually adapt and change according to new experiences and interpersonal exchanges. Such novelistic memories, therefore, never preserve data in the form of permanent inscriptions. This is the case for the novel reader and also for the characters in the novels who talk, and bond, and read. Toby Shandy transacts new memories from the British newspapers that change the original memory of his traumatic war wound. Celestina's memories are influenced by reading mid-century sensibility literature; this affects the way she writes her own history both in poetic contexts and at the level of the novel's plot. Mr. Rushworth in *Mansfield Park* borrows a memory from his wife's desires expressed in conversation, and Jane Austen implies the actions prompted by this memory set in motion the course of Maria's infidelity. The impulse to break with ideological memory in *Evelina* reveals a darker side to transacted memories, but the idea that thoughts run between minds occurs even in this novel. Such accounts of the social origins of memory remind us of Hume's idea of the imagination and the powerful influence that the impressions of other people have on our own minds.

Nevertheless, what happens to these memories as they alter forms in the world extends beyond what even Hume imagined. For memories in each of these novels perform the work they do in specific environmental contexts. Each of the five novels I consider exposes memory's ability to alter forms in the world. It is no surprise that they stage scenes where memory can, as it were, work its magic. On Crusoe's island, on Toby's bowling green, in Mrs. Beaumont's garden, in the wild isles of the Hebrides, on the banks of Sotherton, in Fanny's East room, memory makes a material difference. It changes forms, events, and narratives—how characters and readers act and think.[108] When Eliza Bennet walks into the family picture gallery at the Pemberley estate, she is carrying out an early novelistic tradition that perhaps began when Toby Shandy first set foot on the rood and a half of ground behind Shandy Hall.

In these works, memory is a force that reenvisions and revises form, all the while growing and evolving as the characters engage with new environments, networks, persons, and things. For neuroscience, a memory error is a "fuzzy trace." Developed by Charles Brainerd and Valerie Reynal, fuzzy trace theory explains why memory errors occur.[109] They posit that memory is associational, but also housed in fragmented ways throughout the brain, and thereby combined and recombined over time and experienced ad infinitum. For the literary etymologist, to err is "to wander."[110] What if memories were not confined to a closed system? What multitudinous forms and structures might memories alter as they wander into new pathways, into infinite sets of combination? Throughout the five novels studied in this book, I persistently encounter literary evidence of memory's creative genius. Memory has the power to make, remake, and mend; it alters objects, nature, feelings, and history. It intervenes in systems and worlds, revealing its curious power to heal wounds and suture gaps.

❖ CHAPTER 1 ❖

Accounting for Crusoe's Survival

How Memory Matters

No man is an island, entire of itself; every man is a piece of the continent, a part of the main. If a clod be washed away by the sea, Europe is the less, as well as if a promontory were.
—JOHN DONNE, Meditation 17.

John Donne's famous homily "no man is an island" seems to haunt the narrative of Daniel Defoe's *Robinson Crusoe.* Thanks to Defoe, our fascination with the story of one man lost on a desert island persists in the cultural imagination. Of course, over the past century we have come to read the novel as much more than a history of desertion, individualism, or solitude. As a survival narrative, *Robinson Crusoe* is about the mind's power to overcome the conditions of its physical environment. In this sense, Defoe's fiction stages a dramatization of how the mind interfaces with the world.

Critical readings of *Robinson Crusoe* have come faintly to echo a Romantic philosophy of nature and the imagination. The assumption that "nature requires human ingenuity"[1] to make it serviceable has easily led us down the path of presuming that Crusoe's survival and his penchant for making things should be attributed to the work of imagination.[2] This is the gist of arguments like those of Jayne Lewis, who ascribes an "imaginative background" to the novel,[3] or Michael Seidel, who claims that Defoe's narrative really exists in the "imagined" or "supplemental . . . realm" of the text. Defoe uses the term "imagination," Seidel argues, "to chart a parallel narrative universe that exists in the mind at all times as potential."[4]

And yet not only does Crusoe encounter others on his island—indigenous peoples, animals, and companionate things (becoming the crazy cat lady version of a British colonizer)—but he brings a virtual world of *past experience* to his survival narrative. For someone like John Locke, it would be significant that Crusoe was not born on his island, and even more so that his story does not begin here, that is to say in medias res, with the moment of Crusoe's marooning sea wreckage. Crusoe arrives having traveled the world and colonized the Caribbean.

Neither imagination nor Providence alone can account for Crusoe's survival on the island.[5] Rather, another invisible agent is responsible for Crusoe's uncanny capacity to endure and adapt to conditions and circumstances of distress, and that is his memory. Crusoe's famous "ingenuity" and his instincts toward survival are owing to his memories. What is more, these memories are not entirely his own but are borrowed from other cultures, persons, sites, and social systems.

Crusoe's recollections inform his ability to adapt to new environments; they territorialize and transform. In an effort to make the new look something like the old, they turn the old into something rather new. Nor is memory a mere systematic trope of colonization in the novel. Rather, it lends new cognitive meanings to colonial history, bringing fuzziness to the borderlines that fail to separate nations and peoples, personal and global histories. Defoe gives us a picture of the traveler who comes to be a "clod . . . washed away at sea," showing how a past "Europe is the less" in trying to become something more. In its reflections on colonization, *Robinson Crusoe* likewise adopts the island as a self-canceling metaphor for the mind. Far from home, Crusoe's cognition is subject to constant colonization. Thought is not contained or circumscribed; it is not something personal or entirely *owned*. Rather, Crusoe's memories traverse time, place, and self in surprisingly global ways. This is a story about a man who goes from *taking things* to *making things*. As Crusoe finds his resources running out, memories from his boyhood and his global travels drift into his mind. These memories assist him with the means to recognize raw materials on the island, but they also become legacies of craftmanship that provide him with the knowledge of how to transform those materials into basic, survivalist things. In this, *Robinson Crusoe* tells a tale of how and why memory matters. It speaks of memory's capaciousness—its ability to contain worlds, cross continental divides, and transform the most seemingly trivial things into life-sustaining wonders.

Personal Things

A critical focus on the relationship between mind and matter, person and thing, has long prevailed in studies of *Robinson Crusoe* and has consequently shaped our definitions of how early novels "personate" things. [6] For some, this is a story of man's mastery over things.[7] For others, things, like events, master and triumph over mankind,[8] and persons become reduced to their thinglike status,[9] as things begin to impress themselves on the world of the mind.[10]

In *Defoe's Narratives,* John Richetti insists that a reciprocal structure always exists between the self and the objects perceived by that self. Supposing that the matter at hand in *Robinson Crusoe* is about man's process of converting matter into things, Richetti argues that Crusoe "refines nature into that which sustains and nourishes [him]."[11] This kind of mediation, or assimilation, between the self and its environment is something like Lynn Festa's much later argument about our desire to "fit" into the world of the things. In "Crusoe's Isle of Misfit Things," Festa remarks on the critical discourse as being deeply invested in how objects and subjects "mediate" or "constitute" one another.[12] Like others before her, Festa is interested in the indistinct margins that blur the difference between minds and the objects they encounter in the world. Her argument about how the "heterogenous elements" of the novel attempt to make persons and things "fit" into one another through a logic of description, approximation, and the creative work of the imagination causes us to reexamine the distinction between persons and their possessions. The very idea of human ingenuity as mediation calls into question the role of human consciousness as it relates to animals, objects, and environments. Is human thought simply a matter of fitting into, or fitting together, various other matters?

Annette Baier's essay, "Cartesian Persons," offers an answer to this puzzle by providing us with a less spatial and more temporal account of cognitive reasoning; it refers to a type of memory that captures not facts but "the *history* of a mind."[13] This special form of consciousness is distinct from animal thinking since it is not defined by a responsiveness to stimuli alone but by reflection—a "reference to what is absent ... or could have been once present, so it requires an understanding of the past (and future) tenses."[14] Baier is speaking of what we might call long-term or autobiographical memory. In a related essay titled "Mixing Memory and Desire," she turns to the topic of animal versus human consciousness when she examines what she dubs memory's "personal" facets[15]:

> There is a difference between attributing memory and attributing *memories,* somewhat like the difference between attributing purpose and attributing intentions. The individuation of memories and intentions is what seems impossible in the case of animals.... We can of course speak of the cat's remembering how to do things, of its remembering and so recognizing its former owner, but we cannot separate its memory of him from its recognition of him, and we would not... speak of it having vivid or dim memories. [On the other hand, humans act and think according to a] ... temporally continuous story consisting of intended exercises.[16]

For Baier, human consciousness is "continuous"; it is related to a human capacity for temporal sequencing. She distinguishes between memory as a self-avowed narrative of our intentions and actions and memories as mere recognitions. In doing so, she hits on a special quality of human consciousness that approximates current neuropsychological models.[17] When considered alongside Festa's and Richetti's mediational accounts of matter and cognition, Baier's autobiographical memory, as a temporal theory of mind, ensures that persons will not become exactly like their pets or properties even as they interact with forms in the world.

Thinkers like Baier address a form of conscious memory that amounts to the human capacity for storytelling. Although little work has been done on memory's creative operations in *Robinson Crusoe,* a whole host of critics have addressed the topic of storytelling in the narrative. From J. Paul Hunter's and G. A. Starr's early identification of the text as "spiritual autobiography" to Stuart Sherman's notion of Crusoe's diarylike journal that practices diurnal structures of timekeeping, from Michael Seidel's observation of the text as "memoir" to David Marshall's commentary on the pervasiveness of autobiographical acts in the novel, *Robinson Crusoe* has long been understood as a text that constantly references its own textuality.[18] Metaphors for memory's relationship to the processes of storytelling abound—archetypal mementos and memorandums appear everywhere as indexical objects. Like other critics before me, I address some of these metaphors for memory in the novel, but my focus is less on the physicality of the text itself as a record of events and objects and more on how memory operates to transform things.

I begin by addressing Crusoe's false assumption that he can find deliverance from crisis in appealing to God or in searching his environment in order to demonstrate that Crusoe's mental possessions are the key to his survival. Throughout this chapter, I argue that memory must always inform the cognitive operations of thinking and imagining to make survival possible. I do so by tracking the many necessities that Crusoe makes from the resources of memory. Unlike the other novels I discuss in this book, my account of memory in *Robinson Crusoe* takes its foundation from empiricist ideas of what memory is. I consider Lockean recognition and retention (brought about by sensation) as fundamental aspects of remembrance that allow Crusoe to perceive and comprehend the potential use value of raw materials in his environment. However, I go on to address the narrative components of memory, the moments in the novel when Crusoe links past stories of experience to his present circumstances. In this temporal quality of memory, Defoe begins to exceed empiricist models of sensational recollection within the novel form by revealing how remembrance allows Crusoe to traverse time, make things, survive his present, change history, and project into his future.

This temporal consciousness resembles, but does not perfectly fit with, Locke's idea of time in his *Essay*. Time, according to Locke, is a "measurement" of motion and duration.[19] (Even in his definition of time, Locke cannot get beyond spatial and material analogies.) Duration is another kind of "distance" less permanent than space or matter; it is the "fleeting and perpetually perishing ... Succession" of ideas that pass through the mind.[20] Duration is the distance between any two apparent ideas that organize themselves in our mental landscape sequentially and linearly; we reflect on these ideas and thus "know that we do exist."[21] Amit Yahav has aptly called this moment in the *Essay* Locke's version of Descartes' *cogito ergo sum* wherein Locke posits, "I think therefore I endure."[22] In this sense, duration is a mode of cognition, and cognition is a mode of survival.

In Locke's system, however, thinking endures even as it perishes. His Cartesian maxim only sets Locke up for a theological reflection that soon comes at the end of chapter 15 in book 2 of the *Essay*. Here, Locke distinguishes between infinite God and finite man. Whereas God can see "all things past and to come ... under the same view," man suffers because he has: "Thoughts ... but of yesterday, and he knows not what tomorrow will bring forth. What is once passed, he can never recal; and what is yet to come, he cannot make present."²³ Insofar as Locke has defined memory as an activity of seeing again, the citation from Job ("he can never recal") may strike the reader as a strange interlude. I read this statement as evidence of Locke's desire to separate temporal consciousness (duration and time) from any tangible substance, or real material things. Locke's spatial analogies are emphasized here as *mere* metaphors. We might choose to read the word "make" rather literally; humankind cannot "make" the past a physical presence again, nor can we make much of our future. Locke's meditation on duration thus ends with an almost Puritanical gesture toward predestination.²⁴ Temporal consciousness implies awareness, not control; to endure is to watch our own thoughts passing by. Although we may reflect on our thoughts, we cannot make anything from them; we cannot change them, or even use them to change our future.

Crusoe's creed, *I remember therefore I endure,* posits that memories make material things that allow him to survive and that these memories can thereby charter new pathways into the future. Memory is both emotional and functional in *Robinson Crusoe.* Often, it serves as a secular epiphany in the narrative that leads to self-conscious experience and inspires action. Moreover, memories become useful only when they scale beyond the personal—when they chart global courses so as to revise Crusoe's approach to creation. Crusoe makes many things on his island, but these projects only satisfy his desires when they take the shape of remembered images—and when they are drawn from memories that disturb Crusoe's nationalist ideals of aesthetic value.

Crusoe's memory is the key to his survivalist know-how that quickly becomes a tool of transformation—the journal, more a sketchbook of artistic process than the immutable ink blots it claims to be. I begin by addressing three aspects of Lockean memory—recognition, retention, and recall—that provide for Crusoe when he lacks material things necessary for his survival. By tracking activities of making throughout the journal portions of the narrative, I show how these various aspects of remembrance become entangled in Crusoe's creative projects. But what happens when matter is not merely absent but runs out? As Crusoe's story carries on even after he has expended all the ink necessary for recording his experience, Defoe intimates at something beyond empirical memory as that perfect record-keeper of events in time. The novel in some sense asks us to envision memory's unique tie to works of fiction and imagination.²⁵ As the source of Crusoe's resourcefulness, as the phenomenal force that pervades and produces all things, memory differs from its creations, which themselves take on many tangible forms in *Robinson Crusoe*. But these forms are sourced from what is *not* in, or on, the island itself but rather from several casual and causal thoughts, gathered up in time.

Crusoe's Dwellings: Finders, Keepers

When Crusoe lands on the shore of the island, a pervasive feeling of hopelessness overwhelms his consciousness. This feeling comes from a direct observation of his present surroundings. Overturning an empiricist emphasis on the connection between sight and knowledge, Defoe subtly suggests that the sentiment of survival, along with the capacity to survive, does not necessarily come from a physical observation of one's environment or surroundings.[26] Rather, survival is a state of mind that links the material conditions of our environment to the abstract forces of consciousness[27]:

> I began to look round me to see what kind of Place I was in, and what was next to be done . . . neither did I see any Prospect before me, . . .
> All the Remedy that offer'd to my Thoughts at that Time, was, to get up into a thick bushy Tree like a Firr, but thorny, which grew near me, and where I resolv'd to sit all Night, and consider the next Day what Death I should dye, for as yet I saw no Prospect of Life. (35–36)

In a brilliant pun on the word "Prospect," Defoe disentangles hope, futurity, and imagination from one's physical and immediate sight. Crusoe's narrative begins with a reliance on an empirical system of thought, as action here is predicated on observation: he considers what is "next to be done" through immediate observations of his environment. The assumption is that Crusoe's actions should be anticipated by sight and spatial calculation. However, Defoe quickly overturns this empirical method of mental mapping when, in the face of unfamiliar territory, Crusoe feels easily discouraged: seeing no "Prospect before" him, he imagines no "Prospect of Life."

The discourse of firsthand experience is not enough to buoy Crusoe up in a situation of distress. He fails to navigate new sights/sites, at once foreign and unrecognizable. Thus Defoe begins to hint at a different source for survival, one that demonstrates a subtle yet surprising relational discourse of mind and world wherein one's prospects are not mere derivatives of environment or experiment, since they are not simply found in one's immediate surroundings, or by way of direct, sensory observation. In this manner, Crusoe's literal prospect (i.e., his physical point of view) and his temporal "prospects" (i.e., his future) are no longer synonymous.

The gap between these two readings of the word "prospect," one spatial, the other temporal, functions as a near invisible sign to the unassuming first-time reader since it remains yet unseen by Crusoe himself, whose personal account of survival in its initial stages is forever punctuated by an empiricist rhetoric of observation and a deep faith in the life-giving potential of firsthand matter. In a profane reliance on environment, Crusoe expects his island, like his yet unacknowledged God, to provide for him. In this manner, Crusoe rests his fate on what is given, or derived, firsthand, from immediate observation.

Returning to the site of the sunken ship, he expects to glean hope from waste, provision from wreckage. The result is not one of complete satisfaction, even though matter in some sense will later enable Crusoe to create something from (almost) nothing[28]:

> I first got three of the Seamens Chests . . . and lower'd them down upon my Raft; the first of these I fill'd with Provision . . . there had been some Barly and Wheat together, but, to my great Disappointment, I found afterwards that the Rats had eaten or spoil'd it all; as for the Liquors, I found several Cases of Bottles belonging to our Skipper. . . . While I was doing this, I found the Tyde began to flow . . . and it was after long searching that I found out the Carpenter's Chest. (38)

A first reading of this passage might cause the reader to think that Crusoe is being resourceful. Saving things from the wreckage of his experience that might later serve him; he seems to have a special kind of foresight into future necessity. But Crusoe also plays the part of the grave robber who, like the rats, is a mere scavenger that survives only by depending on the bad fortune of others. Such subsistence defines survival through acts of taking ("I got") or plundering things from an open grave. The predominant verb in these first portions of Crusoe's narrative is "I found," and finding here implies theft. Again and again, Crusoe places his faith in the world of found objects. His imagined future, his listless hopes at survival, are initially erected on an act of giving himself over to the conditions of his environment. Like the novice scientist, he places complete certitude in his findings.

Such language continues in Crusoe's initial explorations of his newfound island:

> I perceiv'd that there was some Indraft of the Water, and consequently I hop'd to find some Creek or River there, which I might make use of as a Port to get to Land with my Cargo.
>
> As I imagin'd, so it was, there appear'd before me a little opening of the Land, and I found a strong Current of the Tide set into it, so I guided my Raft as well as I could to keep in the Middle of the Stream: But here I had like to have suffer'd a second Shipwreck ... for knowing nothing of the Coast, my Raft run a-ground at one End of it upon a Shoal.... I at length found my self in the Mouth of a little River, with Land on both Sides, ... I look'd on both Sides for a proper Place to get to Shore, for I was not willing to be driven too high up the River, hoping in time to see some Ship at Sea, and therefore resolv'd to place my self as near the Coast as I could. (39)

The rhetoric here of the "middle passage" echoes the parable of Crusoe's first decision to go to sea. By putting aside the allegorical implications that critics have previously attributed to this archetype of wandering (its providential, Protestant, and ethical innuendo),[29] we note an important trend emerge in Crusoe's logic of experience, one that lends a different message to the archetype of exploration.

Ilse Vickars underscores how Crusoe's language is akin to that of the laboratory scientist who places faith in the tests of experience, but there is something amiss about the way Crusoe experiences, and experiments with, his environs.[30] Crusoe "perceives" an "Indraft" and "consequently hopes" to "find" a port. Just as in a scientific experiment, expectations arise as consequences of direct, initial perception. (One is tempted to consider Jane Austen's later warning about the nature of "first impressions.") Moreover, Crusoe's powers of perception do not stop here: "As I imagined so it was," Crusoe states. As hope arises from perception, imagination expects a repetition of experience. Crusoe is thinking here by way of David Hume's pattern of relational cognition—that he will continue to "find" on this island what he has always "found" and "known" before. Unfortunately for Crusoe, islands and minds do not work this way in Defoe's novel.

Crusoe's deductions move from perception to imagination and back to perception again; indeed, experience repeats itself, but not in the manner that Crusoe expects it to. Relying on direct observation only leads Crusoe into a situation of a near second shipwreck. Crusoe "finds" his way into dangerous waters only to expect that he will likewise "find" his way into survival and salvation. Floating along, Crusoe's mind gives itself over to his surroundings. Finding himself at the river's mouth, Crusoe "looks" ashore for his "proper Place"; "hoping in time to see some Ship," he stations himself near the coastline. Although Crusoe claims to place his faith in time, it becomes eminently clear that Crusoe's expectations, his beliefs and understanding are all founded on place, on a spatial comprehension of his world. "Self" is something "found" in this passage by way of a mere consciousness of situation. By putting himself in the proper place, Crusoe anticipates that his environment will deliver him from distress. But such expectations are easily frustrated, suspended, and prolonged. Survival, Defoe implies, is no material matter; it cannot be sought in our physical surroundings.

In this manner, Crusoe's initial efforts toward domestic preservation all err in one direction; his work is persistently predicated on the maxim, "Seek and ye shall find." "My next Work was to view the Country, and seek a proper Place for my Habitation," Crusoe narrates (39). This first home is designed as a place to "stow" goods. Unsurprisingly, Crusoe's tent is no safe house in the sense of preserving his life by way of bodily shelter but rather is a container for found things. Even time is described in these initial passages as a "thing" of value, a commodity that can be wasted or gained in the procuring of other goods, and Crusoe boasts that he has "lost no time" in getting "every thing" out of the wreck that might be "useful." Crusoe "fence[s]" himself in, "enclos[ing] all [his] Goods" in a "kind of Dwelling" that derives from having "consulted several Things in [his] Situation." To "dwell" in this instance is to live, and think, through the preservation of things. Crusoe places "all these Things" in his tent before him, and then digresses in his narration, claiming to "go back to some other Things which took up some of [his] Thoughts" (43–45, passim). The life of the mind in these early descriptions harps on the Lockean metaphor of the cabinet or container. Defoe couches Crusoe's thinking in a materialistic rhetoric, as matter is preserved and contained in the name of survival.

Of course, this initial "dwelling" amounts merely to a flimsy tent designed to preserve and protect our hero's material possessions. Crusoe soon improves upon and "enlarge[s]" it. The act of dwelling as thinking in Defoe's novel also quickly gives way to a more sophisticated form of thought, one that is reflective, reflexive, and retrospective in nature. In this manner, Defoe's metaphors for thought and life begin to veer from the famous empirical metaphor of the mind as a collection.

What critics have called Crusoe's famous style of rhetorical casuistry[31] marks a transition in the way things are accounted for on the island. Crusoe's story slides effortlessly into another kind of discourse, one that abstractly searches for "something" beyond his immediate environment, that "check[s his] Thoughts," causing him to consult "Reason" on the "Subject of [his] present Condition." Moreover, Crusoe's "considerations" about Providence describe mental reasoning as fueled by the cognitive work of memory: "Pray remember," Crusoe commands himself in thinking upon his fate, "Where are the rest" of your companions? It "occur[s] to [him] again" how he has been "furnish'd for [his] Subsistence" (47).

This shift in narrative structure and style suggests that remembered experience spurs on the will to survive; it also inspires Crusoe to keep a "Reckoning of Time" and to write about the experience of his condition.[32] The latter account begins as a projected "State of Affairs in Writing," one that mimics economic styles of accounting as the conditions of "Debtor and Creditor."[33] This list of pros and cons is not merely an examination of the works of Providence but, simply put, is a categorical record of "Comforts ... enjoy'd" versus "Miseries ... suffer'd." The famous account of "Good" and "Evil" in fact tells the common story of a mind attempting to adapt itself to the conditions of distress (49–50).

These first accounts in the novel that precede the official journal entries are telling. Crusoe is suddenly motivated to keep a calendrical tracking of time. This unexplained desire magically "com[es] into" Crusoe's "Thoughts," only soon to give way to a contemplation of his distress. In between these two accounts, of time and situation, Crusoe's pattern of thinking begins to shift. In usual fashion, he contemplates his possessions, securing his things by way of a mental stocktaking: "In the next place we are to observe, that among the many things which I brought out of the Ship in the several Voyages, which, as above mention'd, I made to it, I got several things of less Value" (48). As Crusoe reviews his actions (and voyages) through a kind of observational accounting of value, he begins to observe not what is *there*, but what is *not there*. Taking stock causes Crusoe to muse on his lacks, and with that the former rhetoric of the empirical scientist gives way to that of the economist, pulling the narrative into new realms of abstraction. We move from things to *no things*: "And this put me in mind that I wanted many things, notwithstanding all that I had amass'd together . . . [the] Want of Tools made every Work I did go on heavily. . . . But what need I ha' been concern'd at the Tediousness of any thing I had to do, seeing I had time enough to do it in" (48–49). Crusoe's accounts of time and things cause him to think of time as no longer material or finite but as an infinite abstraction that provides when matter does not. Time is the tool that will allow Crusoe to make something out of nothing.

Moreover, as Crusoe weighs evil against good, misery against comfort, like the successful cognitive behaviorialist, he hits on the following insight: "Having now brought my Mind a little to relish my Condition, and given over looking out to Sea to see if I could spy a Ship, I say, giving over these things, I began to apply my self to accommodate my way of Living, and to make things as easy to me as I could" (50). Crusoe's epiphany captures the paradox of hope in hopelessness. By "giving over" the search for "things," he can begin to dwell in new ways upon his self. No longer looking toward the horizon, sight is cast inward, not outward, and the limitlessness of human experience, the capacity to survive in the harshest of conditions, is a kind of mind-over-matter insight. The decision to "accommodate living" not by looking for things but by making them irrevocably alters the account. Through this new self-conscious management of mind and world, Crusoe officially transitions from the keeper of things to the maker of things.[34]

The metaphorical evidence for this change in mental state or perspective is undeniable. Crusoe's manner of "dwelling" transitions from a flimsy tent, open to every shift in his material environment, to a cave, walled in from external distress.[35] Before he begins his journalistic account, he summits another promontory and looks "out to Sea" in hopes of seeing a ship. Seeing nothing at sea becomes an archetype for helplessness. By depending on what he cannot see, Crusoe embodies the psychological metaphor of a man lost at sea. The result is a mind bent on the ever-elusive prospects of an unforgiving "fancy": "Then [I would] fancy at a vast Distance I spy'd a Sail, please my self with the Hopes of it, and then after looking steadily till I was almost blind, lose it quite, and sit down and weep like a Child, and thus encrease my Misery by my Folly" (52). Once again, Crusoe's pure reliance on immediate and direct sight, or perception, leads only to hopeless disappointment. It turns out to be a miserable, errant, and "blind" faith. To be sure, we can read a Protestant ethos into this critical characterization of "seeing and believing," but Defoe also comments on the cognitive facets of surviving conditions of distress. Crusoe attempts to alleviate all "discomposure of mind" by writing a literal *compo*sition, thus exposing the journal as a relic that testifies to the healing powers of memory (51–52, passim). Hope is fruitless, Defoe suggests, when not tempered and composed by the work of conscious recollection.

Of course, "dwelling"—as a cognitive state of thinking, living, and perceiving—is neither exclusively tentlike nor cavelike in Defoe's ultimate cognitive model. Crusoe's thoughts throughout the narrative never run in a unidirectional path; they are not simply cast outward or inward. The journal's testament to the formative powers of memory never leaves physical conditions or sights behind but rather demonstrates a dialectical relationship between mind and world wherein memory shapes and enhances the realities of present and future experience.

Making Things from Memory: Beyond Recognition

A pattern emerges throughout Crusoe's journal wherein memory and time provide the necessary materials for survival, while the mere search for things within one's immediate environment always proves fruitless. However, it takes Crusoe some time to abandon his old methods. In the first pages of the journal, the verb "to find" disappears in frequency, only to be replaced by a similar verb, "to see." "To see," but not "to find," suggests that acquisitions have *mental*, not merely appropriated or *possessive*, value. Nevertheless, Crusoe's approach continues to adopt an empirical understanding of the world (i.e., seeing lies at the foundation of knowing) with this all but slight shift in diction. What is "seen" here is described as something unknown, or not previously seen, since it does not align with Crusoe's English history of experience: "I saw many Sorts of Sea Fowls which I did not understand," Crusoe writes (54). As per John Locke's alignment of memory with knowledge, remembered experience lies at the foundation of understanding. In this manner, Defoe demonstrates how recognition is the first step by which memory begins to render itself serviceable for survival.

These experiences of discovery, however, complicate empiricist accounts of memory once the narrative transitions from observational accounting to the story of making or forming things in order to survive. Crusoe's first effort at making something is rather unsuccessful: "*Nov. 7*. Now it begain to be settled fair Weather. The 7th, 8th, 9th, 10th, and Part of the 12th (for the 11th was Sunday) I took wholly up to make me a Chair, and with much ado brought it to a tolerable Shape, but never to please me, and even in the making I pull'd it in Pieces several times. *Note,* I soon neglected my keeping Sundays, for omitting my Mark for them on my Post, I forgot which was which" (54). The side note about failing to keep the proper time has obvious religious implications, wherein the observation of the Sabbath becomes important for Crusoe's working efforts at making things. As Crusoe destroys objects on his first creative attempts, his frustrations begin to correlate with the forgetting, or omission, of time. Ironically, by forgetting to rest, Crusoe fails to form the object of a chair, designed for resting. The episode begs a question of chicken-and-egg semantics: does Crusoe's failure to make the thing of rest cause him to forget to rest, or is it the other way around? Together, the event and its footnote imply that making is successful not when the "shape," or form, of the thing is "pleasing," or quite fitting, to our aesthetic expectations. Rather, making succeeds when its aims are survivalist in nature. This is key, for the kinds of memories that effectively assist Crusoe undercut his nationalist expectations about form. Use and survival are universal drives, and Crusoe's circumstances require a kind of memory that crosses the borderlines of both place (i.e., nation) and time.

Crusoe is able to make a shovel because he finds the proper wood, but the wood is found only because Crusoe *recognizes* the tree "which, in the *Brasils* they call the *Iron Tree*" that allows him to make a shovel whose "Handle [is] exactly shap'd like ours in *England*" (54). This causes him to point out the shovel's many deficiencies since it only partially conforms to his native expectations of design and fashion. Crusoe's nationalist prejudice implicitly subverts the notion that memory (and creation) can be culturally or personally contained. His ability to identify the iron tree implicates a memory of his time "in the *Brasils.*" As use value trumps aesthetic taste, Defoe all the while hints that the memory of things, both foreign and familiar, is what assists Crusoe in his efforts at survival. Moreover, it is this composite nature of memory, its capacity for universal contamination and influence, that makes it serviceable.

Whether resources are readily available or not, undergirding Crusoe's many efforts at making things is the implicit work of cosmopolitan memory. This deployment of memory involves various related mental faculties: recognition, retention, and recall. All cohere in the creative capacities of memory to alter present circumstances through the making of new forms. Defoe implicates memory's layered powers in Crusoe's expressed desire for a basket or barrow to contain his working tools: "I was still deficient, for I wanted a Basket or a Wheel-barrow, a Basket I could not make by any Means, having no such things as Twigs that would bend to make Wicker Ware, at least none yet found out; and as to a Wheel-barrow, I fancy'd I could make all but the Wheel, but that I had no Notion of, neither did I know how to go about it . . . so I gave it over" (54–55). Crusoe accounts for his initial failures at making things when he complains about the lack of raw materials (recognizable matter) accompanied by a lack of know-how (notions, or "how to" memories), suggesting that things are formed by way of both matter and method. Fancying a thing, or imagining its form, is a useless endeavor of wishful thinking without memory. So the narrative returns to these objects and projects (like this one of the basket) only to suggest that what was lacking all along was not the raw material but rather memory's rewiring methods.

Expecting to find things on the island, even expecting that things must conform to Crusoe's preset notions of English form, sets him up for disappointment and failure. Matter on the island will not appear as it once did in Crusoe's homeland, and thus survival only comes from forgetting one's expectations so as to assume the adaptive powers of memory. Memory becomes the source of Crusoe's resourcefulness when he ceases merely to repeat past experience (habit) and begins to create new forms out of creatively spliced and combined memories.

Crusoe's new environment requires that he create new associations between old things. The reference to Crusoe's recognition of a Brasilian wood from which he tries to make an English shovel begs the question of whether or not Crusoe's imagination (his vision of form) is more at fault than his memory. What if the form were to refit itself to the matter at hand? Memory and imagination must work together, conforming to a new, less familiar logic so as to assist Crusoe in his survivalist endeavors. Memory, Defoe suggests, is reliable only when it is pliable. In this manner, Crusoe is more than a historical icon of the self-made man or the hunter-gatherer.[36] He is an emblem of the creative and cosmopolitan forces of conscious memory.

Retaining Things

The importance of recognition to Crusoe's creative endeavors evinces Defoe's foundational reliance on empirical models of mind, which he ultimately embellishes upon as the journal's narrative of making continues. Memories are first implanted by way of empiricist notions of sight—the attentive glue that allows the mind to retain and recognize information in the world; they then take on evolutionary, transformational, and creative qualities as memories adapt to new environments, feelings, and situations. Take, for example, Crusoe's search for the Cassava root:

> I searched for the *Cassava* Root, which the *Indians* in the Climate make their Bread of, but I could find none. I saw large Plants of Alloes, but did not then understand them. I saw several Sugar Canes, but wild, and for want of Cultivation, imperfect. I contented my self with these Discoveries for this Time, and came back musing with my self what Course I might take to know the Vertue and Goodness of any of the Fruits or Plants which I should discover, but could bring it to no Conclusion; for in short, I had made so little Observation while I was in the *Brasils*, that I knew little of the Plants in the Field, at least very little that might serve me to any Purpose now in my Distress. (72–73)

Crusoe's foraging yields no fruit because his memory is lacking. He knows that recalling his time in the Brasils may assist his present wants. However, having made so little observation then, he has no memories now. This empirical reliance on perception thus explains the failures of Crusoe's remembrance. Matter requires memory to be understood, or recognized. Similarly, Crusoe spends May third through June fifteenth trying to acquire material resources from the wreck, only to end up with pieces that cannot be fashioned into a proper boat because he lacks "knowledge," or rather recognition. When he states in the above passage, "I saw large plants of Alloes, but did not then understand them," he aligns "understanding" with recognition. To see is not enough; knowing usefulness requires a different account of experiential retention, one that relies on the felt, sensory qualities of memory.

As Cynthia Wall has argued, Crusoe's utilitarianism is also characterized by a certain reverence for the pleasure principle.[37] So many of the journal's accounts reveal the connection between memory and feeling. In a pithy record of events, Crusoe writes of June 17: "I spent in cooking the Turtle; I found in her three-score Eggs; and her Flesh was to me at that Time the most savoury and pleasant that ever I tasted in my Life, having had no Flesh, but of Goats and Fowls, since I landed in this horrid Place" (64).

Feeling here is what brings events to mind, and Crusoe's memory of time is influenced by feeling. Clearly, the turtle flesh is not really "the most savoury and pleasant" food that Crusoe has ever tasted in his life. Yet the hyperbole is accurate to the extent that it arises from the interrelationship between time and sensation. Alongside recognition, another foundational quality of memory is retention, and this occurs in the novel as per empirical models of impression. We retain what we feel most. As David Hume would have it, memories are defined by the forces of feeling. In this sensational approach, memory is characterized through its variable vividness—it is a comparative self-scanning device haunted by the echoes of past feelings.

Crusoe marks feelings with temporal tags, and in this manner time is also conceptualized sensorily. The present, the immediate past, and the distant past are all differentiated through registers of felt experience. Memory is both sensory and temporal; it structures and creates time subjectively. Yet Crusoe's experience of the turtle flesh also remarks on how memories revise the shades of feeling with time's passage and the introduction of new experiences. Even turtles taste good when one is starving on a desert island. The new experience of distress thus revises, reroutes and re-relativizes past feelings of pleasure, as memories change with time.

Crusoe's obsessive need to account for time, so as not to *lose it* but rather *put it to its use*,[38] so often leads him to speak of time as having a physical or embodied quality. Much like his predecessor, John Locke, Crusoe treats time as a material entity, marking calendar and seasonal time, and, as he repeatedly says, "dividing" it. This human tendency to account for time's passage not only dovetails with Locke's empiricist concept of durational time as so much mental distance or space but also resembles biblical rhetoric. Such a material approach to time seems in conflict with the passages in the journal wherein Crusoe becomes freed from the matter of things by searching his mind over his environment. However, it also indicates a mind-into-world relationship to one's external environment as time becomes bound up in acts of making. If time is an unwieldy entity, seemingly infinite and of endless supply, unlike the material things found on the island, then Crusoe's impulse is to control time, to give it bounds and make it finite. Hence his conservationist approach to time when he talks about his creative labors: "It cost me a Month," he continually laments. Has time become the new commodity that barely replaces Crusoe's fetish for things?

Not quite. Memory's attempt to organize time may take on the material, sensory, and finite qualities of empirical retention, recollection, and duration, but in Defoe's narrative the relationship between time and memory does not stop here. Memory also has the capacity to traverse time. Crusoe's calendar is an attempt to convert abstract entities such as time and feeling into matter; it is also a method of autobiographical accounting, a way of making memory not just associational but tangible. Thus memory, as so much time, takes on a conscious, intentional quality so that Crusoe can put it to use. In this sense, the calendar expresses a cultural fantasy and fallacy, the ability to make memories into something concrete and true. Of course, memory is not actually tangible; it simply gives rise to necessary materials that allow Crusoe to endure his island stay. It does so by providing (1) the capacity to recognize useful matter on the island and (2) the know-how to *convert* one kind of thing into another. This latter facet of memory (more evocative of Romantic than Enlightenment notions of mind) surfaces when Crusoe links memories of past narrative experiences to his present circumstance. Here is where time ceases to have a material quality and departs from empiricist notions of temporality as evidence of so much thought passing in the mind.

In this manner, the journal exposes time as not merely measured or accounted for but also as a central player in the shaping of Crusoe's self-consciousness.[39] Crusoe literally "finds himself" as resources cease to be delivered to him by Providence, fate, or his immediate environment:

> And now, in the managing my household Affairs, I found my self wanting in many Things, which I thought at first it was impossible for me to make, as indeed as to some of them it was; for *Instance*, I could never make a Cask to be hooped, I had a small Runlet or two, *as I observed before*, but I cou'd never arrive to the Capacity of making one of them, tho' I spent many Weeks about it; . . .
>
> In the next Place, I was at a great Loss for Candle; so that as soon as ever it was dark, which was generally by Seven-a-Clock, I was oblig'd to go to Bed: But I remembered the Lamp of Bees-wax with which I made Candles in my *African* Adventure, but I had none of that now; the only Remedy I had was, that when I had kill'd a Goat, I sav'd the Tallow, and with a little Dish made of Clay, which I bak'd in the Sun, to which I added a Wick of some Oakum, I made me a Lamp; and this gave me Light, tho' not a clear steady Light like a Candle. (57)

Within Crusoe's catalogued desires for things, we find two different types of material absence: there are the things Crusoe has but wants more of, and then there are the things that he simply lacks. Strangely enough, Crusoe cannot make more of what he has already been given; these things never multiply. He describes his inability to "make a Cask to be hooped" even though he already has "a small Runlet or two." Things taken from the external environment lead to an inability to "arrive [at] the Capacity of making." In this manner, Defoe excludes all possibility of subscribing to the politics of a gift economy on the island. Notably, in instances such as those of the cask, time is spent and wasted, yielding fruitless labor. Crusoe's phrase "tho' I spent many Weeks about it" implies an expectation that time, in infinite surplus, can and will supply Crusoe with what he desires. The hooping of the cask, however, also exposes Crusoe's pathological obsession with "it"; an inability to get beyond the things of our immediate environment only frustrates successful efforts at survival.

The next project Crusoe describes is of a different nature: he "wants" a candle in the most literal sense, describing the need for light as "a great Loss." What supplies this loss is not something given. Rather, memory "remedies" the absence of the thing. The want for candlelight triggers a brief narrative of Crusoe's African adventures wherein he remembers how he used to make candles from beeswax. Once again, memory crosses continental divides and is most efficacious when it adopts a cosmopolitan ethos. Realizing he lacks this raw material now does not deter Crusoe, since it is the *method of making*, reignited by memory, that fuels his fanciful search for some alternative thing capable of standing in for what is not presently there. One memory, from the more distant past, leads to another of the recent future, as beeswax gives way to goat tallow.

It is this narrative power of memory, its attentiveness not simply to feeling but to the histories of experience, that allows Crusoe to make, as it were, something from nothing. Memory endows Crusoe's mind with a godlike capacity of creation, and the language Defoe uses implicitly asks us to think about consciousness in this way, as having the ability to elevate the human mind over the stresses of the body or the discomforts of our environment. Memory's capacity to traverse time allows Crusoe to live in a space of the more than present, as the past folds in on his current affairs. Also, the ability to know and mark the hour of day ("Seven-a-Clock") leads to a desire to battle the limitations of natural time, its material strictures and finitudes.

Nevertheless, the passage's implicit revision of an empiricist archetype also revels in the fallibility of memory, in what neuroscience would later call "memory errors." Although memory provides Crusoe with the techniques and materials needed for candle making, his lamp, he says, "gave me Light, tho' not a clear steady Light like a Candle." In this Enlightenment archetype, we are reminded of a metaphor for consciousness from Locke's *Essay*, and yet unlike Locke's lamp, we see here the waxing and waning of the mind. For Locke, the candle's flame represents a defined segment of duration. The flame's endurance becomes a measurement derived from the object that the mind copies and perfectly retains in the memory so as to preserve an *idea* of time.[40] Crusoe's lamp, however, wavers and glimmers unsteadily. As a new metaphor for mind, it gestures toward memory's imperfections, but also toward its inherent strength in flexibility. Though the lamplight is fuzzy, its emblematic usefulness asks us (and Crusoe) to accept that matters have changed. Memory transposes things in time. Moreover, time no longer represents a material thing but becomes an imperfect phenomenology of the mind. From bee to goat, from Descartes to Defoe, the wax finds new form again.

The image of the goat candle takes on even greater significance as the sentence continues with the story of the corn feed, one that famously indicates a false moment of providential wonder. Critics have typically argued that this is where Providence steps into the novel, allowing Crusoe to allay his fears and act rationally, which indicates a sacred need to separate human from divine consciousness.[41] However, what is curious about this passage is that Crusoe's error arises from trusting too deeply in the powers of providential gifts. As in the later Gothic novel, the inexplicable powers of the otherworldly are explained away by mundane human events. Most strikingly, Crusoe's error boils down to an act of forgetting:

> It was a little before the great Rains, just now mention'd, that I threw this Stuff away, taking no Notice of any Thing, and not so much as remembering that I had thrown any Thing there; when about a Month after, or thereabout, I saw some few Stalks of something green, shooting out of the Ground, which I fancy'd might be some Plant I had not seen, but I was surpriz'd and perfectly astonish'd, when, after a little longer Time, I saw about ten or twelve Ears come out, which were perfect green Barley of the same Kind as our *European*, nay, as our *English* Barley.

> It is impossible to express the Astonishment and Confusion of my Thoughts on this Occasion; I had hitherto acted upon no religious Foundation at all, indeed I had very few Notions of Religion in my Head. . . . I began to suggest, that God had miraculously caus'd this Grain to grow without any Help of Seed sown, and that it was directed purely for my Sustenance, on that wild miserable Place. . . .
>
> I not only thought these pure Productions of Providence for my Support, but not doubting, but that there was more in the Place, I went all over that Part of the Island, where I had been before, peering in every Corner, and under every Rock, to see for more of it, but I could not find any; at last it occur'd to my Thoughts, that I had shook a Bag of Chickens Meat out in that Place, and then the Wonder began to cease. (57–58)

Crusoe's mistake arises not only from a failure of perception, or recognition, of "taking no Notice of any Thing," but, more important, from the narrative lapses of self-conscious memory. The "not so much . . . remembering"—that is, Crusoe's failure to account for his past actions—troubles his present faculties of perception. Crusoe's descriptions of time here are fuzzy. He cannot recall exactly how long it is after he casts off the corn feed that the stalks appear: was it "about a Month," or "thereabouts"? This forgetfulness of time and of his own actions, which are always embedded in time, leads Crusoe to false deductions about his immediate environment. The present, Defoe indicates, must always "be flanked by a past"[42] in the experience of human consciousness; otherwise, revelations that are in fact human *seem* divine. Crusoe's thoughts, unsupported by the temporal conditions that shape conscious action, become "confused," and thus time, devoid of its powers, "occasions" what looks like an event but is in fact, to use Jonathan Kramnick's distinction, an action.[43] A superstitious belief in miracles causes Crusoe to expect too much from Providence; he assumes fate will produce for, and sustain, him. But survival on the island is less about events happening to Crusoe than it is about Crusoe's actions.

Crusoe's naïve belief, his lack of doubt, sends him on a wild goose chase that complicates the maxim "seek and you shall find." It is not in searching our environment but in searching our minds, Defoe suggests, that we attain true Enlightenment as a revelation of our own self-governing mental powers. On his search for *it*, Crusoe finds no *thing* but himself: "at last it occur'd to my Thoughts that I had shook a bag of Chickens Meat out in that Place." This "occurrence of Thought" is another phrase in the novel indicative of the faculties of memory, and Defoe's rhetoric for remembrance only highlights the notion that thinking is temporal. Moreover, the immeasurability of time, and Crusoe's inability to remember time with finite exactitude, ties actions to the fluidity of mental phenomena. In recalling himself and what he has done, Crusoe recognizes his capacity to shape his own environment. He thereby places his faith not in God's providing powers but in time: "I carefully sav'd the Ears of this Corn you may be sure in their Season, which was about the End of *June* . . . I resolv'd to sow them all again, hoping in Time to have some Quantity sufficient to supply me with Bread" (58–59). In this manner, Crusoe realizes that time is the only thing that can, and will, supply his wants. Yet this material "hope in Time" fails when time is unaccounted for,[44] or to be more exacting, when it is improperly remembered. "About the end of June" proves an insufficient phrase for deriving corn, some *thing*, from some *time*. Rather, Crusoe insists that he must strictly observe and remember time in order to glean from it his creative powers: "for I lost," Crusoe writes, "all that I sow'd the first Season, by not observing the proper Time" (59). Time is not simply some thing that can be counted, or counted on. Rather, it is the "observation" of time—how it interfaces with the mind and memory—that matters.[45]

The wavering flickers of attention account for times, or memories, lost. Like the lamp's flame, memory is fuzzy, and yet it also figures as the protagonist, the hidden agent, behind the parable of the corn. Although Crusoe ceases to "wonder" at the "astonishing" appearance of his English barley in a foreign isle, his recurrence of thought urges the reader to reroute her gaze. There is indeed something awesome about what Crusoe finally remembers. On his search for some thing, he finds the mundane miracle of memory flourishing in his backyard. What is implanted, what is sown, what is finally recognized, is the product of a memory lost and found again.

Creative Recall: Survival Is a State of Mind

I want to turn now to a passage about basket weaving that occurs midway in the journal. Robinson Crusoe recalls when, as a boy, he would watch basketmakers in the process of wicker weaving. "It came into my Mind," he says, "how they work'd those Things" (78). In his memory of the basket weavers, Crusoe declares, he "wanted nothing but the Materials" to furnish his desires (78). In this distinctive moment in Defoe's narrative, the past uncannily converges with the present to furnish the protagonist's mind with what it lacks. As with the cassava root and the cask, Crusoe's first attempt at basketmaking fails because he begins by trying to acquire things from his immediate external environment. Raw materials are not given, or firsthand, and thereby memory fuels the imagination to supply Crusoe with what he lacks. Notably, retention is again made possible by way of feeling. An interesting implication begins to emerge in this passage that helps us better understand the role of time in the narrative. In the end, we realize that time is not merely a material commodity, or thing, despite Crusoe's impulse to make it so. Rather, time travels through the filters of memory, becoming the operative force of human cognition that allows the mind to move from a pattern of ingesting experience to extending into the world so as to shape and form natural environments:

> This Time I found much Employment, (and very suitable also to the Time) for I found great Occasion of many Things which I had no way to furnish my self with, but by hard Labour and constant Application; particularly, I try'd many Ways to make my self a Basket, but all the Twigs I could get for the Purpose prov'd so brittle, that they would do nothing. It prov'd of excellent Advantage to me now, That when I was a Boy, I used to take great Delight in standing at a *Basket-makers*, in the Town where my Father liv'd, to see them make their *Wicker-ware*; and being as Boys usually are, very officious to help, and a great Observer of the Manner how they work'd those Things, and sometimes lending a Hand, I had by this Means full Knowledge of the Methods of it, that I wanted nothing but the Materials; when it came into my Mind, That the Twigs of that Tree from whence I cut my Stakes that grew, might possibly be as tough as the *Sallows*, and *Willows*, and *Ossiers* in *England*, and I resolv'd to try. (78)

Objects become subordinated to time in Crusoe's efforts at survival when he realizes that he can create "any Thing as [he] had occasion" by way of the powerful operations of time and memory (79). In describing his utilitarian efforts at basket weaving, Crusoe declares, "[I] employ'd a World of Time about it, I bestirr'd my self to see if possible how to supply . . . [my] Wants" (79). What intervenes to aid the survival of mind and body is a cognitive dependence on the past's ability to inform the present. The passage begins with a pun regarding the dual nature of time. Labor, or "employment," like thinking, takes time. Therefore, we can, as per the Lockean model of duration, think about time as a mere map, or representation, of thought passing. But Defoe suggests that our labors are also shaped and limited by time, as in Crusoe's allusion to seasonal activities; moreover, these labors are frequently tied to mental states. There are times, as in the memory of his boyhood musings, that labor is desirable for Crusoe—because it entices or distracts his mind from other wanderings; time informs labor, just as it informs mind. In this way, time shapes both action and thought. Crusoe begins his narrative digression into the avenues of time and memory with the recollection of a feeling: "I used to take great Delight," he writes, "to see them." Unlike many of Crusoe's remembrances, this memory is expository in nature; it rolls on, becoming revivified in Crusoe's mind while it also becomes pleasurably accessible to the reader. Memory is infused with the details of both sight and feeling. What Crusoe calls "full Knowledge" is derived from a felt memory of a felt action.

For this reason, it is not the material of the baskets that first comes to mind when Crusoe remembers his childhood interactions with the basket weavers but rather "the Methods of it." A past version of Crusoe observes not things themselves but "how they work'd those Things." *It* is subordinated to *time* here, but also to *action*. Things are wrought and made; memory, however, shapes thinking and acting while giving humans the power to form things. Crusoe's "resolution" implies that actions are derived from our powers of recollection. In accounting for the use of the baskets, wrought by way of memory, Crusoe describes them as having the capacity to "carry or lay up any Thing as I had occasion" (79). We are herein reminded of Locke's memory storehouse, as baskets, like minds, "lay up" things, actions, impressions, and events. From the foundation of memory, Crusoe "bestir[s]" himself "to see if possible how to supply" his "wants." Thus we might choose to read the baskets as a metaphor for the mind's retentive capacities that cause Crusoe to carry on, to exist and persist, on the island. However, retention is simply the blueprint for a memory that then lends Crusoe the ability to think within and across multiple temporalities so as to alter his present circumstances. And here, in this depiction of memory's narrative and nonlinear powers of creation, Defoe begins to depart from his often cited empiricist predecessor.

Crusoe's recollection, with its full-bodied narrative, uses memory as the launching pad for imagination. Resolution arises from a vision of new "possibility"—one in which his island tree "might" be recognized as strong enough to match his memory of English arbors. The revelation of the basket, which eventually will carry and contain, is a tapestry of woven memories, jointed together through the cross sections of time. Crusoe splices a long-term autobiographical memory, vivid and rich in attentive details, to memories of "English *Ossiers* and *Willows*," and again to a more recent recollection of "that tree" on the island from which he has cut his "stakes." Memories cross and rewire. From here, matter, born from memory, is remembered into a new object of retention. The basket is a thing that weaves together memories from across temporal landscapes; it layers time in ways that exceed empiricist metaphors of mind and linear structures of time.

In this manner, memory does not contain but transforms what it holds; and this brings me to clay vessels. Among the many wants in the journal that Crusoe supplies himself with by way of his "great Mind" is the famous earthenware pot (another vessel that could be aligned with Locke's metaphor for consciousness as a container). It is perhaps no surprise that this passage, which so many readers have found compelling since the time of Virginia Woolf, also delivers a direct interpellation of the reader that is rare in Crusoe's narrative: "It would make the Reader pity me, or rather laugh at me, to tell how many awkward ways I took to raise this Paste, what odd misshapen ugly things I made, how many of them fell in, and how many fell out, the Clay not being stiff enough to bear its own Weight" (87–88). Engaging the reader's mind in what might be read as a metaphor for mind, Defoe subtly underscores the story of Crusoe's endeavors at pottery as addressing the Enlightenment archetype of retention. Like a collection or a conservatory, the empirical mind holds a reservoir of memories, copied feelings, observations, and mental states. Pots and baskets remind us of how Locke's mind *lays up* and layers things. The wicker baskets and the corn come up again in the following paragraph, creating in the reader's mind an association between the three parables of consciousness: the corn, the basket, and the pot. This interaction between three things that all originate from the creative powers of memory, however, also reveals the secrets to Crusoe's survival: a composition as mental exposition that is evidence of the text-as-mind's ability to use memory to make things.

What appears to be a metaphor for retention is also a biblical archetype for creation (Genesis I). The clay, despite its extraordinary ugliness, intimates the most sublime aspects of memory's generative nature. Though not beautiful, the pot is a malleable thing, ever altering and misshaping its own form. Thus it fails to hold things perfectly. Folding in on itself, it proves a poor container. With things that fall in and out of its grasp, the earthenware pot is a better metaphor for novelistic memory than Locke's storehouse. Although not ideal, it allows Crusoe to shift his ideals.

As with his other creative endeavors, Crusoe's frustrations with pot making are often delayed by a lack of readily available materials: "This was a most difficult Thing," he whines, "so much as but to think on; for to be sure I had nothing like the necessary Thing to make it; I mean fine thin Canvas, or Stuff, to search the Meal through." *Making it*, Defoe suggests, is not about a search for *stuff*, and *some things*, Crusoe tells us, are *difficult* even to *think on*. But when it comes to the creative powers of the mind, where contemplation and imagination fail, memory inevitably assists. Again, the "Remedy" lies in a moment when Crusoe "at last . . . remember[s]" (89).

Crusoe's trial-and-error methods of making continue along a familiar pattern in his project of the stone mortar. The passage begins with an assumption that things can be "got," or acquired, from nature, and yet the island again fails to provide Crusoe's wants by way of such methods. Rather, the world of matter is again supplemented by the abstract, "infinite stores" of labor. Time too is an infinite, abstract resource, yet it is lost when the mind expects nature alone to satisfy necessity and desire:

> My next Concern was, to get me a Stone Mortar, to stamp or bear some Corn in; for as to the Mill, there was no thought at arriving to that Perfection of Art, with one Pair of Hands. To supply this Want I was at a great Loss; for of all Trades in the World I was perfectly unqualify'd for a Stone-cutter, as for any whatever; neither had I any Tools to go about it with. I spent many a Day to find out a great Stone big enough to cut hollow, and make fit for a Mortar, and could find none at all; except what was in the solid Rock, and which I had no way to dig or cut out; nor indeed were the Rocks in the Island of Hardness sufficient, but were all of a sandy crumbling Stone, which neither would bear the Weight of a heavy Pestle, or would break the Corn without filling it with Sand; so after a great deal of Time lost in

> searching for a Stone, I gave it over, and resolv'd to look out for a great Block of hard Wood, which I found indeed much easier, and getting one as big as I had Strength to stir, I rounded it, and form'd it in the Out-side with my Axe and Hatchet, and then with the Help of Fire, and infinite Labour, made a hollow Place in it, as the *Indians* in *Brasil* make their *Canoes*. After this, I made a great heavy Pestle or Beater, of the Wood call'd the Iron-wood, and this I prepar'd and laid by against I had my next Crop of Corn, when I propos'd to my self, to grind, or rather pound my Corn into Meal to make my Bread. (89)

Time is lost in "searching" his environment but is found to be more useful in the avenues of memory, a kind of retrospection that allows Crusoe to reengage with his world in new ways. Initially, the raw material of the found stone does not suit, or "fit," the desires of Crusoe's imagined project, and so the mind adjusts to the concept of a wooden mortar. It is easy to read this adaptive shift as the work of the imagination, which would imply an original method of making things, a creative force of the mind that projects into the future and is self-inspired. To be sure, Crusoe's projects are all self-authorized; "I proposed to my self," he writes, at the start of narrating his bread recipe. Lurking behind the text's narrative of a mind adapting to its world, of a self that survives situations of distress and tackles unfamiliar challenges, however, is another mental faculty. Memory is the implicit resource that provides Crusoe with new solutions and resolutions. I "made a hollow Place in it, as the Indians in *Brasil* make their Canoes," Crusoe writes. The wooden mortar is in fact inspired by something Crusoe has observed before in his travels. His vision comes from the resources of memory, as does his capacity to recognize new methods of making "it." "I made a great heavy Pestle or Beater," he narrates, "of the Wood call'd Iron-wood." The recognition of a raw material that already has a name and language of its own indicates that the "Iron-wood" is found, acquired, and deemed useful because it is recognizable to Crusoe, because he remembers it as having material value. His English project of a mortar readapts itself to a Brasilian one because of Crusoe's fund, his variety, of previous experience. Making is an insight that involves no direct perception but a revisionary method of *seeing again*. Crusoe's creative genius relies on a memory serviced by the cultural ideas and things of various nations and peoples. Things, or ideas, are "found in the mind" only to be re-cognized, rearranged, and reenvisioned in the world. Thus Crusoe acquires things from his global memory only to reshape and reform them. In this manner, the objects tailored to Crusoe's mind forever shift with, and adapt to, his ever-accruing memories and surroundings. Like an earthenware pot, memory lays aside ideals to make imperfect things; it is the "tool" most perfectly suited to Crusoe's survival.

Running Out

As the journal comes to a close and peters out, Crusoe comments on his new state of affairs, which is one of a life sustained, not lost: "I had now brought my State of Life to be much easier in itself than it was at first, and much easier to my Mind, as well as to my Body" (95). Circumstance affects both mind and body, and both are causally united in Crusoe's journal, which I posit might be read as a story of memory's survivalist powers. The organic closure of the journal, which critics have so often noted as seamlessly bleeding out into the remaining narrative, is due in part to a running out of resources, since Crusoe has no ink left to write.[46] This text that exists beyond the text again owes to the forces of memory that curiously live on past the natural end of matter. Whereas matter is finite, memory, like fiction, continues even when Crusoe's method of recording is gone.

The reader imagines this post-journal record to be in and of itself owing to Crusoe's imperfect memory of events. Notably, it occurs in a supposed state of relative ease, since we presume Crusoe to have adapted successfully to the conditions of his new environment. Yet the narrative continues to comment on the powers of the mind to survive a lack of resources; if Crusoe's initial problem was in "finding" the necessary thing, he now encounters the tragic and mundane reality of the fact that things decay long before the mind or body ceases to need them:

> The next Thing to my Ink's being wasted, was that of my Bread. . . .
> My Cloaths began to decay too mightily . . . and tho' it is true, that the Weather was so violent hot, that there was no need of Cloaths, yet I could not go quite naked . . . [because] I could not bear the heat of the Sun . . . the very Heat frequently blistered my Skin. (97–98)

Since the island is no Eden, Crusoe finds himself confronting an immanent world wherein matter is definitively finite and subject to the conditions of nature. Things as resources thereby take on the rhetoric of the body; they "waste" and "decay" in time.

The mind, however, continues to provide and create, to survive and adapt long beyond the demise of most things. And so memory comes to fund Crusoe with new clothes, just as it provides his readers with an after-journal, a text beyond the text:

> I have mentioned that I saved the Skins of all the Creatures that I kill'd, I mean four-footed ones, and I had hung them up stretch'd out with Sticks in the Sun, by which means some of them were so dry and hard that they were fit for little, but others it seems were very useful. The first thing I made of these was a great Cap for my Head, with the Hair on the out Side to shoor off the Rain; and this I perform'd so well, that after this I made me a Suit of Cloaths wholly of these Skins, that is to say, a Wastcoat, and Breeches open at Knees, and both loose, for they were rather wanting to keep me cool than to keep me warm. I must not omit to acknowledge that they were wretchedly made; for if I was a bad *Carpenter*, I was a worse *Taylor*. However, they were such as I made very good shift with . . . I was kept very dry. (98)

As Crusoe narrates a survivalist project of keeping his body both dry and cool, conditions necessary in eighteenth-century medical discourses for humoral health, he notes the "unfitness" of objects to conform to his personal needs and desires. Once again, imagination when not ballasted by the forces of memory fails to provide. Some things "seem" more useful than others, however, and so Crusoe's project of making highlights the foundational power of mental recognition. As per an empiricist model, judgment is derived from sight, and perhaps this accounts for Crusoe's descriptions of his work as that of a poor tailor. The articles of clothing are all described in the English fashion and style; thus they are brought home to the English reader's imagination as things both recognizable and legible. The "wretched" aesthetics of these less than fashionable items are owing again to their use value; they must be designed for keeping the body cool, not warm. Thus Crusoe adapts an English model to an island need. Still, the English mode is the inspiration here, and so memory reveals itself again as the providing force that allows Crusoe first to recognize a resource and then to re-fit and re-form it to his needs and desires. The mental capacities of recognition, judgment, and know-how all take us back to a memory of an England now long gone from Crusoe's physical purview, but this is an England that survives on in Crusoe's mind as only one guiding force of his memory.

The same structure undergirds Crusoe's need for an umbrella,[47] his next project after making himself a new suit of clothes:

> After this I spent a great deal of Time and Pains to make me an Umbrella; I was indeed in great want of one, and had a great Mind to make one; I had seen them made in the *Brasils,* where they are very useful in the great Heats which are there. And I felt the Heats every jot as great here, and greater too, being nearer the Equinox; besides, as I was oblig'd to be much abroad, it was a most useful thing to me, as well for the Rains as the Heats. I took a world of Pains at it, and was a great while before I could make anything likely to hold; nay, after I thought I had hit the Way, I spoil'd 2 or 3 before I made one to my Mind. (98–99)

When England, Crusoe's native and thereby most sentimentally remembered place, fails to provide him with the memorial blueprint for his projects, his travels to the Brasils always step in. Nor, in this case, are the Brasils a mere back-up plan, for the current climate of the island conforms more fittingly to his experience there. The umbrella is a product of a memory shaped by bodily, sensorial experience. The idea of the umbrella is recollected from a feeling of heat. The feeling of the past correlates more or less to a feeling now, and thereby memory allows Crusoe to imagine and execute his object-oriented desire. Past, present, and future, dictated by their correspondent feelings, align to inspire production, and use value is likewise determined by a felt desire to alleviate sensory pain.

Crusoe's oft-repeated phrase "I had a great Mind" is one way of articulating "want" or desire, yet the phrasing also brings to mind the relational distinction between mind and brain. As Crusoe states here, his "great Mind" is suited to the activity of making; its power is creative, and creativity is inspired by an effortful desire to realign time according to volition—to conform desire to memory. In this sense, the thing of the umbrella becomes useful (i.e., not a product of wasted or "spoiled" labor) only when it is made according to memory's map of what a Brasilian umbrella or parasol actually is. The verb "hold" here means "stay," the capacity of the object to stick to a form, but what that form holds is derived from a mental picture held, so to speak, in the memory alone. Satisfaction, like survival, arises from a shaping of world to mind.

The passage thereby begins and ends in a now familiar fashion—with an allusion to time, as something both measured and infinite that leads to a project of uniting and conforming mind with world. Time again has that *seeming* quality of an economic resource or commodity when Crusoe talks about "spending a great deal of it"; however, this illusion is quickly overturned when we realize that time, like space, is always traversed or exceeded in Crusoe's mental abstractions. Like his global travels (from Brasil and England to the island), Crusoe's memories crisscross over temporal and spatial boundaries to make his current environment livable. Crusoe inhabits the conditions of a physical place, with its own temperatures and temporal rhythms, but that space is altered as it confronts a mind bent on endurance. Survival, like the parasol, is achieved by way of a remembered feeling that takes shape, shading and protecting the body, only when it "holds" fast to the fluid intersections of memory. The collision of past, present, and future, the various time frames of the mind, produces a thing that separates the self from its sensory environment so that it may safely inhabit it. The brain, a sensory organ, feels the world; the mind, a temporal abstraction, navigates and forms it. Although mind and brain function differently here, they exist collaboratively and in concert with one another.

Accounting for the origins of things in the avenues of memory and time allows Crusoe to exercise his thinking on his environment. In this manner, we could argue that Defoe accounts for the past's ability to return Crusoe, by way of mental abstraction, to a present engagement with worldly matter. The relationship between these two temporalities would thereby seem to follow a dialectical, looping trajectory. To return to the story of the earthenware pot, thinking is endlessly fertile. As Crusoe says, "All the while these Things were doing, you may be sure my Thoughts run many times upon the Prospect of Land which I had seen from the other Side of the Island, and I was not without secret Wishes that I were on Shore there, fancying the seeing the main Land, and in an inhabited Country, I might find some Way or other to convey myself farther, and perhaps at last find some Means of Escape" (90–91).

By finding in memory the means to supply his many wants, Crusoe's self-agency only fuels desire, pushing the text from a kind of past and/as present into the consciousness of one's futurity. Here we might consider

Crusoe's desire for a different place, a different "dwelling" and abode, as evidence of consciousness's capacity to occupy multiple temporalities. "All the while" that Crusoe is "doing things" (linking past and present in his mental exercises), he is also thinking about his future "prospects" for escape. Characterizing this desire as "a secret wish," Crusoe's confession to the reader looks something like an infraction against the supposed laws of Providence to be content with one's station in life. And yet something about human consciousness reveals the inevitability of a "grass is always greener" mentality; felt desire, like felt memory, fuels fancy and allows us to "convey ourselves" into future states, to have prospects, plans, and projects that extend beyond the here and now. This manner of thinking, of course, runs against the grain of a survival narrative, wherein immediate necessity takes precedence over a distant future, and yet Defoe suggests the mind cannot so easily be reined in.[48] In the end, Crusoe's nagging need to catapult himself into "farther adventures" wins out over his desire to abide by what he deems the laws of Providence, a strained effort to remember and accept his allotted place in the world. "Composing one's mind" into a restful state proves a useless endeavor. Likewise, memory, as an agent of survival, cannot account for the moments in life when we desire more than what is necessary, or useful, to our subsistence.

As the narrative strays farther and farther from the text of the original journal, we lose the sense of memory's presence, the origin whence all things come from. Imagination comes to replace memory in Crusoe's repeated references to the mind once Crusoe encounters the footprint, an episode that critics have long read as a transitional moment in the narrative.[49] Imagination forever seems to be "filled" and "filling" things[50]; it haunts all of Crusoe's physical surroundings. So often imagination becomes the inspiration for a thing, but memory is its origin, the avenue through which it is made or achieved, and it remains a foundational force in a text so invested in the qualities of self-conscious experience. Crusoe's remarks on the event of the footprint serve as a reminder of the enduring relationship between mind and world, memory and imagination: "To think there was really nothing in it, but my own Imagination" (115). Things, as products of thought, are "real" only because they are imagined *and* remembered. In the incident of the footprint, the "it" of the "thing" retains only an abstract, insubstantial sense of its origin, and thus turns out to be no-thing more than a mental image. Perhaps it is no surprise that when the ink used to supply Crusoe with a means of record-keeping runs out, his story turns increasingly to the activity of imagination. Nevertheless, the periphery that marks the boundary between the journal's close and the story that runs on points to the instrumental collisions between memory and imagination.

Crusoe's last account of making some thing in the journal is the ship that he abandons. He writes of his first attempt at launching the boat to water: "The Boat was really much bigger than I ever saw a *Canoe*, or *Periagua*, that was made of one Tree, in my Life" (93). Unsurprisingly, the project that fails to conform to Crusoe's memory also fails him in his intentions. The boat never achieves use value as an agent of escape and survival but rather remains a mere inanimate, aesthetic object, since it is derived from imagination only: "I could not have had the least Reflection upon my Mind of my Circumstance, while I was making this Boat," Crusoe writes, but "I pleas'd myself with the Design, without determining whether I was ever able to undertake it" (92). "Design" here not only implies form, an aesthetic or artistic intention for the projected shape of the thing, but also a blueprint for the object's *imagined* futurity. However, a future that is unmoored from past precedents, like imagination without memory, proves null and inert. The boat becomes a useless thing that cannot launch itself or serve a purpose beyond the trivial gratifications of sentimental value. In fact, this is precisely the meaning that Crusoe's boat eventually comes to occupy (99). As sentimental remembrancer, it serves as a static and enduring symbol within Crusoe's world.[51]

In remembering (or reflecting on) his memories and experience, Crusoe contemplates things as commodities of life and endurance, and yet things often come to mind by way of imagination informed by memory: "I had no room for Desire, except it was of Things which I had not" (94). This seems like an odd, tautological phrase. However, it places the definition of desire within an account of reflection. We only know the absence of the thing by way of its loss. Crusoe's doctrine of things is no mere diatribe for or against materialism, but rather it reveals a story of how mind and body operate in situations of distress. This survival narrative places things in between the realm of imagination and memory. Once things remembered come to life, they only sustain an ever-persistent desire, a hope, for life itself.

Not being able to "bring" his ship "to the Water," Crusoe leaves it as "a *Memorandum* to teach [him] to be wiser next Time" (99). This memorandum reveals the true memorialized thing of the ship as a signifier of memory's ability to carry Crusoe forward into the realm of his future prospects. Like Crusoe, who calls himself a "*Memento*" to "Mankind," the boat is both object and metaphor—one that underscores how memory fuels and reifies the desires of our imagination (140–41). As a thing, the boat remains stuck and still on the island's periphery. As a metaphor, it implies a crossing over. Resting on the shoreline, the inert ship spans the middle passage. It is a note to self that asks readers to remember the creative powers of memory and its potential to spur the imagination. Time and time again, Crusoe revisits the ship, wrestling with his escapist desires. Time marked by, and as a marker of, things, Defoe suggests, has the ability to free us from our station; it is the force by which consciousness crosses over into a less material and finite state of being. Memory, like desire, for Crusoe, proves infinitely useful this way.

❖ CHAPTER 2 ❖

Re-membering the Real

Uncle Toby's Maps and Models

—Inconsistent soul that man is!—languishing under wounds, which he has the power to heal!
—LAURENCE STERNE, *Tristram Shandy*

In the previous chapter, we saw how *Robinson Crusoe* both borrowed and departed from Locke's theory of recollection as it began to envision a kind of memory as craftmanship that relies not just on personal experience but on the collective histories of diverse cultural narratives as well. Defoe's work subtly sets the stage for a new way of thinking about memory and survival in the eighteenth-century novel. Laurence Sterne's *Tristram Shandy* offers a more radical and direct challenge to empiricist accounts of mind. It is likewise in this work that we encounter the eighteenth century's most famous fictional attempt to illustrate a theory of mind-body relations that demonstrates the human ability to overcome crisis. "The desire of life and health is implanted in man's nature," Tristram writes. "These my uncle *Toby* had in common with his species" (75).

Critics have typically characterized Toby's attempts to grapple with the physical pains of his wound from the battle of Namur as an early example of the psychological structures of trauma, wherein a repetition of the event leads to a pattern of associative thinking that traps Toby's mind in a habitual cycle of pain.[1] Tristram warns the reader that dwelling on past events can distress the mind and "exasperate ... symptoms" of the body (73). Yet this warning comes when Toby is still in a state of confinement, and the same paragraph paradoxically speaks to the mind's powerful abstracting and alleviating qualities. In an effort to make sense of his past, Toby reads into his history so as to "forget himself, his wound, his confinement, his dinner" (72). In fact, Toby's recovery is brought about by a decision to construct a physical model based in the "rood and a half of ground" adjacent to Shandy Hall (78).[2] This project reveals the reifying powers of the mind to heal past injuries and construct new futures. Much like his predecessor Crusoe, Toby makes a fortification "sloped" and tailored to his mind (78). As Corporal Trim says, the form of the model is "not much matter" at all (78), but a "bewitching" thought (79) that leads to the "manage[ment of] ... matter" (76, 78, 80). The model both complicates materialist accounts of mind-body relations in the eighteenth century and challenges approaches to trauma in the early novel. What critics have called Toby's trauma is in fact a revelatory act of conscious memory that subdues pain and underscores the mind's powers to overcome the conditions of its physical environment and body.

In the same manner that scholarship on *Tristram Shandy* has historically divided around the issue of whether the novel appropriates the philosophical empiricism of John Locke or David Hume,[3] recent critical accounts have debated whether the novel is a satire or a triumph of the eighteenth-century new science and philosophical materialism.[4] These debates underscore the slippery nature of the text itself as a vast system of endless reference.[5] Somewhere in the muddle of thought upon thought, this modern novel makes it difficult to distinguish satirical object from ideal, inside from outside, cause from effect, subject from object.

The novel's affinity for mixed references, what critics have called its "encyclopedic" structure,[6] alongside its gifted use of metaphor and aposiopesis draws attention to one significant distinction that must be made for anyone attempting to unravel the Shandean maze of mind and matter: that is, the distinction between the reader's and the characters' mental points of view. What is elided in the text is not necessarily elided in the minds or memories of its characters. Rather, *Tristram Shandy* upholds the notion that thought is a private matter—private, that is, until it is penetrated through bodily, or objective, reference. Nothing is mere matter in this text unless it is perceived as such, for Sterne delivers a complex dialectic between mind and world that cannot be reduced to any one eighteenth-century philosophical treatise. The novel's semiotic system provides the reader with objects as signs that allow us to access mental thought, *to some extent*.[7] For what is referenced in Sterne's metaphors of body and mind is not simply thought or sensation but imagination's delightful embellishment of memory. For Sterne, the conditions of the material world, though always imposing themselves on the body, often are overturned in the lawless universe of the mind. As Judith Hawley writes, Sterne's "characters are at once influenced by external forces, and determined to blaze their own trails."[8] The novel's world of possibility thus motivates minds to alter the conditions of matter, sometimes beyond what is seemingly possible.

The critical divide on the relationship between mind and matter in *Tristram Shandy* likewise can explain why scholars have tended to describe the novel's relationship to physiological pain as embedded in the rhetoric of psychological trauma. In describing literature's unique role in psychoanalytic studies of trauma, Cathy Caruth emphasizes the linguistic powers of the text to become the "voice that cries out" or the thing that bears "witness" to the catastrophe of a wound.[9] To this extent, Caruth envisions the language of trauma as something inexpressible that finds its voice in the avenues of literary representation. Anna Sagal has deployed this notion of trauma in literature to argue that the story of Toby's wound is an "unspeakable" event made comprehensible through Toby's world of objects.[10] My method bears some resemblance to Sagal's, for I focus on the relationship of mind to environment by attending to Toby's indexical world of appropriated things. In my reading, however, this system of mental reference is the manner in which Toby's truth becomes known to the reader—not to Toby. Moreover, the objects of the novel do not typically reference the trauma itself, as in Sagal's reading, but rather metaphorically indicate the wound as something healed, or at least psychically overcome. Such references reveal a mind-over-matter approach to distress in the novel, which diametrically opposes trauma's defining character.

As Caruth reminds us, the word "trauma" comes from the Greek term for a bodily "injury," and only in Sigmund Freud's time does it take on psychological associations.[11] Of course, *Tristram Shandy* is rife with bodily traumas, and though it may appear anachronistic to seek mental trauma in a narrative that comes before its time, it is no surprise that critics have done so, for as Helene Moglen demonstrates, association may be read as a precursor to the psychoanalytic subconscious.[12] Caruth explicates Freud's definition of "traumatic neurosis" as an "unwitting . . . reenactment" of an event. This repetition is "unconscious," "unwished-for," "unassimilated," "inadvertent."[13] As a mental wound, trauma signifies the "breach in the mind's experience of time, self, and world" that cannot be healed until it exposes itself to consciousness.[14] In other words, the temporal structure of trauma, and even its etymological shift over the course of history, tracks the movement of a physical (external) event that slowly announces itself to the awareness of the psyche. In this manner, the structure of trauma shares much with Sterne's satire on empirical associationism: it depends on the temporal and linguistic deployment of repetition and is obsessed with mental, not just physical, "breaches" in time. Toby's model, however, takes a different course, for the project begins as a physical structure tailored or suited to what is in the mind—to what is *already known*. As Jonathan Lamb states, "The circular tracks of happiness imprinted on Toby's bowling green perfectly correspond to those in his brain.... [His] garden ... [is a] perfect ... picture of his mind."[15] *Consciousness comes first.*

To add to Lamb's observation, I would underscore that Toby's creation does not necessarily re-present the reality of the past but rather rewrites it. Like the text itself, the model is a fiction that heals. It references a history of a rewritten and replaced (not a represented) past. Toby's "trauma" is not in fact a trauma at all but something like its antithesis: a consciousness that allays distress, a sealing, not a "speaking," of the wound that covers up pain by transforming it, by converting it into pleasure.

This chapter focuses on a genre embedded in Laurence Sterne's *Tristram Shandy* that resembles the work of the novel itself. In an effort to reproduce the past, Uncle Toby's maps and models result in a craftwork that ultimately fictionalizes and alters his reality. The model that reconstructs experience nevertheless begins as a map of Namur that attempts to represent Toby's physical trauma or injury. I read the first draft of this early map as a memory trace that serves as an object of satire on representational models of empirical recollection. Neither the map nor the model dovetails with Freud's notion of traumatic neurosis in *Beyond the Pleasure Principle*, in which actions are "unwished"-for "reproductions" of the past unknowingly carried out in present actions or in our dreams.[16] Yet the social and reconstructive nature of memory that Toby and Trim finally carry out on the bowling green does in some sense have a Freudian legacy. For here memory's reconstructive nature is in part due to the transactive processes of sympathetic transference.

In "The Wolf Man," or "An Infantile Neurosis" (1914), Freud details an analysis of a neurotic's dreams and phantasies that show how various memories in the mind flow together to form a patchwork tableau not of real past events but rather of mental fictions. As the patient's memories of sense perceptions combine with his memories of the stories of family members and tales from childhood picture books, they produce a startling effect: "What supervened during the . . . excitement of the night of his dream was the transference on to his parents of his recently acquired memory-picture, with all its details, and it was only thus that the powerful emotional effects which followed were made possible."[17] Both Freud and Sterne approach memories not simply as reiterative but as reconstructive. For Freud, the implications of "screen memories" like this one are twofold. First, they hint at a typically unacknowledged source for memory formation: "I cannot help concluding that what I am dealing with is something that never happened at all but has been unjustifiably smuggled in among my childhood memories," cries the patient in "Screen Memories."[18] Memories are not replicas of our own experiences; rather, they are "smuggled in" from the accounts, stories, and supposed feelings of other people. Second, screen memories produce new feelings, impressions, memories, and narratives as they are emotionally transferred, or redirected, onto other persons. This is to say that both memories and feelings shuttle between people; they follow sympathetic and social trajectories. On Toby's bowling green, memories are transacted and transposed in a similar fashion, and they likewise produce new feelings and even ardent passions.

Yet for much of the account of "The Wolf Man," Freud approaches memory as pathological. This signals a key difference between Freud's analysis of reconstructive memories and how I address memory in *Tristram Shandy*. The Freudian patient suffers from memory's inaccurate entanglement with fiction and other people. Toby, on the other hand, heals by the same process that renders Freud's patient hysterical. Many would underscore that the resolution at the end of "The Wolf Man" is one of an imaginary trauma now healed. Nevertheless, Freud cures his neurotic patient of a reconstructed memory by bringing his latent fantasies into plain sight. The implication is that therapy is a clinical attempt to get back to the real. In *Tristram Shandy*, however, the truth hurts. Freud's clinical process never delights in the pleasures of memory fiction; Sterne, on the other hand, offers us a hypothetical realm wherein transacted memories triumph to heal the wounded body.

For many critics to date, Toby's world has been dismissed as a mere illusion,[19] and for some the novel itself amounts to "a fallacy" that delusively "expects" a pain-free existence.[20] In this manner, Sterne criticism has given fiction a bad name. In a rhetoric akin to something like the eighteenth-century realist's distaste for romance, Toby's fiction has been relegated to the status of pathology or a common "adaptive" coping mechanism.[21] However, I'm compelled to take Toby's mental system seriously. With matters made from externalized thought, Toby's mind manages to alter instead of adapting to his past, and this seems a key difference. Toby's maps harbor a history of "what passes in a man's mind" that asks us to give the "smoakstack" another turn. Somewhere in this illusory system of fiction is a very real pleasure that emphasizes the mind's great powers to interface with matter. For as the past is turned into smoky ephemera, one consciousness gives way to another when memories are mediated, embellished, reimagined, restructured, recreated, and rewritten.

The Happy Reader

Sterne's novel begins by overturning early eighteenth-century conventions of dedication when it sacrifices the desire for critical fame in favor of a more personal aesthetics of reading. The circulation of print provides not consumption but consolation. Sterne is in good company with other late eighteenth-century novelists who appeal to the emotional over the commercial powers of reading. Yet the dedication's peculiar version of consolation is, in the end, self-interested:

> SIR,
>
> NEVER poor Wight of a Dedicator had less hopes from his Dedication, than I have from this of mine; for it is written in a bye corner of the kingdom, and in a retired thatch'd house, where I live in a constant endeavour to fence against the infirmities of ill health, and other evils of life, by mirth. . . .
>
> I humbly beg, Sir, that you will honour this book by taking it—(not under your Protection,—it must protect itself, but)—into the country with you; where, if I am ever told, it has made you smile, or can conceive it has beguiled you of one moment's pain—I shall think myself as

happy as a minister of state;—perhaps much happier than any one . . . that I have ever read or heard of.

. . . THE AUTHOR.

As Melvyn New has suggested, Sterne's allusion to the salutary nature of "mirth" stems from Shaftesbury's notion of humoral reading in *The Characteristics*.[22] Indeed, Sterne's dedication resembles Shaftesbury's *Letter Concerning Enthusiasm* in more ways than one. As in Shaftesbury's *Letter*, the writer imagines his audience; the narrator then latches on to his conception of a laughing reader when he projects himself into the reader's imagined "state" of personal "happiness." Laughter, like enthusiasm, is contagious, and so the novelist relies on publication to render the imagined feeling real.

The purpose of *Tristram Shandy* the text is essentially to "beguile . . . pain." Its inspiration is "ill health." "In a retired thatch'd house," the writer lives by a "constant endeavour to fence against . . . infirmities." Tucked away in the solitude of his inspired grotto, Tristram figures the patient as the proverbial inspired author. The double figure characterizes a textual "endeavour" to ward off pain through the activity of the imagination. In this manner, the catharsis of writing is not a simple matter of externalizing one's feelings onto the page. Rather, happiness is registered, is known, through a doubly imagined transaction. As the author borrows mirth from his imagined reader, he then compares his mental state to that of other imagined characters he has "heard or read of."

Happiness here boils down to a shared fiction. To imagine happiness is to become happy because happiness signifies more than a mental state, it is a nation state—albeit a fictional one. Sterne's imagined community of mirth alleviates the physiological pains of the writer's consumption when the writer's imagination alters his reality through the mental project of fiction making. By imagining how others will read him, and by *remembering* what he has read, the author exchanges real pain for fictional pleasure. Publication is a self-healing transaction—one that substitutes sensations through a process of imagining, remembering, reading, effecting, reifying, and adopting the happy fiction of others.

In a novel where so many characters suffer from physiological ailment (Walter's sciatica, Tristram's asthma, Trim's knee, Toby's groin)[23] and "accidents" are events that must be endured or "sustained" (10), Tristram's satire attempts to overturn the fatal effects of gravity through satirical levity or "jest." As the dedication notes, the satire's effect is what truly matters in this Shandean world. Yet its cause, alluded to here and throughout the novel, points to a subtle interaction between memory and imagination, one that helps us better understand Sterne's unique philosophy of mind and matter. Another allusion to the material transactions between author and reader appears in a conceit at the start of chapter 12 of volume 1:

> The *Mortgager* and *Mortgageé* differ the one from the other, not more in length of purse, than the *Jester* and *Jesteé* do, in that of memory.... The one raises a sum and the other a laugh at your expence, and think no more about it. Interest, however, still runs on in both cases;—— the periodical or accidental payments of it, just serving to keep the memory of the affair alive; till, at length, in some evil hour,——pop comes the creditor upon each, and by demanding principal upon the spot, together with full interest to the very day, makes them both feel the full extent of their obligations. (24)

Tristram's analogy suggests that the jest of the text survives through memory just as the financial account of a mortgage survives on credit. In Tristram's pun on "interest," the author must demand something from the reader's memory ("keeping all tight in his fancy") as a way of sustaining his interest.[24] The success of the satire thereby depends on what is remembered and what is forgotten. Returning to the dedication, we recall the author's pains are endured because readerly interest (or laughter) is "sustained." The exchange of pain for pleasure relies on keeping up the jest. Tristram's conscious manipulation of our memories seems to counteract the unconscious accidents of universal reality, and thus fiction endures through a species of memory-making (akin to what today is called memory science).

Sterne's choice of metaphor here is also key. The remembered jest, like the monetary payment of a loan, represents a transaction that is also a material transformation. The credit, when given, is literally *no*-thing— like the imagination, it represents nothing more than an airy prospect, a gesture toward the future. But ultimately the credit becomes substantial; the money must be paid. A similar transaction occurs in the shared fiction between author and reader as what was initially imagined, or conceived, becomes remembered. This transaction represents Sterne's concept of a different kind of realism wherein fiction actually produces real outcomes through the act of reading.[25] In this case, it is the memory that represents the substantial thing as the reader brings about the desired effects of the author's imagination.

Sterne's concept of memory in the novel operates much like his imagined transactions of public readership. Memory in *Tristram Shandy* is a process of fiction-making, one that selectively replaces the pains of past realities for the happy prospects of a more sustainable future. The exchange largely depends on what is remembered and what is forgotten—and this makes a very material difference, as Tristram warns us at the start of the novel with the unfortunate accident of his conception. Notably, the scene also underscores the distinctions between unconscious matters and conscious thought processes:

> I wish either my father or my mother, or indeed both of them, as they were in duty both equally bound to it, had minded what they were about when they begot me; had they duly consider'd how much depended upon what they were then doing;—that not only the production of a rational Being was concern'd in it, but that possibly the happy formation and temperature of his body, perhaps his genius and the very cast of his mind; . . . Had they duly weighed and considered all this, and proceeded accordingly,—I am verily persuaded I should have made a quite different figure in the world. (5)

Tristram's wish for a different origin emphasizes the dangers of association as habitual thinking. When minds operate like clocks, reality is "bound" to accidental production. The "form" of Tristram's "body" and the "cast" of his "mind" follow from an accidental event (not an intentional action). He "proceeds" from a gap in time. We might say that Tristram, like the text, represents a rupture in the empirical system of Locke's duration,[26] as so much thought passing progressively through the annals of the mind. The novel thus begins with the overturning of time's diurnal mechanics, and many critics have argued that in its wake, we encounter an emotional or psychological conception of time as associative memory.[27] But I want to focus less on the trials and tribulations of Tristram's textual or bodily form and more on what the novel, or the character, *might have been*. For the text opens with this possibility, this gesture, perhaps toward satirical reform. Tristram posits a very different kind of universe at the start of the novel from the one that the text "figures in the world." This imagined reality is one wherein actions are born out of intentions, and intentions give rise to "happy . . . forms."

Chapter 1 of volume 1 commences with a lament, a wishful yearning for a system of conscious thought; when it comes to creating forms, our "duty" is to "mind what [we] are about," to "consider," "weigh," and "proceed accordingly" to the activity of "production." If we are to read the text, as so many critics have done, as a satire on materialism and empiricism, then Tristram's happy alternative envisions matter born from mind. The catastrophic accident of Tristram's conception produces the history of a decrepit body, and the accidental form that *is* Tristram results from a perverse act of forgetting. Tristram's father famously forgets to wind the clock, his parents forget what they are doing, and accidents give way to more accidents in a "train" of events something like Locke's notion of habitual thinking (5). Tristram sets up a universe wherein everything falls into ailment and decay. This is the stuff born out of forgetting, from mechanistic cognitive processes.

Forgetfulness, like illness, pervades the novel of *Tristram Shandy*, and its tragic effects suggest that one accounts for the other. The episode of the sash window is a perfect example of this. Walter, like Jane Austen's later Sir Walter, is perpetually lost in a book. With a mind that resembles an extensive and musty library collection, Walter is myopic in respect to the present. His (and Susannah's) forgetfulness not only leads to Tristram's catastrophic castration, but Walter apparently forgets to write the episode down in the *Tristrapaedia* (307). The oversight leaves the task to be taken up by Tristram, indicating that Walter's forgetting must become Tristram's memory. For the reader experiencing Tristram's memory, this literally becomes the case when the episode is finally described in volume 6, for it is symbolically elided through Tristram's signature style of aposiopesis (348). What is forgotten by one character can only be remembered by another as an unalterable absence. Forgetfulness has its own social network—a communal power to mar both physical and textual bodies.

But a much less tragic alternative introduces itself implicitly at the narrative's beginning—the conscious memory of "happy forms." This silver lining produces the novel's subtext. While so many characters in *Tristram Shandy* are busy forgetting—Walter, Mrs. Shandy, Yorick, Susannah—and we are left to lament the tragic scars of that forgetfulness on Tristram's body and mind, Uncle Toby is intent on a very different task: remembering. The parallel between the narrator's and Toby's injuries undeniably haunts the novel at every turn, right up to the finalizing touch of "the Cock and Bull Story."

But the parallel is not exact, for Toby's story also shifts the paradigm of memory in the novel.

In the critical reception of *Tristram Shandy*, Uncle Toby has come to represent a kind of memory as radical association. For this reason, he has become a symbol of Hume's sentimental epistemology,[28] a satire on Locke's rationalism,[29] a parody of philosophical materialism,[30] an example of eighteenth-century pathologies of madness,[31] and an embodiment of the later Freudian conception of trauma.[32] The focus on Uncle Toby in the critical imagination is no surprise; despite his seemingly secondary role, he takes up the vast majority of Tristram's attempts at plot-based narrative. Indeed, the novel is bookended by Toby's stories of love and war. Moreover, Toby's memories and designs are responsible for the remembered story of Tristram's birth (7) and the manner of Mrs. Shandy's birthing experiences (35, 37). In essence, Toby is the subtext of the novel that becomes the text itself.

Of course, the predominant reason why "My Uncle Toby" has received so much critical attention over the past thirty years is the novel's famous narratological reliance on the hobbyhorse, which has redefined the manner in which literary studies approaches issues of mind and brain. In volume 8, chapter 31, Tristram reminds us of the distinction between the "passions" and his use of the term "hobbyhorse":

> For many years of my father's life, 'twas his constant mode of expression—he never used the words *passions* once—but *ass* always instead of them—So that he might be said truly, to have been upon the bones, or the back of his own ass, or else of some other man's, during all that time.
>
> I must here observe to you, the difference betwixt
>
> My father's ass
>
> and my hobby-horse—in order to keep characters as separate as may be, in our fancies as we go along.
>
> For my hobby-horse, if you recollect a little, is no way a vicious beast; he has scarce one hair or lineament of the ass about him—'Tis the sporting little filly-folly which carries you out for the present hour—a maggot, a butterfly, picture, a fiddle-stick—an uncle Toby's siege—or *any thing*, which a man makes a shift to get a stride on, to canter it away from the cares and solicitudes of life—'Tis as useful

a beast as in the whole creation—nor do I really see how the world could do without it. (471)

For all the attention given to Sterne's hobbyhorse in the critical literature—its associationist operations, its scientific basis in materialism,[33] its literary reference to Hamlet and the concept of memento mori,[34] its psychological[35] or mechanical[36] systems—there is a tendency to gloss over the main purpose of Sterne's invention.

At this late moment in the novel, Tristram asks the reader to recollect his definition of the hobbyhorse from the end of volume 1. The interjection comes in the midst of a comical miscommunication between Walter and Toby wherein the word "ass" (Walter's euphemism for the passions) is taken literally by Uncle Toby to mean his rear end. Uncle Toby is thinking about the blister that has broken on his backside—an incident that occurs, as the cheeky pun reveals, while he is riding his horse. In the context of Uncle Toby's "innocent" mind, the blister signifies his falling in love. In the context of the narrative, it represents a transition in Toby's hobbyhorsical affairs from the miniature wars on the bowling green to his mock-heroic attempt at romantic love. When Walter asks his brother how it goes with his "ass" (meaning his love affair with widow Wadman), and Toby assumes he means the physical part of the body connoted by the word, the comedic effect is doubly satirical. Ironically, the miscommunication turns out to be an effective communication: both men through different mental pathways, have confused "asses" for "love."

Sterne's choice of euphemism is also archetypal, signaling the shared emblem of satire for the early eighteenth-century Augustans.[37] (The ass famously formed the frontispiece of Alexander Pope's *Four-Book Dunciad*.) This symbolic allusion to satire captures the tenor of the hobbyhorse described in the above passage as a "sporting little fill-folly"—in other words, "*any thing*" rendered in the tone of the light and playful. The form of the hobbyhorse is comic, but its intent carries a much more serious and critical "use" that sustains the "whole creation" (of both the "world" and the work itself). On offering up a list of potential examples, Tristram ends with "Toby's siege," the quintessential hobbyhorse that is the novel's own central investigation into the matter. Accordingly, Tristram defines the hobbyhorse as a kind of distraction, an escape from distress, "the cares and solicitudes of life."[38] Carol Houlihan Flynn has argued that the hobbyhorse's medicinal purpose was to "distract" splenetic minds through the bodily mechanics of "diversion."³⁹ I would add that this boon to suffering also signals the temporal powers of the mind to abstract the body from physical pain. The path of the hobbyhorse as digression or diversion is to "canter . . . away" not merely from place but from a moment in time. It "carries you," Tristram notes, "out of the present hour."

When Tristram thereby asks his reader to "recollect" the essence of the hobbyhorse, he essentially urges the reader to *remember memory*. So as not to confuse hobbyhorsical memory with the passions, with the materialism of the body, or with the mechanistic system of association, Tristram defines memory here as a distraction, or better yet, an abstraction, from *present pain*. Literally, it is "man's nonsense" (5) or his non-sense—a countervailing mental force that pushes back against empiricism's sensationalism. Moreover, hobbyhorsical memory takes on intentional qualities in Tristram's definition when he gives it a use value. If in reading we have failed fully to understand the phenomenon of Toby's sieges, then Tristram ensures we get the gist of the hobbyhorse now: it is an effort, and a playful one at that, to alleviate care. *Tristram Shandy*, like Toby's siege, attempts to heal the wounds of the past through a new novelistic vision of memory.

Mental Mapping

The story of Uncle Toby's hobbyhorse begins with a physical injury: "a wound" in his "groin, which he received at the siege of Namur" (62). Toby returns to England for medical intervention, and this takes the form of "four years" of "total . . . confinement." The time is described as one in which he "suffer'd unspeakable miseries." The wound, we are told, has been got by "gravity" as opposed to "projectile force" (62). Critics have aptly noted the new scientific parody here on Newtonian physics.⁴⁰ The motion, however, insinuates a problem with the current medical approach even as it hints at a better healing method to come: by confining Toby, the doctor is fighting gravity with gravity (which he ironically describes as a "great happiness"). What will ultimately heal the suffering of the past is a future project of "projectiles." Sterne's pun on "gravity" and "humor" as emotional as well as physiological systems begins to suggest the potential power of the mind to heal when bodies become inert or ineffectual.

The end of the first volume tries to account for the wound itself. The diagnostic process proves just as elusive as the wound's origins when Uncle

Toby is at a loss to communicate the full story of his injury. This is problematic, for the text promises that "the history of a soldier's wound beguiles the pain of it" (63). As per Adam Smith's model of sympathy, Toby "receive[s] great relief" from conversing about the wound and telling his story, but since the account is incomplete, so is the relief. For "three months together," Toby cannot "extricate himself" from "unforeseen perplexities" (63). Added to this are "four years" of suffering (62). The ambiguity that "retards" the healing process would seem to suggest a potential castration, a concern on Toby's part that is withheld from the reader's and his visitors' view (63). In this manner, Sterne satirizes the effects of representational memory. At the end of volume 1, Toby's attempts to reproduce the real story of his wound causes his mind to ail with his body, contributing to the temporal duration of his pain.

It is no surprise that critics have read this scene as one of mental as well as physiological trauma. The initial language that feels so Freudian to the twentieth-century reader of trauma studies wherein Toby encounters "insurmountable difficulties" in communicating "his story" to his "visitors" (67) is due to Toby's first, failed attempt at history telling—that is, merely to retrace and repeat the movements he was taking during the attack of the counterscarp. Toby's mental entanglement mirrors the physical entrapment of his real history. Volume 2 continues in this vein with the account of Toby's healing process as a struggle to locate his injury geographically. Although the initial narrative elides the word "impotent" from the text, it has memory (almost) to a fault. Toby's problem is his attempt to reconstruct events too exactingly: "—the ground was cut and cross-cut with such a multitude of dykes, drains, rivulets, and sluices, on all sides,—and he would get so sadly bewilder'd and set fast amongst them, that frequently he could neither get backwards or forwards to save his life" (68). The internalization of war (through empirical imprinting) only mires Toby's mind in temporal stasis. The wording is key, for life, Sterne suggests, is only preserved through memories that defy the properties of realism. Toby's first attempt at a personal-historical accounting leads to an "inward . . . fret[ing] and fum[ing]" that condemns the mind to the same "hourly vexations" of the body. The wound is aggravated by repetitive mental motions that try to replicate personal history. In fact, what critics have identified as traumatic neurosis could easily be read as Sterne's attack on empirical ideas of mimetic memory.

Yet this is only the beginning of Toby's story: one that alludes to a potential difference between minds and bodies. Bodies are forced to adhere to the diurnal progress of time. Locked into Locke's system of duration, Toby suffers for calculated "years" and "months" in a physical and temporal confinement that imposes on his mind as it entangles mental processes with physical matter.

This first map initiates a process of progressive externalization wherein the wound no longer situates itself in the mind or body. Once externalized, it becomes a site that can be pinpointed and indexed:

> He was one morning lying upon his back in his bed, the anguish and nature of the wound upon his groin suffering him to lye in no other position, when a thought came into his head, that if he could purchase such a thing, and have it pasted down upon a board, as a large map of the fortifications of the town and citadel of *Namur*, with its environs, it might be a means of giving him ease.—I take notice of his desire to have the environs along with the town and citadel, for this reason,—because my uncle *Toby*'s wound was got in one of the traverses, about thirty toises from the returning angle of the trench, opposite to the salient angle of the demi-bastion of *St. Roch;*—so that he was pretty confident he could stick a pin upon the identical spot of ground where he was standing in when the stone struck him.
>
> All this succeeded to his wishes, and not only freed him from a world of sad explanations, but, in the end, it prov'd the happy means, as you will read, of procuring my uncle *Toby* his HOBBY-HORSE. (68–69)

The first map harbors the most exact signs of Toby's original wound. The details form a referential system of displacement. In drawing out the spatial signs, we imagine a traverse, and our eye moves upward to the nearby "returning angle of the trench" to the "demi-bastion," whose design pictorially represents a half phallus. On the one hand, Sterne underscores the importance of textual systems of reference in storytelling. Speaking about reality is a pain at once alleviated through the use of metaphor and aposiopesis, which tell the story in a way that renders the publication of impotence bearable by subjecting it to the legible status of probability. Yet the metaphor proves all too real.

Studying a representation of his original experience causes Toby to feel his wound again. Whereas the mapping of the wound serves as a kind of bodily displacement and a mode of distraction, it can conjure up early empirical notions of the "memory trace" when it veers too closely to a realist account: "In the latter end of the third year, my uncle *Toby* perceiving that the parameter and semi-parameter of the conic section, angered his wound, he left off the study of projectiles in a kind of a huff, and betook himself to the practical part of fortification only; the pleasure of which, like a spring held back, returned upon him with redoubled force" (74). Staring into a schematic mirror of his injured member (the "semi-parameter of the conic section") causes Toby to re-present and feel his wound again. Toby's attempts at delivering an exact, realist account—complete with all the gory details of the wound's occurrence—always leave him in an exacerbated physical state. This is the case for both the earlier and later stages of Toby's recovery. On the other hand, the selective evocation of pleasing memories allows Toby to forget his wound. Thus he consciously returns to the moment in history that brings pleasure, not pain: the fortification building that was designed to protect the soldiers' bodies. The change in mental focus causes a brief shift in bodily sensation. By mapping "fortifications," Toby is fortified from recumbent pain into pleasurable action.[41]

The first draft of the map is a composition akin to what Frances Yates has called the classical art of memory; it describes a mnemotechnic process of imprinting an original place or image on the mind.[42] Sterne describes Toby staring at his map like the dutiful scholar who uses pictures as mnemonic devices to commit things to memory: "WHEN my uncle *Toby* got his map of *Namur* to his mind, he began immediately to apply himself . . . to the study of it; for nothing being of more importance to him than his recovery, and his recovery depending, as you have read, upon the passions and affections of his mind, it behoved him to . . . make himself so far master of his subject, as to be able to talk upon it without emotion" (72). Falling in love with the map of his own making, Toby's study becomes a near Pygmalion complex as "the more . . . *Toby* pored over his map, the more he took a liking to it" (72). In this, the map is meant to signify a reproductive copy of what is in the mind. Once Toby becomes "master" of his memory, the text suggests that his constitution may shift. If Sterne's irony is not readily apparent in this passage, it quickly becomes so; Toby's healing is nearly stymied when he tries to acquire knowledge of the "geometric rules" of the parabola of his own wound, described as a "breech upon an horizontal plane" (73). This resolution, Tristram warns, will only "exasperate

[Toby's] symptoms" (73). To enclose the mind in the physics of realism is to deploy a regressive, gravitational kind of memory that entraps us in our past and thereby repeats it. Memory as repetition will "evaporate thy spirits,—waste thy animal strength,—dry up thy radical moisture,—bring thee into a costive habit of body, impair thy health,—and hasten all the infirmities of thy old age" (73). Tristram suggests that the origin of the wound is less important than the effect of it when he pushes back against what we might now call trauma therapy. In this manner, Tristram suggests "HYPERBOLA" for the memorialization of history; a fictionalized account that exaggerates is better than a story that attempts to replicate one's past (73).

Toby's initial attempt to commit his map to memory (to get "the map of *Namur* to his mind," 72) might be read as a satire on philosophical empiricism's idea of memory as a faculty that inscribes and preserves images in the mind. His study of the map of Namur describes a mnemonic technique of recalling a memory to mind. "In a fortnight," however, something else happens to Toby's memories and studies:

> In a fortnight's close and painful application, which, by the by, did my uncle *Toby's* wound, upon his groin, no good,—he was enabled, by the help of some marginal documents ... together with *Gobesius's* military architecture and pyroballogy, translated from the *Flemish*, to form his discourse with passable perspicuity ... before the first year of his confinement had well gone round, there was scarce a fortified town in *Italy* or *Flanders*, of which, by one means or other, he had not procured a plan, reading over as he got them, and carefully collating therewith the histories of their sieges, their demolitions, their improvements and new works, all which he would read with that intense application and delight, that he would forget himself, his wound, his confinement, his dinner. (72)

Finding his own memory incomplete and ineffective, Toby supplements it with the histories of others. Once he "procures" the plans of Italy and Flanders, he reads "the histories of their sieges" with a different effect. The narrator implies that Toby was not an "eye-witness" (67) to these attacks as he was at Namur, and Toby quickly goes on to purchase more volumes about military warfare and architecture (adding to "*Gobesisus's* pyroballogy") in the very next paragraph that starts the second year of his confinement. Reading the memories and histories of others rouses Toby with "intense . . . delight" that becomes a nearly addictive pleasure in his solitude. The rote style of reading as a mimetic system of knowledge formation, which initially allowed Toby to remember with "no emotion," has quickly been replaced by another type of reading entirely. As the stories of others overpopulate Toby's memory and begin to get "collated" or folded in with his personal perceptions, they generate a different feeling about Namur. Insensibility becomes passionate pleasure.

Toby's hobbyhorse is founded on transacted memories. Even in these initial stages of hobbyhorse formation (for Toby becomes, in the language of the hobbyhorse, emotionally "be-pictur'd,—be-butterflied, and be-fiddled," 72), distraction is the predominant effect of Toby's obsession with his map and explains the nature of his love. Toby's infatuation with mapping leads to an important and blissful erasure, one that alleviates the present circumstance of pain. As Toby forgets his wound, his dinner, and his self, the ecstasy of forgetfulness has an effect that we never encounter elsewhere in the novel: it heals instead of harms. This has something to do with the fact that this act of forgetting is more like a mental shifting of memory's gears: "It was in this year that my uncle began to break in upon the daily regularity of a clean shirt,—to dismiss his barber unshaven,—and to allow his surgeon scarce time sufficient to dress his wound, concerning himself so little about it, as not to ask him once in seven times dressing how it went on" (74). The selective evocation of pleasing, transacted memories allows Toby to forget the painful circumstances of his present confinement. The wound too is forgotten. By consciously redirecting memory, the change in mental focus causes a shift in bodily sensation. The mind does not allow the material brain to feel what is unpleasant. Toby commences the process of mapping as an iconic new brand of history-making. What's added here to his personal experience of Namur are other histories. The account of the wound is soon embellished and altered as Toby escapes into other fortifications. Such reading also requires imagination. Conceptualizing his escape into a different story that then becomes bound up with his own history, Toby allows himself to alter his memories through intersubjective layering, through global storytelling. Reading history is not merely a matter of "collating" or organizing events in time but is the "procuring of a plan"—a creative project whose intent will be to remap matter and space. As Tristram implies, the purpose of history is to demolish and then improve through "new works."

Ever the satirist, Tristram's ideal memory is like his ideal account: "Writers of my stamp have one principle in common with painters.—Where an exact copying makes our pictures less striking, we choose the less evil; deeming it even more pardonable to trespass against truth, than beauty" (74). This self-conscious digression on his writing process, inserted in the middle of Toby's story, is less a digression than an interpretive aside to the reader.

In returning to the notion that the "history" of the wound may "beguile [its] pain," we should consider the various potential meanings of history at the time. On the one hand, a historical account might represent, through an exacting realism, the events of the past. In this system of storytelling, history is essentially relived through mimetic processes (as per Freud's later notion of trauma). But Sterne's novel is also a fictional history of what passes in the mind, one that signals the power of fiction to alter historical accounts.[43] If we return to the novel's dedication, wherein the author promises a history that will "beguile . . . pain" through the shared "happy forms" of reading, we see that our narrator, like Toby, is in a removed state of confinement. However, his pain is "carried off" through the transports of the reader, who has been asked to take the book away into the country. The distracting force of the hobbyhorse's canter promises to carry us from present concern. Although the body is trapped in the circumstances of the present, the mind is free to range about time.

What if the mind could assist, convert, or change the sensations of matter? Toby's hobbyhorse, which grows up through the text of volume 2, conceives of an imaginative kind of memory that shifts the pathways of materialism's mind-body dialectic—one that has the power to alter the initial account. It is vital that we keep Tristram's dedicatory appeal to the reader in mind when we arrive at Toby's history, for the story, and the potency, of this new kind of memory to reconstitute bodily vigor has much to do with the manner in which Toby's memorial account is mapped and read. As Tristram says, Toby's preference is for geography over chronology (454–55), and thus Toby's mental state of perplexity over his wound is fixated on the "where" more than on the "when" or "how" of the injury. This is not simply a jibe at Locke's chronological duration; it also suggests the power of transacted memories to reconstruct forms in the world. The infamous error of communication between the widow Wadman and Uncle Toby makes this distinction clear; it is significant that Toby searches for the site of his wound outside (not inside) his body.

It is, therefore, no surprise that, after reading so extensively about the histories of other "fortified" bodies of war, Toby experiences a "sudden . . . change . . . as quick as lightning" wherein he begins to "sigh heavily for his recovery," becomes "impatient with his surgeon," "shuts up his books," and essentially takes his recovery into his own hands (74). Tristram explains this sentiment as Toby's "desire to get well and out of doors," which is the same as "the desire of life and health . . . implanted in man's nature" (75). Toby's desire for health and the outdoors essentially results in an attempt to go out of his mind. Yet this cannot be characterized as madness, for Toby shares this vital urge "in common with his species" (75).[44] As Alva Noë has suggested, this is the truly defining feature of consciousness: it is not something that goes on inside us; rather, consciousness is about "our interaction with the wider world."[45]

The Birth of a Bowling Green

The movement outward to the green shifts the art of memory away from a two-dimensional process of mapping to a three-dimensional activity of making things in the world. The map of Namur is a satire on empirical retention that envisions memory as a transactive process, but it is not until the bowling green model that memory's truly creative arts come to the fore. As Toby realizes that his confinement provides insufficient space for his routines, his movement outdoors foreshadows the reconstructive potential of memory to alter the materials of our environment. It turns out that the bowling green, a conscious plan or "design in execution," is the only cure for Toby's wound (76). As Trim suggests when he proposes the project, this sea change promises infinite space with which to "manage . . . matter" (76). Trim's plan is successfully seductive:

> These ravelins, bastions, curtins, and hornworks make but a poor, contemptible, fiddle faddle piece of work of it here upon paper, compared to what your Honour and I could make of it, were we in the country by ourselves, and had but a rood, or a rood and a half of ground to do what we pleased with: . . .—and I will be shot by your Honour upon the glacis of it, if I did not fortify it to your Honour's mind. . . .—For if your Honour . . . could but mark me the polygon, with its exact lines and angles, . . .—I would begin with the fossé, . . .—I would throw out

the earth upon this hand towards the town for the scarp,—and on that hand towards the campaign for the counterscarp . . .—and when I had sloped them to your mind,—an' please your Honour, I would face the glacis, as the finest fortifications are done in *Flanders,* with sods, . . . whether they are gazons or sods, is not much matter. . . .

Your Honour understands these matters. . . . I would work under your Honour's directions like a horse. . . .

. . .—We might begin the campaign, continued *Trim,* on the very day that his Majesty and the Allies take the field. . . .—Besides, your Honour would get not only pleasure and good pastime,—but good air, and good exercise, and good health,—and your Honour's wound would be well in a month. Thou hast said enough, *Trim,*—quoth my uncle *Toby,* (putting his hand into his breeches-pocket). . . .—Say no more, *Trim,* quoth my uncle *Toby,* leaping up upon one leg, quite overcome with rapture, . . . go down, *Trim,* this moment, my lad, and bring up my supper this instant.

Trim ran down and brought up his Master's supper,—to no purpose:—*Trim*'s plan of operation ran so in my uncle *Toby*'s head, he could not taste it.—*Trim,* quoth my uncle *Toby,* get me to bed:,—'twas all one.—Corporal *Trim*'s description had fired his imagination,—my uncle *Toby* could not shut his eyes.—The more he consider'd it, the more bewitching the scene appeared to him;—so that, two full hours before daylight, he had come to a final determination, and had concerted the whole plan of his and Corporal *Trim*'s decampment. (78–79)

Trim's version of military landscape gardening imagines the pleasures of three-dimensional form as vastly superior to the "fiddle faddle" two-dimensionality of paper. Like the first map, the bowling green is "marked" as an external reference to Toby's inscape, but here puns on marking and marksmanship ignite the potent firing of the imagination, reinvigorating a part that seems to have borne all the deadly marks of impotence. The polygon, transfigured by earthy matter, takes an imagined memory and gives it form. The bowling green is matter that stems from mind. "Sloped to [Toby's] mind," it transforms thought into "gazon" and "sod." Matter is both "started" (as Tristram says "fresh matter may be started," 31) by mind and "managed" by mind. Between Trim and Toby, the bowling green is also something "understood," a secret that binds them together like the referential system of satire itself.

After three years of failed medical recovery, Trim's project promises to restore Toby to health in a mere month. The short interval of time envisions a mind freed from the slow, progressive operations of Locke's durational existence; the mind liberates itself from matter by creating new matter, and thus time ceases to be the oppressive convention that imposes itself on mind and body.[46] One could argue that Trim's plan takes much less time even than a month, for the alleviating effects are apparently instantaneous for Toby. His mind catches the vision "painted, all at once, upon the retina of . . . [his] fancy (80)." What ensues is a couple of parenthetical references that tell the reader the truth of the subtext: Toby's wound no longer matters. "Leaping up upon one leg," Toby is cured of his need for the cane, and the potency of his member seems reignited by the sexual allusion to Toby "putting his hand into his breeches pocket." Rapture, ecstasy, enthusiasm all "fire" and "bewitch" the imagination so that Toby is abstracted from the late material concerns of his injury. He literally senses nothing but the scene projected by his mind: he "cannot taste" his food or fall asleep. Trim's inspiring image of "a rood and a half of ground to do whatever [they] are pleased with" provides Toby with a map that may be marked and filled according to his greatest mental desire. In this manner, Toby continues to rewrite personal history by appropriating the ideas of other persons and organizing matter as he goes so as to fit it to whatever his mind "determines." "The whole plan" of the three-dimensional map bears all the marks of conscious thinking; it is "concerted" and "determined" upon. As a matter that references the most fanciful kind of memory- and history-making, this second map is formed from the greatest of all intentions: Toby's desire to overcome personal distress. In this manner, the men begin to *re-member* a potentially traumatic war history.

Notably, the plan for the bowling green takes effect before it is even put into action. At the very birth of Toby's hobbyhorse, we see the capacity of the mind to alter reality:

> Never did lover post down to a belov'd mistress with more heat and expectation, than my uncle *Toby* did, to enjoy this self-same thing in private;—I say in private;—for it was sheltered from the house, as I told you, by a tall yew hedge, and was covered on the other three sides,

> from mortal sight, by rough holly and thickset flowering shrubs;—so that the idea of not being seen, did not a little contribute to the idea of pleasure preconceived in my uncle *Toby's* mind.—Vain thought! however thick it was planted about,—or private soever it might seem,—to think, dear uncle *Toby,* of enjoying a thing which took up a whole rood and half of ground,—and not have it known! . . . my uncle *Toby* and Corporal *Trim* managed this matter,—with the history of their campaigns, which were no way barren of events. (80)

From first to last, the narrative never explicitly confirms or denies whether Toby's bodily wound is ever healed. However, our narrator sets up our readerly expectations alongside Toby's through a parallelism that depends on reading external objects as an indirect system of signs. The language is all masturbatory: the map is described as a "mistress" that Toby "enjoy[s] . . . in private." But the mistress is also a material, "self-same thing," a reference, of course, to Toby's member. The scene of the bowling green, like the scene of Toby's first map, shows the reader what is covered up from every character's sight (including the widow's).

The landscape tracks the sublime form of the erect and "immortal" phallus. Like a scene out of John Cleland's *Fanny Hill*, the large and straight-lined tract of smooth garden walk is introduced by a hairy tangle of "rough holly" and "thickset . . . shrubs." The allusion to masturbation, "unknown" to the public, is a shared secret between men.[47] The matter at (or in) hand may not be expressed, but it is "managed" by the mind and most especially by "the history" of both mind and nation. In the end, Tristram subtly assures us that the bowling green, Toby's phenomenal hobbyhorse, is the cure to Toby's wound, and what remains once healed is "in no way barren of events." Fertile, potent, and re-membered, Toby's bowling green alludes to his mind's capacity to alter, embellish, and re-form events in time.

Volumes later, Tristram reminds his reader of the bawdy image of the bowling green,[48] badgering the reader into the work of both memory and imagination: "If the reader has not a clear conception of the rood and a half of ground which lay at the bottom of my uncle *Toby's* kitchen garden . . . the fault is not in me,—but in his imagination;—for I am sure I gave him so minute a description, I was almost ashamed of it" (355–56). While Toby's memory fictionalizes experience so as to alter historical events, the reader's memory and imagination are imposed upon. In effect, we become the mechanism of the fiction, *Tristram Shandy,* itself—our interest and perceptiveness are what make the bowling green mean, what ensure it becomes a legible object.

As masculinity is recuperated through the power of the metaphor, the effects of the project as a healing routine are all the while left to subtext. As the two go on through volume 6, carrying out their improvements on the bowling green, the reader registers what is not there as the most important effect of the whole scheme. Not once is Toby's wound mentioned, or, more important, felt.

Although a "private matter," the bowling green also demonstrates the intersubjective nature of memory. The model is constituted of Toby's memory *and* Trim's ingenuity and labor, for the work of the campaigns always follows this trajectory. Before the "storm of the counterscarp" between "*Lower Deule* . . . and the gate of St. *Andrew,*" the Corporal vows to "give away [his] Montero-cap . . . if [he does] not manage this matter to his honour's satisfaction" (361). What Trim calls Toby's satisfaction is, in essence, his memory: "As this was the most memorable attack in the whole war . . . my uncle Toby prepared himself for it with more than ordinary solemnity" (361). What is remembered and how it is remembered—what becomes matter and how that matter is fashioned—is stylistically crafted to Toby's memory and desire. Trim simply "manages" to make the "matter" possible.

This method of improvement tells us how Toby's memory serves to render his wound absent from the purview of history:

> My uncle *Toby* came down, as the reader has been informed, with plans . . . of almost every fortified town in *Italy* and *Flanders;* so let the Duke of *Marlborough,* or the allies, have set down before what town they pleased, my uncle *Toby* was prepared for them.
>
> His way, which was the simplest one in the world, was this; as soon as ever a town was invested—(but sooner when the design was known) to take the plan of it, (let it be what town it would) and enlarge it upon a scale to an exact size of his bowling-green; upon the surface of which, by means of a large role of pack-thread, and a number of small piquets driven into the ground, at the several angles and redans, he transferred the lines from his paper; then taking the profile of the place, with its works, . . .—he set the corporal to work—and sweetly went it on: . . .

CHAPTER XXII

When the town, with its works, was finished, my uncle *Toby* and the corporal began to run their first parallel—not at random, or any how—but from the same points and distances the allies had begun to run theirs; and regulating their approaches and attacks, by the accounts my uncle *Toby* received from the daily papers,—they went on. . . .

When the duke of *Marlborough* made a lodgment,—my uncle *Toby* made a lodgment too. (356–57)

As Jonathan Lamb has aptly argued, uncle Toby's "parallels" are exact parallels of the duke of Marlborough's every action.[49] For the strict empiricist, the bowling green may seem like no object of memory at all, for it lacks the foundation of personal experience. As Robert Chibka has argued of Tristram's narrative,[50] the green is composed of the memories of others. Toby's plans and designs take shape from a socially networked model of history.

His creation is an effective plagiarism that takes to heart Locke's greatest anxiety about language (that the experience of others will override personal sensation) and turns it into something fruitful. Toby's method fits and rescales the memories of others to his purpose of altering personal history. Events are "enlarge[d] . . . upon" to accommodate the "exact size of his bowling green." Let us not forget that the long track of green itself serves as a replacement phallus that stands in for the wound and thereby invigorates and heals Toby's body. Personal history is elided and a new history adopted, making Toby's constitutional fortification possible. This surreptitious mental theft carefully and exactly enacts a "transference" from the newspapers to paper, to the garden's material model member. Adopted and adapted, the experience of someone else's potent, fortified body of war is another "account" that Toby assimilates into his mind and body. Fiction-making proceeds from fiction reading; what is read is re-membered, self-appropriated and newly formed.

Toby's method of making and remembering history funnels in a sensation of "sweetness" that overrides the pain of the wound so that it no longer imposes itself on his mental or physical experience. Unlike Walter's reading habits, which often lead to forgetfulness, Toby's reading heals and creates. Truth is recast and fiction reclaimed through a slippery network of ever-evolving sensory experience, one that dispenses with the necessity of personal origins and laughs at the notion of genius as originality. Herein the stories of others, taken on as one's own, are requalified as healing and benign pleasures:

> To one who took pleasure in the happy state of others,—there could not have been a greater sight in the world, than, on a post-morning, in which a practicable breach had been made by the duke of *Marlborough*, in the main body of the place,—to have stood behind the horn-beam hedge, and observed the spirit with which my uncle *Toby*, with *Trim* behind him, sallied forth;—the one with the *Gazette* in his hand,—the other with a spade on his shoulder to execute the contents.—What an honest triumph in my uncle *Toby*'s looks as he marched up to the ramparts! What intense pleasure swimming in his eye as he stood over the corporal, reading the paragraph ten times over . . . lest . . . he [Trim] should make the breach an inch too wide,—or . . . too narrow. (357)

Tristram figures the two men, with spade and newspaper in hand, as collaborative artists who form their creation by reading and transacting the histories of other persons. The voyeuristic placement of the narrator who witnesses these events on the bowling green is likewise strategic. Sterne implies that the novel reader's pleasure (like that of the observing narrator) arises from a sympathetic transference in which the joy of others, their "happy state," becomes his own. Toby's habit of turning events from paper into clay-clod matter brings on a contagious "intense pleasure" that erases pain and sutures the "practicable breach" between the text and "the main body" of its reader. The narrator describes this science of "improvement" as an enduring "track of happiness" wherein even waiting for the news becomes "the torture of the happy." "Improvement," for Toby and the corporal, "open[s] fresh springs of delight in carrying them on." The borrowed origin of new matter is glossed over and redeemed as a self-fulfilling good in favor of its happy effects. Along with the stories from the *Gazette*, Trim's ingenuity helps in an implicitly social project of converting Toby's painful memories into newly remembered pleasures of military glory and bodily vigor. Much like Tristram's dependence on the reader, the art of reconstructing or "improving" memories relies on aesthetic receptivity. Toby's willingness to change his mind so as to heal his body is what sustains and actualizes the pleasing fiction.

In this way the design behind the material construction of the model towns becomes a metaphor for both the shared fiction of memory and the elasticity of the mind. Although Toby's creation may be said to defy principles of originality by heralding a realist system of exact representation, it leaves matter flexible, allowing for a constant "change of mind." In chapter 23 of volume 6, Trim has the idea of making a model of the besieged towns that allows the houses to "run up together" so as to "serve" as a unified and universal representation. Toby's improving additions to Trim's idea render the act of replication a paradoxically flexible affair: "The one was to have the town built exactly in the stile of those, of which it was most likely to be the representative.... The other was, not to have the houses run up together, as the corporal proposed, but to have every house independent, to hook on, or off, so as to form into the plan of whatever town they pleased" (359). Since the bowling green is an aesthetic object that is never published or circulated, unlike the novel or newspaper, it may be subject (like the mind itself) to endlessly fluid alteration. Toby can form and re-form his plans as he pleases; the diversely styled houses, like the aesthetics of the green, become ductile designs that give endless pleasure. In this way the plastic mind takes over when the body fails to render physical pain ineffectual. Here, Sterne also indicates his method for writing and for the aesthetic properties of the novel. Both the bowling green and *Tristram Shandy* are objects of prolific reference, which depend on the shared stories of others, but they are organized in such a manner that entertains notions of independence. Every part can be "hooked on, or off" at the pleasure and will of the writer/director/maker. The composite network of other people's memories and ideas takes a new form once personally appropriated and rearranged so as to reflect the "slope" and "stile" of the author's mind.

In this manner, the hobbyhorse is a fiction of infinite externalization, transference, and remembrance designed to sustain the pleasures of memory as imagination. In every material (ex)change enacted on the green, from the "converted" matter of the gates to the "addition" of the sentry box, memory fiction allows "Toby to take the field [once again] with great splendour" (358).[51]

The Pipe in the Box

The case of Uncle Toby's memory is reminiscent of a neural circuitry that rewires bodily impositions on the mind to reroute sensation from pain into pleasure. Moreover, the bowling green is not the only player in Toby's attempts to alter historical feeling; various objects become sources of potential fecundity in the text, activated by the mind's sensational desires. As memory and imagination work to form a bowling green model that is sloped to the desires of Toby's mind, objects take on qualities of mental agency in the grammatical signs and syntax of the text. One example is the matter of Uncle Toby's pipe, which seems always to stand in when his "great artillery would not bear powder" (360). The mind exchanges one inert object (or part) for another, active (or activated) one in a mentally infused rhetoric of vitalism that starts, or ignites, matter at will. The problem with the artillery (a metonym for Toby's wound) is solved when Trim turns his inventing mind to the pipe: "SOMETHING therefore was wanting, as a *succedaneum* . . . to keep up something like a continual firing in the imagination" (360). The replacement of one object by another is an exchange described as "one of the great *desiderata* of my uncle *Toby's* apparatus" (360), and thereby the willing transaction depends on the intentions of one man's inventiveness and the other's desires. The object itself activates Toby's brain through the vitalist rhetoric of matter in motion, as his "imagination" is continually fired by the pipe so as to forget the inertia of his wound. Mind and matter are mutually constitutive and dialectically related. Moreover, they are continually wired together in a cognitive system of social consciousness.

Objects map the exchange from one mind to another. When Trim offers the pipe to Toby's activating mind, it becomes the locus for intersubjective feeling. The pipe is passed back and forth, and, of course, the pipe itself is a thing that requires human agency to do its work. An instrument that alludes both to inspiration and to phallic potency, the object becomes an allegory for the hobbyhorse itself and the relationship between mind and matter: "Give me hold of the ivory pipe, *Trim,* said my uncle *Toby*—my uncle *Toby* put it to his lips,—drew it back directly,—gave a peep over the horn-beam hedge; never did my uncle *Toby's* mouth water so much for a pipe in his life.—My uncle *Toby* retired into the sentry-box with the pipe in his hand . . .—there's no trusting a man's self with such a thing in such a corner" (365). Through a kind of mock-heroic miniaturization, the smoke from the pipe replaces the full-blown smoke of military artillery, so that violence is rescaled into a diminutive, benign satire on war and masculinity.[52] But something happens when Toby borrows Trim's pipe: it is as though the pipe becomes a conduit for a type of masculine potency transferred (to use a Freudian term) sympathetically from Trim to his needful companion.

As the object of the pipe stands in for the wounded soldier's member, Toby regains the ability to activate this new matter (if not the old) by breathing life into the hollow instrument. The high biblical activity of making is rendered low into the bawdy affairs of the human body, but the mock-heroic effect, rife with homoerotic innuendo, is not grotesque. As man interfaces with matter, his desire "for life and health" is rekindled. The artillery fires again when the imagination turns the pipe into a full-scale military cannon. The masturbatory allusion of Toby sneaking off to the sentry box with the pipe rekindled references the capacity of the mind to render the body restored to its original powers.

Just as the pipe becomes the re-membered phallus that symbolizes the power of transference, the sentry box represents the mind that activates or directs the body. With a structure tailored to the body of the soldier, and a peephole for the eyes, the box is something like an empirical mind that takes in perceptual experience and directs the matters of the bowling green. Sentry boxes were typically shaped in the same style of a full (not a demi) bastion and looked like erect phalluses. The combination of both metaphors, however, may be read as a satirical attempt to reform the laws of empirical perception. By retiring with his new stand-in-artillery-machine-in-miniature to a box-as-mind-and-member, Toby signals the powers of transacted memories to activate and interact with matter. What occurs in the box, left to the reader's imagination, is also rendered material through the symbolic medium of the text, as objects become metaphorical references to Toby's mental landscape. In this manner, the reader-voyeur can peep behind the curtain without lifting a thing. Somewhere between pipe and box, Toby's physiological machinery aligns with his mind so that his body can carry out its natural passions.

Critics have often characterized the affairs on the bowling green as "war games." In frowning at the paradox of a man of sympathy who is obsessed with destruction, they have read Toby as an object of satire and not a reformative ideal.[53] My reading views Toby's hobbyhorse as less of a passionate obsession than as a means of carrying out the passions and bodily health. The text, in fact, answers this very paradox when in an oration to his brother, Walter, Toby attests to the nature of war not as a violent end in itself but as the natural role of the solider who is an instrument of nation. The nation's aim being one of "liberty," the soldier's intention, by extension, is one of liberation.

However, the liberty that arises from the bowling green wars pertains less to the body national than to the body natural. Toby's speech comes to a flourishing conclusion that suggests some motive unperceived by Walter (the ever-faulty "motive-monger," 367). Behind Toby's habit of mapping sieges, we find not a perverse addiction to violent destruction but another thing entirely: "The pleasure I have taken in these things,—and that infinite delight, in particular, which has attended my sieges in my bowling green, has arose within me, and I hope in the corporal too, from the consciousness we both had that in carrying them on, we were answering the great ends of our creation" (370). These wars in miniature resemble war in form alone—not in content or effect. Whereas war wounds and destroys, Toby's sieges heal, reconstitute, and reconstruct. They answer "the ends of our creation" as a matter of creation itself. Toby underscores the purposes of the sieges in the bowling green as the production of "infinite delight." Their end is "pleasure," and pleasure alone.

Aesthetic pleasure is "taken" from "things," underscoring the paradoxical temporality of the aesthetic: "infinite" feeling comes from the experience with a finite object. The effect is not merely emotional but physiological. Pleasure "arises *within*" Toby; it is internalized in the body once it is transfused, Toby opines, between the bodies of the two men. The rhetoric of the rising activity references the phallus but in the manner of a medical need to sustain the body's circulatory system. Most important, the pleasure of action (i.e., the siege) is derived not so much from body as from mind. It comes "from the *consciousness*" of "carrying on . . . creation." The creation of matter, like Tristram's commentary on the creation of a rational being through coitus, is moral and pleasing when it is consciously done and consciously felt. The literal and figural re-membering that Toby's war memorial performs depends on the conscious activity of a mind bent on pleasure over pain.

Nothing Matters in Love as War

If the plot of *Tristram Shandy* is essentially Toby's story of love and war, then the paradox of the novel is that forms are not what they appear to be. Toby's wars turn out to be a subliminal act of love. On the other hand, his love turns out to be a sublimation of war.[54] The comic-tragic shift from the pleasures of the bowling green to the perplexities of the affair with widow

Wadman occurs during the peace treaty of Utrecht, an event that "creates a shyness betwixt my uncle *Toby* and his hobby-horse," forcing him to "dismount." Aesthetic form and effect are misaligned in these events, and Tristram characterizes Utrecht as a "Fatal interval of inactivity!" (371-72).

It is during this period in the novel that Tristram subtly and intermittently reminds the reader of Toby's wound: "In cases like this, corporal, said my uncle *Toby*, slipping his right hand down to the middle of his cane, and holding it afterwards truncheon-wise, with his forefinger extended—. . ." (372). The phallic reference of the cane becomes a mark of returning impotence. As the reader remembers what he was wont to forget, Toby too struggles with a tyrannical memory that recalls pleasure only to remind him of its loss: "A DELUSIVE, delicious consultation or two of this kind, betwixt my uncle *Toby* and *Trim*, upon the demolition of *Dunkirk*,—for a moment rallied back the ideas of those pleasures, which were slipping from under him;—still—still all went on heavily—the magic left the mind the weaker" (373). Memory here operates something like David Hume's system of recollection wherein the memory of an impression is an "idea" of pleasure that causes a secondary impression, a reiterated experience that carries with it new forces of sensation. The conversation distracts in the "delusive, delicious" manner of the hobbyhorse that recalls pleasures to carry us away from pain. The problem is that the pleasure is fleeting. It lasts but "a moment." Ideas may be "rallied back," but as they signal the loss of what once was and is now "slipping" away, remembrance fails to invigorate the body as the mind returns "still—still" to the stasis of the present. "The magic" of a kind of memory that embraces the "delusions" of fiction and reconstructs events in the mind still risks temporal closure, that moment when the fiction must come to an end and can no longer sustain us, leaving the mind "weaker" than before.

But for now, at least, the text makes up for the temporal problems of Toby's feeling mind in time. Tristram goes on to catalogue and review all the masturbatory pleasures of Toby's wars in chapter 35 of volume 6, with dreams and prospects that "hurried on the blood," causing Toby to fall asleep and reawaken with ideas of glory "streaming" (373). These sexual innuendos reenact a memorial record of the mind's capacity to revitalize the body. The chapter ends with another exchange of metaphorical objects: when Toby's hands release the "trumpet of war," they take up the "sweet . . . lute" of inspired love (373). At the moment that Toby's mind risks slippage back into inactivity, the text keeps memory's fiction going by recounting pleasurable events. Like the substitution of the phallic lute for the equally phallic trumpet, the replacement of narrative recollection for the character's personal memory lends a fruitful hand. This very substitution becomes a way of carrying out Toby's love of war, albeit with new instruments.

In many ways, the referential role of objects in the episodes of Toby's amours expose the affair as a war between two minds. Although the tale seems obsessed with Toby's potentially impotent body, it might as easily be read as a story of the many miscarriages of the widow's imagination. The history begins when Toby is obliged to take a bed in the widow's house:

> A daughter of Eve, for such was widow Wadman, and 'tis all the character I intend to give of her—
>
> —"*That she was a perfect woman;*" ... or any thing you please—than make a man the object of her attention, when the house and all the furniture is her own.
>
> There is nothing in it out of doors and in broad day-light, where a woman has a power, physically speaking, of viewing a man in more lights than one—but here, for her soul, she can see him in no light without mixing something of her own goods and chattels along with him—till by reiterated acts of such combinations, he gets foisted into her inventory—. (440-41)

Widow Wadman's fancy effectively turns Toby into an object that can be owned.[55] Like the bed he sleeps in, Toby becomes an inert piece of mental and physical furniture in the context of the widow's mind. The problem returns to Locke's anxiety about unnatural (though habitual) association, and it likewise borrows his mind-as-storage cabinet metaphor. The widow perceives Toby through such a light, or filter, that "mixes" furniture, "chattel," and "goods" with the man himself through a cognitive process of "reiterated acts of ... combination." Much like the associations of Jonathan Swift's poor Strephon ("The Lady's Dressing Room"), the widow's faultily wired wit makes a fatal inventory that frustrates her ability ever to carry out her passionate objectives. By turning Toby into parlor furniture, the widow's imagination re-renders what was just revitalized back into inert matter.

In her efforts to make Toby Shandy fall in love with her, the widow not only imaginatively projects new figural forms onto the object of her affections but enacts her own siege on Toby's mind:

> Whatever town or fortress the corporal was at work upon, during the course of their campaign, my uncle Toby always took care on the inside of his sentry-box, which was towards his left hand, to have a plan of the place, fasten'd up with two or three pins at the top, but loose at the bottom, for the conveniency of holding it up to the eye, &c . . . as occasions required; so that when an attack was resolved upon, Mrs. Wadman had nothing more to do, when she had got advanced to the door of the sentry-box, but to extend her right hand; and edging in her left foot at the same movement, to take hold of the map or plan, or upright, or whatever it was, and with outstretched neck meeting it half way,—to advance it towards her; on which my uncle Toby's passions were sure to catch fire. (447)

I previously noted the metaphor of mind that the sentry box represents. By following the archetype, we might read this scene as an attempt on the part of the widow Wadman to change Toby's mind—one wherein the figure is made literal. The attack is essentially on Toby's "plans" or "projects." Reaching into the proverbial sentry box, the widow steals Toby's plans of war in an attempt to exchange them for her own plans of carnal love. Parts of the passage are written in what might be read as a precursor to free indirect style, for it is the widow, not Tristram, who presumes "Toby's passions . . . sure to catch fire." Toby's map is hung so as to be easily eyed from within the box/mind. For whoever is willing to enter into Toby's hobbyhorsical mental state, the map is left in a precarious position—easily seized by any passerby who gets the reference. In this manner, reading opens up the space between minds.

Of course, the widow, in inviting Toby into her house of inventories, also trespasses on fallow ground. The bowling green is a secret, hidden love affair of fruitful labors, hedged in and walled off like the sentry box or any metaphor of a mind bent on illicit thoughts. In a novel wherein the meeting of minds is a rarity, and interpretation is always subjective, penetrating another's mind proves a dangerous affair. Whereas Trim's ingenuity succeeds, the widow's vexed Lockean system fails.

We might read Mrs. Wadman as a satire on objectification and materialism, for her attempts to move matter turn out to be something like the activity of moving furniture around. She places her hands, her legs, her fingers near to Toby's body, but when these "pushings, protrusions, and equivocal compressions" put Toby's "centre into disorder" (448), it is not Toby's phallus or mind that participates in the disorienting pleasure. Rather, like a mere object knocked down, Toby again falls prey to Newton's gravity. In this manner, the widow's attacks are perpetually frustrated in a battle of wits, wherein she never fully penetrates Toby's unique way of thinking:

> When the attack was advanced to this point;—the world will naturally enter into the reasons of Mrs. Wadman's next stroke of generalship—which was, to take my uncle Toby's tobacco-pipe out of his hand as soon as she possibly could; which, under one pretence or other, but generally that of pointing more distinctly at some redoubt or breast-work in the map, she would effect before my uncle Toby (poor soul!) had well march'd above half a dozen toises with it.
>
> —It obliged my uncle Toby to make use of his forefinger.
>
> The difference made in the attack was this; . . . she might have travelled with it, along the lines, from Dan to Beersheba, had my uncle Toby's lines reach'd so far, without any effect: For as there was no arterial or vital heat in the end of the tobacco-pipe, it could excite no sentiment—it could neither give fire by pulsation—or receive it by sympathy—'twas nothing but smoak. (447–48)

In the end, the joke is on Mrs. Wadman, and in this manner she becomes an object of satire that threads through the final volumes of the novel. The widow touches the object that stands in for Toby's phallus, only to find out the mereness of the metaphor. The pipe, without "arterial or vital heat," cannot receive the sympathetic sensation of touch from her. The widow commences an assault on Toby's passions, assuming that that passion (in the manner of a sympathetic materialism) can be transferred or transfused by hands alone. What the widow fails to see is that Toby's hobbyhorse is less a corporeal passion than a corporeal distraction—a system of mind over matter perceptions. In capturing the pipe, the widow's materially inspired imagination causes her to steal what is essentially no thing. Inert in the widow's hands, the pipe is in no way the same vital matter that it is when it lies within Toby's own grasp. Only there may it be ignited by Toby's memory and imagination. Through perverse combinations, the widow confuses mind with matter, but the relationship between the two is not so monolithic. Left empty-handed, the widow finds the affair "'twas nothing but smoak."

For Toby, falling in love essentially takes the form of a flesh wound when he confuses the breaking of the blister on his backside for a wound to his heart (468). Walter likewise defines love as a "SITUATION" not a "SENTIMENT" (475). In this manner, love is not of the mind but of the body, and like the widow Wadman, it follows a materialist trajectory in the novel that is dependent on the environment that the mind lives in.

Nevertheless, the objective world that comes to represent the affairs of love always, in a shadowy way, recalls the sweet memories of the bowling green for the reader. For example, Toby's belief that he can bear children is evidence, like the blister, that he has been mounting his horse for so long that he no longer feels the material effects of his wound (472–73). The powerful mental forces of Toby's hobbyhorse are always a backdrop to the novel, and, as with the periodic return of Toby's pipe, our readerly expectations are always prepared for their comeback. When the corporal flourishes his cane in a diatribe on liberty, we, like uncle Toby, cast an "earnest look" back to the "bowling green" (491). The "inactivity" of the period of Utrecht (372) and the widow Wadman affair signals a shift in the way minds interface with the world. Of course, the plot itself never did constitute much action at all. As Tristram states, Uncle Toby "seldom went further than the bowling green" (487). With the bowling green in no need of improvement, however, the "inactivity" after the peace treaty articulates a particular species of mental inertia that poses risks to Toby's healing process.[56] The philosophical materialism rhetorically satirized in the love affairs also seems to underscore what is missing, or lost, in empirical systems of memory's relationship to mind and world.

The lost love of the bowling green is best captured in the military attacks of Trim and Toby on the house of the widow Wadman wherein the form of the military hobbyhorse, in some sense, is kept alive. Now it is Walter and Mrs. Shandy, not Toby in his sentry box, who peer through the peephole to espy the event. Tristram seizes the occasion to explain his unique system of narrative digression as a response to empiricism: "When issues of events like these my father is waiting for, are hanging in the scales of fate, the mind has the advantage of changing the principle of expectation three times, without which it would not have power to see it out" (500). Looking on every new attitude and shifting pathway of the corporal's trajectory, Walter Shandy, who is ever the student of empiricism, finds vexation in the need to change his course of mind. But this frustration of expectation is precisely the system that Sterne's novel is built on. The hobbyhorse even trespasses against the logic of David Hume's radical skepticism as it defies all expectations in rendering any matter possible through its swift, unprecedented changes of mind. Volume 9, chapter 10, ends with a march down an avenue "diametrically opposite to [Walter's] expectation" (501). We note here a rift in the mental states of both brothers as the source of Walter's "soreness of humour" is the very spring for Toby's happy remedy (501). Still, the difference of the various cognitive systems in the text begs the question, what happens to Lockean duration or Humean expectation when events do not proceed from like causes? Instead of viewing *Tristram Shandy* as an attack on John Locke or David Hume, we might, as Cristina Lupton has suggested, read the text on its own terms.[57] Walter's frustration and Toby's hobbyhorse borrow from the stuff of empiricism and materialism, but Toby's way of thinking generates new possibilities for the circuitous relationship between mind and world, memory and matter.

Toby's cognitive process may never throw the associative mechanisms of empiricism out the window, but it does add something to the equation. The hobbyhorse re-forms historical experience, and as it does so, the embellished fiction, the adoption of the potent, successful histories of others, becomes appropriated in such a way as to replace Toby's initial ("real") memory. Fiction itself, more so than philosophy, is the most apt of forms, Sterne realizes, to demonstrate the strange narrative phenomenon in which the mind reroutes memories by creating matter from mind and assimilating matter back into mind again. Given this dialectical pattern, it is no surprise that in the end, the story returns to where it began. Finally, Toby's love of war wins out over the widow's war of love:

> —but when Mrs. Wadman went round about by Namur to get at my uncle Toby's groin; and engaged him to attack the point of the advanced counterscarp, and *pêle mêle* with the Dutch to take the counterguard of St. Roch sword in hand—and then with tender notes playing upon his ear, led him all bleeding by the hand out of the trench, wiping her eye, as he was carried to his tent—Heaven! Earth! Sea!—all was lifted up—the springs of nature rose above their levels—... and had he been worth a thousand, he had lost every heart of them to Mrs. Wadman.
>
> —And whereabouts, dear Sir, quoth Mrs. Wadman, a little categorically, did you receive this sad blow?—In asking this question,

> Mrs. Wadman gave a slight glance towards the waistband of my uncle Toby's red plush breeches, expecting . . . that my uncle Toby would lay his fore-finger upon the place—It fell out otherwise—for my uncle Toby having got his wound before the gate of St. Nicolas, in one of the traverses of the trench, opposite to the salient angle of the demi-bastion of St. Roch; he could at any time stick a pin upon the identical spot of ground where he was standing when the stone struck him: this struck instantly upon my uncle Toby's sensorium—and with it, struck his large map of the town and citadel of Namur and its environs, which he had purchased and pasted down upon a board by the Corporal's aid, during his long illness—it had lain with other military lumber in the garret ever since, and accordingly the Corporal was detached into the garret to fetch it.
>
> My uncle Toby measured off thirty toises . . . from the returning angle before the gate of St. Nicolas . . .
>
> Unhappy Mrs. Wadman!—
>
> . . .—but my heart tells me, that in such a crisis an apostrophe is but an insult in disguise. . . .
>
> CHAPTER XXVII
> My uncle Toby's Map is carried down into the kitchen. (529–31)

The passage of the final attack leading to the famous miscommunication between the widow and Uncle Toby posits various possibilities for the way physical trauma may be assimilated in the mind. Critics have mostly focused on the linguistic gap of communication that leads to the lovers' failed consummation.[58] However, if we consider that this is an amour with all the Machiavellian strategies and tactics of war, we might consider this final breach between Toby and the widow in a different light.

The passage returns to the hobbyhorse in a manner that triumphs the notion of memory's healing and distracting capacities. We begin with a reenactment of Toby's wounding at the battle of Namur that exactly replicates the scene, with one significant addition—the widow as a spectator. The scene is written as though it is relived in Toby's mind: he even bleeds when coming out of the trench. The relived experience of the war trauma, its mimetic repetition, which culminates in the sympathetic gestures of Mrs. Wadman, is what begets Toby's love. Sympathy, for Toby, with its shared language of tears and soft whispers, is understood. And, as a shared mode of communication, it does the trick. Yet there's something unsettling about the fact that the widow must reinvoke Toby's wound to obtain his love. Her amorous attack is rife with a palpable, physical violence that the "war" episodes on the bowling green never quite see (even with their mock-epic miniaturization of "smoak" and military cannons). The first part of the passage mixes the rhetoric of sympathy with what critics have considered to be a precursor to the structures of Freudian trauma: the physical pain is repeated and relived by way of the mind's subliminal reevocation of an idea. But the passage does not end here. The miscommunication that supplants the sympathetic communication in a manner saves Toby from a kind of memory that merely repeats painful events. Mrs. Wadman's question regarding "where" Toby received the wound sends his memory straight back to the period of his confinement, during which his visitors barraged him with the exact same inquiry.

Everett Zimmerman has deftly argued that this moment in the narrative threatens to reopen Toby's wound after the healing activities of the bowling green. By sending for his map, however, Toby renders the wound "historical and documentable but not present."[59] I would add to this argument that the document of memory that prevails also references a transacted, embellished, or fictionalized history made real. In this moment, the communication between the lovers is breached, and Mrs. Wadman's expectations are frustrated in the same manner as Walter's. The language that follows exactly reiterates Tristram's initial description of the wound in the novel at the start of volume 2. Again, memory becomes a vehicle of relived experience for both Toby and the reader, but that experience is embedded within the language of the fiction, both Toby's fiction on the bowling green and the fictional narrative of *Tristram Shandy* itself. As Tristram repeats the manner in which Toby "got his wound" and how he could pinpoint it on the map, the narrative tautology "strikes" Toby's "sensorium." The association is complete and Toby's memory is rewired, not to the original traumatic event but to the map. As we track the repetition of the word "strike," the grammar of experience takes a dramatic turn, acquiring new direct objects as it careens through Toby's mind. In lieu of the struck groin, we encounter the "struck sensorium" (presumably where the ghost of the wound lives upon the mind). But this mental injury too quickly becomes displaced. Finally, the striking ends when the "struck" sensorium again gives way to Toby's "striking" up of the map. The secondary memory of the map has replaced the sensory original.

It is important to recognize how the tautology operates here as a system of reference for the reader. I have argued that the map is an object in the text that eventually allows Toby to externalize his pain and alter his history into the pleasures of the potent body. Throughout the affair, and even throughout the superior pleasures of the bowling green, the initial paper map that began Toby's healing process and ultimately freed him from his confinement has been forgotten. Like a dead soldier lying "with other military lumber in the garret," the forgotten map has become like the widow's furniture or the books of Walter's library: an inert object in a mental collection of mere matter. Brought back to mind, the map is revitalized alongside its sentimental association as the thing that led to the idea of the bowling green in the first place. In this manner, a practice of mental remapping surfaces at the end of the love affair when Toby's pleasing memory of the map overrides the painful memory of his wound.

Associations strike—but into new neural territories. Fiction, freely felt, is the real rerouted thing that prevails. Toby's mind chooses the fictional, healing memory over the original painful wound, but this, I would argue, is not a repression, to adopt a Freudian anachronism for Sterne's investigation into how the mind and body may relate in scenarios of distress. Rather, Toby's change of mind, simply put, is a shift in mental focus. The original imprint (to use an empirical term) of the wound has not been erased, but more probably it has been altered. Returning to chapter 3, volume 2, we recall that Toby cannot fully remember or map his wound from personal experience; thus a potentially traumatic memory soon gives way to a less personal, or fictional, history transacted from books like "*Gobesius's military architecture and pyroballogy*" (72). By associating the site of his wound not with his "eye-witness" picture of the siege at Namur but rather with a map constructed in part through plans purchased and procured from other historians, Toby's memory pathways in *Tristram Shandy* tell a story different from Freud's trauma. By departing from direct perceptual data as the empirical source for memory, Sterne's joke has serious implications for memory in intellectual history. Toby's associations might be better likened to Freud's earlier, reconstructive model of memory. Nevertheless, unlike a Freudian patient, Toby's cultivated habit of pleasure rewrites history and distracts us, as Tristram would say, from the present "cares" of life. The attack ends with the "unhappy Mrs. Wadman." The epithet indicates another loss for the materialist widow in a battle of wits that reenvisions the complex sensory relationships between memory and the worlds it inhabits. Likewise, the version of mind that triumphs here is a carefree Shandean exertion of mind over matter; it escapes present sensation and chronology by choosing to live in the preferable space of the fiction. The final apostrophe to the widow, as Tristram confesses, is no real lament but a satirical jibe, an "insult" thinly disguised. Indeed, this is not the kind of love story to be wished for, wherein Toby, retraumatized, is relegated to the status of someone else's furniture.

As we follow Toby's mind in time, scanning history to locate the best moment of "sensory" focus, the narrative too begins to grow even more radically disorganized than before. Toby calls for the map in chapter 26, and the corporal accordingly fetches it, so that before the end of the chapter, Toby is already measuring out thirty toises in order to reference his wound. In the next chapter we are again thrust back to the fetching of the map, and narrative history seems to follow an ever-backward impulse. It is significant that these repeated throwbacks always return to the map as the referential thing that supplants the real. Time, it seems, is not mapped like space, measured by way of exactly thirty toises. Rather, it follows the mental trajectories of memory's favored haunts. Although Toby's cognition is anything but chronological, it is not necessarily disordered. Rather, mental time moves so as to emphasize the most fanciful and pleasing of memories—evolving by willfully returning to neural sites of distracting delight. The maps of paper and garden that Toby makes out of memory alter history and time, resetting Toby's "tracks" and "trains" toward happier destinations.

Reading Minds: It's All Hypothetical

Undergirding the end of the novel is also another commentary on fiction itself. The love as war that the widow seeks out is fueled by a nosy desire for "truth"; she is bent on investigating the rumor of Toby's impotence. The widow's attempt to access truth by way of parallels explains the affair between Bridget and the corporal. The concurrence of both love affairs, incidentally, becomes the shared formal strategy of amorous battle; Toby and Trim and the widow and Bridget sit on opposite sides with similar plans of attack. Although their forms align, through a kind of parallelism, the mental intentions behind these coterminous designs (and readerly interpretations of them) diverge. As we follow these battles for information, it seems as though Bridget and the widow will win the day when the corporal discovers the "true" status of Toby's groin to the housemaid in the middle of sexual intercourse (532). However, this communication marks a fair exchange, for it sets Trim on guard as to what the widow is actually about. The source of the whole inquiry is a matter of gossip that circulates back to Susannah and Mrs. Shandy (537). Concerned for Toby's feelings, Trim withholds the information of the widow's motives from his friend (534). But when Toby lauds the widow for her sympathetic frame of mind, Trim can no longer let the ruse go on: he lets out the truth of the whole affair, informing Toby of Mrs. Wadman's motives, a carnal lust that has caused her to question Toby's bodily fitness.

This is where the affairs between the widow and Toby seemingly drop from Tristram's story. However, the "secret articles" of Toby's "siege" (is he impotent or not?) are never revealed to the reader except as a matter of gossip, and the quest for information gives way to Walter's diatribe against women and the passions in a manner that upbraids both the widow and the reader for their interest. Here, Tristram comments on his father's tendency to "crucify TRUTH" by turning a natural "event" into "an hypothesis" (537). This is the very status of Toby's groin at the end of the novel—a mere "hypothesis," or supposition, that masks the truth in favor of upholding the fiction. Like Toby's memory, Walter's antirealist preference for history hovers on the line between true events and fictional embellishments. When Walter's "eloquence [is] rekindled" (537), so too is Toby's pipe, and we see him smoking it again in the final chapter of the novel. The talk of the town, a violent assault against privacy that seeks out "truth" at all costs, gives way to the referential object that masks the real by simply turning it into a "hypothesis."

The novel's famous ending with the allegory of a "COCK and BULL" story replaces one tale of potential impotence with another. The story's focus is on the bull's reputation: whereas the town suspects the bull of being impotent, Walter suspects the cow of coming before her time (539). As per eighteenth-century medical beliefs about conception, Walter assumes it is thereby the cow who fails to calve. The silly cow, like Mrs. Wadman, becomes the satirical scapegoat that diverts attention from the question at hand. The story that masks (and references) Toby's affairs parallels it in both content and structure, for, like the text's other controversial tales, it is dropped. Even at the end, the novel keeps up a referential system of metaphorical parallelism and elusive aposiopesis. *Tristram Shandy* abruptly ends with two perspectives hanging in midair, the talk of the town hovering beside Shandean hypothesis. Whichever way we choose, truth is crucified.

Hence we are left with Mrs. Shandy in a vexed state of confusion. Yet what is alluded to in the world of objects at the end of *Tristram Shandy* provides the reader with a form of silent communication, and here again, form, not language or conversation, is the signifying thing. Just as Toby is free to take up or set down his pipe at will, Tristram takes up and sets down the written text as it pleases him. A cock and bull story is a fiction, and fiction overrides truth, or at least it is the favored choice of this Shandean world.

The pipe and the story of the bull share a formal reference to Toby's groin. The former stands in for the phallus as an object that assists and allows artillery to fire; the latter is the scapegoat for sexual reputation, the digression that conceals the truth of Toby's wound through another narrative diversion. Toby's and Tristram's hobbyhorses in the end collide in an attempt to mask reality and divert our attention toward the revelries of fiction. In realizing the hypothesis, we thereby cross the divide between objective reference and fictional mind. By suturing the gap, our witty remembrance lends credence to the fiction's greatest desires. This, after all, is the hobbyhorse's "useful" intention (471). Through memory and imagination, it entertains the hypothetical as a state of mind that abstracts us from a world of distressing cares into new and pleasing matters.

Novels like *Tristram Shandy*, and to a lesser extent *Robinson Crusoe*, demonstrate how socially networked and transacted memories can intervene to alleviate physical trauma or distress by allowing subjects to alter their personal histories and environments. But what happens when a culture's collective memory itself takes on traumatic structures? The next chapter takes up this very question in turning to Frances Burney's innovative revision of the *Bildungsroman* novel. *Evelina, or, The History of a Young Lady's Entrance into the World* exemplifies how individual memories can shift historical expectations by challenging ideologically ingrained patterns of thinking and acting.

❖ CHAPTER 3 ❖

Evelina and the Virtues of Memory

> Monimia. "Am I then grown so cheap, just to be made
> A common stake, a prize for love in jest?" . . .
> Monimia. ":indeed my nature's easy;
> I'll ever live your most obedient wife,
> Nor ever any privilege pretend
> Beyond your will; for that shall be my law;—"
> —THOMAS OTWAY, *The Orphan*

In Thomas Otway's famous she-tragedy, "the beauteous orphan, fair Monimia" (93) identifies herself in a manner that has come to characterize two salient features of the genre's heroines in Restoration drama: the "passive protagonist" whose sexuality "facilitates a process of female commodification."[1] Monimia's fear that she will become a "common" thing in the game of love smacks of a self-fulfilling prophesy. For today's reader, she seemingly seals the deal in a profession of her love that equates feminine passion with the relinquishing of agency. Prized and reprised throughout the play, Monimia's "easy nature" threads law and life to another person external from herself. Emptied of the weights of will, she opens herself up, as it were, to a narrative of impending rape and tragedy.

Mindlessness, Otway warns, poses a threat to the body. And bodies survive by a much less easy virtue: that is, the hard business of consciousness. Although absent, intention lies at the heart of the she-tragedy's dramatic arch. As Frances Ferguson reminds us, rape becomes a crime only "on the level of mental states."[2] Monimia's "easy nature" flourishes as a feeling, but not as a mental state in the philosophical sense, for it renounces intentionality. How can one rape, or take away, what has already been relinquished—what is no longer there? Without intentions of her own, Monimia lacks the capacity to consent. Enter in what would become a long-standing fascination with the legal and mental complexities of rape in eighteenth-century literature and patriarchal culture. The theatrical tradition of the she-tragedy took on myriad redactions in the newly emerging genre of the eighteenth-century novel, as did the figure of the orphan. Again and again, fictional women of the eighteenth century, adrift from their homes or parents, encounter constant threats to both their virtue and life. In *Love in Excess, Pamela,* and *Clarissa,* in *The Monk, The Mysteries of Udolpho,* and *Celestina,* in *Sense and Sensibility*—even in *Fanny Hill*—Monimia's fate haunts her fictional successors.

Frances Burney's *Evelina,* however steeped in this tradition, makes an interesting addition to this long (and much abbreviated) list. Eighteenth-century readers might easily have identified the heroine's archetypal passivity, and scholars often speak to those budding desires that quickly propel Evelina forward into an infrastructure that forever subjects women to systematic impulses of commodification. Evelina, however, overturns the social status quo when she avoids rape, changing novelistic archetypes of lost female virtue in the eighteenth century.

Most compellingly, Burney reimagines the parameters of the she-tragedy by wedding it to another emerging novelistic genre. As a story of personal growth and/as social assimilation, Evelina's "entrance into the world of manners and mores" is easily classified as an early *Bildungsroman.* Franco Moretti defines the genre as one that synthesizes the formation of one's individuality with her integration into the social system.[3] According to Moretti, the drama of the classical *Bildungsroman* is one wherein individuals must in the end "consent" to give up the more enticing story of their "individual" self-becoming in order to assimilate into society; we might equate this moment of integration with Evelina's marriage.[4] Yet this patriarchal reading of the marriage plot novel savors a little too heavily of Monimia's dangerous love. It not only reduces the idea of consent to its relinquishing, it fails to underscore the gendered implications of such a contract. A man who is integrated into the public sphere in the historical period during which the *Bildungsroman* genre flourished might enter a world of social thinking, but a woman's societal assimilation would mean giving up her newfound education and agency to become a sold commodity, another man's property.

Indeed, this is Evelina's challenge when she enters into a world replete with marketable commodities and social forums: how to make herself into something more than a mere object? By rehinging bodies to minds, Burney's feminist project provides a boon to Monimia's tragic monism. By crossing her archetypes, Burney challenges our assumptions about both womanhood and personhood in eighteenth-century literature by taking the great paradox of the Enlightenment to heart: how to be an autonomous agent living in a world that takes social thinking as our greatest modern privilege. The novel is a voicing of consent, and dissent, that makes intentions possible for women in the public sphere.

It does so by revising the narrative and ideological notions of the *Bildungsroman* by recasting it as a story of memory growth. Typically, we might place narratological emphasis on the *Bildungsroman*'s orientation toward future outcomes. For Franco Moretti, this structural trend dovetails with the genre's emergence in the late eighteenth century:

> Youth is . . . modernity's "essence," the sign of a world that seeks its meaning in the *future* rather than in the past. . . . But while hope looks ahead, towards the future, the valorization of the existing order by the classical *Bildungsroman* prompts hero and reader to look back, towards the past. The refusal to consider the future still "open," we have seen, is presented as an indication of maturity. *Bildung* is concluded under the sign of memory, or *mémoire voluntaire*, of the rationalization of the accomplished journey.[5]

By proposing a teleological structure for the *Bildungsroman* narrative, Moretti equates "memory" with an unalterable past; it is the sign of the novel's ending, and its association with closure explains his use of the term memory as what one "already knows."[6] This attitude toward memory is one that we have seen before in this book; it conjures up ideas of recollection's meaning in early eighteenth-century empiricism as an archive of unchanging mental imprints. My focus on the significance of memory in Burney's early novelistic construction of self-consciousness reconsiders theories of the *Bildungsroman* by complicating our sense of the narrative mind in time. In this chapter, I attempt to demonstrate a theory of *Bildungsroman* subjectivity that depends as much on memory as imagination in its framework for self-consciousness throughout the main body of the novel's narrative. Most significantly, Burney's *Evelina* does not end with a teleological account of memory, in which her personal history and agency come to a close that has no bearing on the "'future of the species.'"⁷ Rather, my reading of *Evelina* will more closely resemble what Mikhail Bakhtin has identified as the most complex version of the *Bildungsroman* in his classification system. In this, "man's individual emergence is inseparably linked to historical emergence."⁸ *Evelina* tracks the growth of a character's memory that allows her safely to integrate into the social and public sphere, but the end result of this process signals the historical emergence of a new kind of feminine virtue and agency in the culture of modernity.

Previous chapters have shown the various ways that memory becomes involved in processes of making. Altering personal things, accounts, and histories, memory's creative force in novels such as *Robinson Crusoe* or *Tristram Shandy* takes social and global pathways to alleviate personal crisis and alter individual experience. Frances Burney's early *Bildungsroman*, *Evelina*, however, reverses the direction of this oft-chartered course: herein, personal memory changes so as to alter history and culture on a social and global scale. To return to Samuel Taylor Coleridge's definition of mentality, intelligent "forces" are dynamic and dialectical; they "find" themselves in nature, transform nature, and also "grow" within themselves.⁹

This chapter explores memory's emergent self-conscious faculties in the *Bildungsroman*, a genre that seeks to capture memory's evolution. How does memory grow so as to become no mere organic thing but a force of consciousness that alters our situations and expectations, among other things? To answer this question, we must confront a rather baffling paradox that resides in memory's intellectual history: if we do not so discretely or entirely *own* our memories, how do we come to act as though we do? How is memory self-appropriated so as conform to our desires of self-preservation and satisfaction? Put differently, this chapter explores how memory develops its uncommon creative powers on common grounds.

Evelina's *Bildung* reveals an increasing narrative turn toward the work of the conscious memory. What is more, memory facilitates a process of the self-made woman that allows the protagonist to avert harm and distress, to flourish both socially and mentally, even though her feelings so often reach Monimian heights. When Frances Burney's early *Bildungsroman* (1778) entered London's literary scene, it supplied readers with more than a narrative invested in its protagonist's social maturation. The novel is also a developmental account of the young heroine's self-conscious faculties. Initially, the narrative grounds itself in an attempt to represent Evelina's thoughts through her emotional relationship to her surroundings; volumes 1 and 2 delineate paradigms of self-consciousness as embodied awareness. However, these momentary reflections, akin to feelings of shame and mortification, prove fleeting and problematic in relationship to Evelina's actions. It is only in the final volume, when Evelina reflects on her experience with objects and others in time, that she attains agency and independence. As Evelina's thinking becomes less reactive and automatic, she gains an ability to survive and overcome situations that pose unremitting threats to her female virtue. Evelina's mind evolves, adapting to new environments, so that she can avoid the personal harm of rape and change the reader's social expectations. Burney's novel invokes archetypes of the she-tragedy to posit a feminist message that reveals how memory mediates and overturns historical outcomes.

What's Mine Is Yours: Sympathy, Memory, Self-Consciousness

Evelina's acquisition of self-conscious subjectivity emerges specifically in the course of the narrative through her engagement with time, and through the insertion of her own consciousness into the processes of temporality. The tendency in recent critical discourse has been to move away from what has been dubbed "interiority," "inwardness," or even in vague terms the "psychology" of literary characters to a concept of modernity that equates persons with matter, and subjects with objects.[10] My understanding of the development of self-consciousness in *Evelina* counters these object-oriented readings of novelistic subjectivity not by repeating the age-old story of "individualism" but rather by promoting a new attention to the significance of temporality in the representation of subjectivity in this period.[11]

In his transformative work *Actions and Objects*, Jonathan Kramnick draws an important distinction between "actions" and "events," associating the former with "mental causation": "the topic of actions involved mental terms (including intentions) as a particular kind of cause. A close look at all kinds of [eighteenth-century] texts shows that these causes move in several directions, sometimes from within but just as often from without."[12] At the heart of Kramnick's investigation into the nature of causality and action is an essential truth about empiricist discourses of mind: "*Actions extend mind into the world,*" but "compatibilism brought the world into the mind."[13] Kramnick discusses how causation unites mind and world, but his investigation into actions demonstrates how the exact relationship between the two is under constant debate in eighteenth-century theories of consciousness. He writes, "Attempts to resolve the problem of mental causation came in a variety of forms: from the idea that mental states or properties might have no causal role to play—*epiphenomenalism* as it is now called—to the notion that external objects and events do the causing for us; from accounts of the mind's free and independent force on the material world to a recognition that causal relations are best inferred from an outsider's stance."[14] In other words, causation is always a part of action—but the real question for eighteenth-century investigations into consciousness is about the origin of causes, whether they come from our internal "self" or from our external environment. Sometimes, for Kramnick, the origins of causality are left ambiguous, as in his reading of Samuel Richardson's *Clarissa*. For the most part, however, Kramnick's readings favor the externalist approach. In this way, his work is very similar to Sandra Macpherson's *Harm's Way*, which complicates presumptions about intention and moral responsibility by revealing the often externalized forces of causality through a novelistic approach to accident that demonstrates how it is possible to cause harm without having agency or even personhood.

Both Macpherson and Kramnick seek to move beyond a conventional character analysis focused on ideas of interiority or psychology and toward an understanding of the relevance of materialism in relation to persons and objects. This trend in equating subjects with things,[15] alongside new materialist approaches to science and literature in the Enlightenment, may leave us with a "shudder"[16] when contemplating the true nature of ourselves as beings in the world. But it has also changed the way we view modernity and the rise of the novel by revealing a new story, a new facet, of eighteenth-century life. While attending to this engagement with objects and "things" as developed in recent accounts of the subject-as-object in Burney criticism (especially Julie Park's and Deidre Lynch's notion of the woman-automaton), I hope to contribute a new understanding of the status of temporality in Burney's unique approach to the novelistic engagement with consciousness.

In *Evelina*, Burney's heroine moves from a thing that is *acted on* to an *acting agent* who causes (or rather prevents) events from happening. To use Kramnick's terms, the novel shifts from a concept of consciousness as the absorption of world into mind to one that triumphs in "actions [that] extend mind into the world."[17] This move is closely tied to Burney's feminist project, but it also interjects into the debate about consciousness in the eighteenth century. How, Burney asks, do subjects arise from objects? How might one's consciousness transform to achieve independence of mind, to become a self that acts of its own accord on the world?

What psychology calls mental growth or development and in literary criticism is better known as *Bildung* depends on a move from externalism to autonomous agency. But this development is not strictly linear (as in the Lockean sense of duration or the existence of a consistent subject) so much as it is dialectical. Subjects emerge from their engagement with, and status as, objects through a kind of consciousness that uses memory as its basis for agentive action. Once the subject gains the ability to see herself in time (across past, present, and future), she can abstract herself from the more immediate threats of her environment and thus act on that environment in new ways.[18]

Lurking behind this argument about memory's necessary relationship to the development of consciousness is also an investigation into sympathy as a problematic category in the dialectic between mind and world. This critique poses an important complication in discussions of eighteenth-century consciousness, for the tendency simultaneously to associate Enlightenment culture with the emergence of autonomy (whether such autonomy is a fallacy or not) and the social context of the self's relationship to others is an ongoing paradox that defines this period in literary history.[19] Recent critical accounts show that although Enlightenment philosophies of empiricism allowed for sympathy's reliance on the imagination because of the moral and vitalizing effects of the sympathetic response, literary models reveal more troubled portrayals of the sympathetic mind.[20] What is interesting about Burney's novelistic engagement with philosophies of sympathy is the author's anxiety about how mind and world interact when one wholly exists in a present state of mind. In sympathy, the mind both absorbs and projects onto its environment, but often, Burney demonstrates, in inaccurate ways. The slippage that can occur in sympathetic consciousness, for Burney, might be defined as a momentary awareness of ourselves existing, and inhabiting a place within, our present environment. Another less problematic form of consciousness arises, however, from the work of memory and reflection and urges us to consider ourselves as products, and inhabitants, of time.

In *The Things Things Say,* Jonathan Lamb describes Adam Smith's moral ideals for a model of sympathetic understanding: "Imagination acts on us like a real event and metamorphoses us into another person, but the moral value of the change is known in the end by an agent conscious of what has been performed, and of what belongs to whom."[21] Lamb's assertion keys into the metamorphical properties of sympathy and its reliance on the imagination while realizing the instrumental role that consciousness plays in acts of sympathetic exchange. The reference to "what belongs to whom" (or perhaps we might say who belongs to whom) alludes to that ever-present anxiety in Smith's *The Theory of Moral Sentiments* about what would occur if the boundaries between subjects were to dissolve. In using the term "conscious" here, Lamb signifies not only awareness but agency. Agency predicates ownership, a knowledge of the distinction not only between self and other but between the self as a subject and the objects that the self is capable of owning, or acting on, in the self's environment. As Adam Smith states in the opening pages of *The Theory of Moral Sentiments,* "It is the impressions of our own senses only, not those of his, which our imaginations copy."[22] Implicitly, sympathy thereby involves not simply imagination but *memory* to uphold the illusory, or metaphorical, nature of the exchange. David Hume likewise stakes his definition of sympathy as the "double relation of impressions and ideas" on the understanding that this passion is "not the present sensation alone or momentary pain or pleasure" but "the whole bent or tendency of it from the beginning to the end."[23] These early philosophies of sympathy cautiously and carefully depend on the history of personal experience. In their subtext, we encounter not the immediacy of associational memory as recurrent emotion but the complex temporal and relational work of conscious memory, an indexical mental faculty that allows the subject to think of herself according to various reference points in time.

But what if the consciousness brought on by sympathy indicated merely a rudimentary and fleeting form of awareness? What does it mean to say that I am "self-conscious" simply because I am aware that I am being looked at? This is the kind of consciousness that Burney entertains in the early portions of her novel. Sympathetic self-consciousness in the first three quarters of Evelina's narrative looks something like shame or embarrassment; it is a transient feeling of self that is constituted wholly in the observer's gaze and is dependent on someone, or something, external to the self. In this case, sympathy transforms the observer into a mere spectacle or object.

Such self-consciousness is not really indicative of agency, and it highlights the problem of a kind of subjectivity defined by the movement of world into mind. The sympathizer becomes an object acted on by an "event." To use Kramnick's distinction, we engage in "action" when we attain a capacity for mental causation, when we ourselves become the agent, as opposed to the effect, of an "event."[24] Burney's novel investigates various definitions of self-consciousness in order to arrive at a dialectical concept of mind and world brought about by the work of memory and a notion of the self in time. Part of Evelina's struggle toward independent action entails her triumph over the temporal trappings of a sympathetic constitution. She must become an actor or agent in the world, not the victim of events. To abstract herself from the present and immediate dangers of excess sensibility, Evelina must attain a kind of consciousness that practices self-awareness across multiple time frames. She must become conscious, not in the transitory sense of a present, sensory feeling that one is the object of another's perceptions but in a transhistorical sense wherein the difference between self and other arises from recalling, imagining, and referencing various versions of one's self in and through time. This is her *Bildung*, her narrative rise to a type of self-awareness that relies on conscious memory.

Feeling Things

Volume 1 of Burney's novel focuses on debates about taste and aesthetic judgment. As Melissa Pino has argued, this portion of the novel presents us with both innate and learned concepts of taste, and this is simply one way in which the novel engages with a whole gamut of topics within the discourse of eighteenth-century aesthetics.[25] To be sure, Evelina possesses an innate and refined type of aesthetic taste; from her first arrival on the London scene, she is moved by spectacles, performances, and music, returning in "raptures" and "extacy" from first witnessing Garrick act in the theater (20). At this early stage, Evelina is predisposed to the novelties of sensory experience; everything around her is new. In fact, she experiences pleasure, even as she wishes for it, awaiting for the sanctioning judgment of her parent/guardian to see her first play: "I cannot, for my life, resist wishing for the pleasures they offer me,—provided you do not disapprove them" (18). "To wish," to feel, to be moved, Burney suggests, is merely to be alive, but even as the aesthetic implies the vital movement of life forms, it does not by any means render Evelina a complete person or judge. As volume I progresses, Evelina occasionally begins to form aesthetic judgments, remarking on the inertia of others and their lack of aesthetic feeling. To this extent, Evelina is conscious in the sense of being awake to her own sensory enjoyment and to a very visceral experience of her physical surroundings.

Yet this basic form of consciousness is problematic if we consider how, if at all, it distinguishes Evelina from the things she experiences and sees. As several critics have recently argued,[26] Evelina is, at this juncture in the novel, rendered as much an aesthetic object as an aesthetic observer. "When Frances Burney dispatches her heroine to London's Pantheon . . . and when she positions Evelina against the backdrop formed by the building's statues of gods and goddesses, she puts her heroine's selfhood at risk," Deidre Lynch writes. Lynch's analysis of Orville's description of architecture at the Pantheon is that sight-seeing renders "both the woman and the Pantheon" into "sights." Entering into spaces of public consumption, she argues, allows persons to become representations or spectacles. In this reading, Lynch acknowledges a conflict between "story" and "spectacle" in Burney's fiction, but argues that it is the transformative power of commerce, the sights/sites of consumption themselves, that prompt the reader of Burney's fiction to grant her heroines an "inner self" different from their aesthetic backdrops.[27]

I would like to propose a different way of considering the tenuousness of personhood and character in this text. We might read the confusion of Evelina-as-subject with Evelina-as-object at this early stage in the novel as indicative of the incompleteness of our protagonist's mental development. In a rather misogynistic attack upon the proposed participation of women in the public sphere, the brutish Captain exclaims to his daughter in volume 1, "I charge you . . . never again be so impertinent as to have a taste of your own before my face" (91). Claiming that women should be seen and not heard, the Captain renders women into spectacles—not authors or agents. Of course, Burney is making an implicit feminist argument for the inclusion of women in the world of aesthetic judgment; after all, we know Evelina has opinions here, even if they remain silent to all but her readers. However, there is also a serious value to something the Captain says in this passage, a literal message embedded deep within Burney's satirical bite. "What signifies asking them girls?" the Captain asks. "Do you think they know their own minds yet?" (91). If for a moment we set aside the gendered rhetoric of this statement, we are left to contemplate a very important temporal tag in the Captain's wording: the girls do not "know their own minds" because they have not "yet" attained a certain level of self-conscious thinking. A possibility for voicing her mind, the attainment of self-authorized judgment and action, remains for our young heroine. A moment does come when Evelina triumphs over her status as spectacle, as aesthetic, or even as legible/textual object. However, this moment is *yet* to come.

Make Up Your Mind in Time

Recent attempts among scholars of the eighteenth-century novel to align readership practices with movements in contemporary neuroscience have extended the eighteenth-century concept of sympathetic understanding to what cognitive studies calls "mind reading." Lisa Zunshine connects mind reading to the work of perception when she writes, "We engage in mind-reading when we ascribe to a person a certain mental state on the basis of her observable action."[28] Blakey Vermeule uses a slightly different rhetoric to define the term: "Boiled down, mind reading simply means representing to ourselves the mental states of other people."[29] We see the work of the imagination at play in the neuroscientific model as in the sympathetic one: the mind's representational, or image-producing, faculties are key to helping us to understand what goes on in other people's thoughts.[30] We might think of mind reading, like sympathy, as dependent on an ability to infer immediate information from physically observable sights. These theories of mind reading highlight its empirical, scientific qualities as a practice of visual semiotics that promotes the survival of the subject.

For Frances Burney, mind reading has a close affinity to sympathy, most especially in how it impinges on the work of developmental self-consciousness. Evelina's subjectivity is constantly at risk when she is placed within aesthetic scenarios and sympathetic relations, and her often faulty and failed attempts at mind reading only add fuel to an ever-increasing fire. Mind reading is a vital part of human life and survival. As with sympathy, it relies on the representational faculties of the mind, on empirical understandings of the world, and on a constant reading of others as objects. However, this mental faculty is a weak one for Evelina in the early stages of Burney's narrative, mostly because mind reading is a problem when it is embedded in a language of immediacy—of instinct and desire. To return to Adam Smith and David Hume's implicit warnings about the stages of sympathetic self-consciousness, when the empirical activity of mind reading is unaccompanied by memory, or the cognitive benefits of time, it is risky business.

This is the lesson Evelina must learn in volume 3, wherein she fails on so many occasions to read the thoughts of others, only finally to triumph over the utter messiness of her interpersonal relationships through the attainment of a more autonomous agency and higher-level order of self-consciousness. Letter 2 begins:

> Oh Sir, Lord Orville is still himself! still, what from the moment I beheld, I believed him to be—all that is amiable in man! and your happy Evelina, restored at once to spirits and tranquility, is no longer sunk in her own opinion, nor discontented with the world;—no longer, with dejected eyes, sees the prospect of passing her future days in sadness, doubt, and suspicion!—with revived courage she now looks forward, and expects to meet with goodness, even among mankind:— though still she feels, as strongly as ever, the folly of hoping, in any *second* instance, to meet with *perfection*. (229)

Thinking occurs instantaneously here and is directly related to sight. As Evelina recalls the "moment" she "beheld" Orville, the text subtly implies that it is the sight of Orville, with his irresistible gentlemanly demeanor, that excites the writer's imagination and desire. Evelina attempts to map thinking here along the lines of time and memory but fails to do so with accuracy. Her thoughts are all cast into a fleeting temporality that hinges on the structures of desire and whimsical expectation. As with Jane Austen's later heroine, Elizabeth Bennett, judgments are formed "at once." The past disappears in a "moment": "no longer" does Evelina allow her past experience to inform her vision of the future. Rather, futurity here is conditioned by immediate feelings, as Evelina elides Orville's alleged past error and ignores the reflective potential of her young mind.

Prospects become fueled with a romantic enthusiasm that renders the clause "still she feels, as strongly as ever, the folly of hoping" somewhat ironic. For Evelina does hope, but what she hopes for is Orville's love; "still she feels" for him and thus cannot imagine a different romantic "prospect." Feeling here is defined by "folly," and one might argue that to feel one's folly is a rudimentary form of self-consciousness as love, shame, embarrassment, or mortification. These are passions that place us in a transient version of self-awareness that shifts with the feelings, behaviors, and gaze of the other. Pages later, Evelina writes, "All my perturbation returned at the sight of him! . . . on *my side* was all the consciousness, for by him, I really believe, the letter was, at that moment, entirely forgotten" (231). Evelina's reference to consciousness here reveals the necessary role of memory in the developmental stages of sympathy. The passage denotes a rudimentary sympathy as the feeling of being looked at, or a passing self-awareness, that arises when Evelina understands herself to be the object of another's aesthetic and moral judgment. Another class of consciousness, however, is sacrificed: one that indexes past errors, that judges and checks feeling by way of memory. In the end, the letter is "forgotten," ironically, not by Orville but by Evelina, who quickly and happily elides Orville's past affront. Such forgetting poses a risk to her virtue. In this manner, conscious memory gives way to associative remembrance, to the mere repetitions of feeling and feeling again, as seeing reproduces, but is never compared to, past sensation. Evelina stands in defiance of Hume's warning. Thus her attempt to read Orville's mind accepts the transitory mechanics of feeling, so that what poses as remembrance in fact amounts to nothing more than forgetfulness. As in Adam Smith's first stage of sympathetic exchange, the sight of Orville's gaze initiates within Evelina a sudden notion of herself as spectacle. In a moment, "struck" by Orville's appearance, his physical image, Evelina "endeavor[s]" to perform a lack of emotion, to recall the contents of the unsettling letter (232). Yet these attempts to inform present action through the work of conscious memory prove insufficient when placed against the force of Evelina's present desires.

Performance fails, devolving further into mechanism, as Evelina moves automatically; she "know[s] not how it [is]" but her "reserve insensibly" melts away, and her "intention" holds no bearing on her actions (232). Plans, "endeavors," "intentions" give way to instinct and feeling when the memory of Orville's offensive letter is quickly supplanted by the present "thought" of seeing him in front of her. Thoughts are not retained but transplanted here as action is founded on the motions and mechanisms of one's present environment. As Julie Park and Deidre Lynch have demonstrated, the figure of the automaton is alive and well in these moments of the novel when Evelina struggles to overcome her passions.[31] In the early portions of volume 3, Evelina's consciousness vacillates between instinctual sensory urges and momentary glimpses of self-awareness that depend entirely on the objects and others within the immediate purview of her environment.

Evelina's conscious awareness, devoid of reflection and memory, is here defined by how she appears to others; it is better termed embarrassment or "feeling very foolish" (236).[32] "I feel extremely uncomfortable in finding myself considered in a light very inferior," she writes (238). To "find oneself" in the gaze of another, a temporary status or location, is quite different from a self-consciousness that enacts and constructs the self through memory or time. Using the former method of awareness without the latter condemns Evelina to a rather crude existence: she is an object, or a feeling, at once found and lost again.

Moral feeling has the potential to grow over time into a more mature independence of mind—of judgment, thought, opinion, and action. However, at this stage in the novel it is ensconced in the structures of basic identification. Burney suggests that the supposedly virtuous sensibility of sympathy has its trappings, thwarting even as it fuels (by way of experience) Evelina's progress toward psychological independence. The reappearance of Mr. Macartney in Bath further reveals a problematic lack in Evelina's mental development. Evelina's "accidental" meeting with Mr. Macartney causes her to make a "private appointment," which she immediately regrets, underscoring her uncertain ability to act according to the conditions of self-authorized thinking:

> "I will come, my Lord," said I, rather embarrassed, "in two minutes." Then, turning to Mr. Macartney, with yet more embarrassment, I wished him good morning.
> He advanced towards the garden, with the paper still in his hand.
> "No, no," cried I, "some other time."
> "May I then, Madam, have the honour of seeing you again?"
> I did not dare take the liberty of inviting any body to the house of Mrs. Beaumont, nor yet had the presence of mind to make an excuse; and, therefore, not knowing how to refuse him, I said, "Perhaps you may be this way again to-morrow morning,—and I believe I shall walk out before breakfast." (246)

Overwhelmed with a kind of self-consciousness as the feeling of being looked at (what Evelina describes as an increasing form of embarrassment as she juggles the intersecting gazes of her two onlookers, Lord Orville and Mr. Macartney), Evelina loses her ability to think rationally or reflectively. "I had not the presence of mind," she says; she does not *know* "how to refuse him." Like the accidental event itself, Evelina's consciousness is conditioned by the coincidence of her physically circumscribed circumstances. Knowledge, Burney implies, arises when the mind abstracts itself from its present environment. This allows for the ability to reflect on, or recogitate, events, experiences, and felt moments in time. In this manner, self-consciousness as a mere sensation of self-awareness—the embarrassment that arises when one considers that one is, at that moment, a spectacle, an object of another's aesthetic or rational contemplation—leads to the dissolution of thought and action. When Evelina feels self-conscious shame, she resumes a pattern of mechanistic or automatic behavior. These actions are derived from feeling and instinct, and they inevitably lead her astray when it comes to following the mores of polite society.

As a kind of misguided reparative to this form of self-consciousness as sensation, Evelina asks Orville to do her thinking for her: "My meeting with Mr. Macartney was quite accidental; and if your Lordship thinks there is any impropriety in my seeing him to-morrow, I am ready to give up that intention. 'If I think!' said he, in a tone of surprise; 'surely Miss Anville must best judge for herself!'" (247). Orville's urgent request that Evelina think for herself calls into question the text's own patriarchal paradigm (wherein Evelina moves from acting under Villars's guidance to acting under Orville's). The substitution of Orville for Villars (a decision that Evelina seems implicitly and unwittingly to make in the middle of volume 3) does more than question gendered concepts of the mind within the structures of patriarchy and polite society. It also highlights a crucial moment in Evelina's mental *Bildung*. Will she attain the ability to think and act of her own accord? Or is this "young lady's entrance into the world" merely a matter of *marrying* one's actions to the thoughts of another?

The following page shows Evelina wrestling with this very question:

> I could not help asking myself what *right* I had to communicate the affairs of Mr. Macartney; and I doubted whether, to clear myself from one act of imprudence, I had not committed another.
>
> Distressed by this reflection, I thought it best to quit the room, and give myself some time for consideration before I spoke; and therefore, only saying I must hasten to dress, I ran up stairs: rather abruptly, I own, and so, I fear, Lord Orville must think; yet what could I do? unused to the situations in which I find myself, and embarrassed by

the slightest difficulties, I seldom, till too late, discover how I ought to act. (248)

Dawning in Evelina's mind is a subtle ability to "reflect" on events in time, on the circumstances of her potential actions. This fledgling mental development seems almost implicit and automatic (she "could not help"), but it is not, in fact, the work of a moment. In Evelina's language, we see Burney's authorial intentions, a scheme that reveals the novel's approach to self-consciousness as a narrative progression and also suggests that this capacity for reflection has grown up throughout the novel, has reached a crux, a developmental crossroad, as it were. Here, thought is ballasted by the stressful work of "reflection"; thinking, Burney argues, takes time, and Evelina's actions are thereby characterized by a need for time. The work of the conscious memory, as reflection or "consideration," leads to action: Evelina's phrase "I thought" is represented as an intention that *causes* her to leave the room. By quitting her present environment, Evelina avoids the spatial and circumstantial dangers of self-consciousness as embarrassment—the crippling feeling of Orville's gaze—so that she may think before acting. Through the avenue of time, which enables her to abstract herself from the pressures of a present that demands immediate action, Evelina intimates another form of self-consciousness, in which one's actions are indeed reflections of one's self and will.

This is the first moment in the novel that represents the potential for what Amit Yahav has called an "off-the-clock break," a temporal pause in narrative time that paradoxically is in itself "decidedly durational."[33] In her reading of Richardson's novels, Yahav describes these pauses as opportunities to "judge with duration," to make ethical decisions in time. Unfortunately, at the juncture of this mental crossroads, Evelina takes yet another wrong turn. Ascending the stairs, she cannot leave the memory of Orville's gaze behind. She has internalized his thoughts and opinions; what he "must think" thus thwarts and muddles her reflections. She remembers not her "own impressions"[34] but his. Evelina confesses that "embarrassment" is the guide to her actions. Too acutely invested in the thoughts of others, she mind reads (but, according to Adam Smith, does not sympathize) to the point of eliding her own self-authority. "Finding herself" in new environments and "embarrassed" by the "slightest difficulties," Evelina cannot "discover" how to "act" until it is "too late."

Of course, it is not too late, and Burney implies that the circumstance of a new environment is exactly what Evelina needs in order to attain a self-authorized form of thinking that is paradoxically dependent not so much on space as on time. Thinking, Burney imparts, should not be merely habitual, but it should be historical. Evelina wrestles to free herself from self-consciousness as embarrassment and thereby to embark on self-reflection. Indeed, she begins to think here about her past errors and what has led to these missteps. In contemplating her past and worrying about her future, Evelina exemplifies the dawning of a kind of thinking about herself in time, a more sophisticated order of self-consciousness that relies on memory to actualize her desires. Memory paves the way to intention, allowing Evelina to become an acting agent in the world who might influence the outcome of events and own her actions. Over the course of the letter, Evelina describes a struggle to disengage herself from her company so as to reflect: "the more I reflect, the more sensible I am of the utter impropriety" of publishing Mr. Macartney's affairs (249). Notably, Evelina's reflections here take place over the course of her writing a letter to Villars. She laments his absence and wishes to "be enlightened" by his "counsel" (249). This suggests an internalization of her patriarchal teachings, a semi-autonomy that is tied more to indoctrination than independent thought and action. Such doctrinal forms of thinking prove ineffective and problematic in the realm of everyday life and the demands it places on thinking and acting.

In the following pages, Evelina's intentions to be "guided" and "enlightened" by Villars in his absence are constantly complicated by a war between resolution and desire. Evelina vacillates between the language of duty and that of passionate feeling, revealing an inconsistent version of the self. Statements such as "after a thousand different plans, not being able to resolve . . . I thought"; "My first impulse was to call him back, and instantly tell him the whole affair; but I checked this desire"; and "with all the resolution I could assume" reveal an attempt to conform to an indoctrinated sense of duty, the externally authorized judgments of her priest/father figure (249–50). These "judgments" are the remnants of a rote style of education that thinks of memory as a faculty that reiterates knowledge, or fact, and inscribes it on the mind. They nonetheless give way to the language of feeling, the overwhelming instincts of Evelina's desires: "affected by an attention . . . and forced to turn away my head to conceal my emotion"; "Determined as I was to act . . . I yet most anxiously wished"; "abashed";

"I found myself much at a loss"; "I spoke so hastily, that I did not, at the time, consider the impropriety of what I said" (250–51). Evelina's struggle between obligation and desire reveals two equally dangerous versions of the woman as automaton: the puppet/monkey of patriarchal doctrine who imitates her masculine counterparts versus the animal/machine that moves only in accordance with its impetuous and instantaneous desires.

By pitting these two troublesome versions of consciousness against one another, Burney implies a difference between duty and true, self-authorized judgment. The latter is a secular alternative to patriarchal or religious education, one that affirms independent thought as the combination of judgment (or reasonable reflection) and feeling. This self-authorized thinking occurs when she contemplates her self in time, remembering past experiences and situations. Of course, Evelina fails to achieve such independence of mind in her effusive story of warring passions. Rather, her hasty "resolution" is in itself troublesome: "Do you think, my dear Sir, I did not, at that moment, require all my resolution to guard me from frankly telling him whatever he wished to hear? yet I rejoice that I did not; for added to the actual wrong I should have done, Lord Orville himself, when he had heard, would, I am sure, have blamed me. Fortunately, this thought occurred to me, and I said, 'Your Lordship shall yourself be my judge'" (252). Evelina's "fortunate thought," a near mechanical occurrence, again arises from an act of misguided mind reading (not from long-term, conscious memory). This "thought" leads to a decisive moment in the text when she essentially asks Orville to do her thinking for her. Although Orville gladly accepts the offer, we recall his earlier exclamation of astonishment at such a proposal, warning us against the temptation to rely on others for our judgment.[35] All the while, Orville's implicit message lurks beneath the action of the text. By deferring to Orville, Evelina not only replaces Villars as her patriarchal guide, she only temporarily resolves the problematic tension between duty and desire. In this manner, she can perform her duty by conforming to the doctrines of patriarchy and polite society while also gratifying her desire to please Orville. The secret impetus behind Evelina's inescapable habit of faulty mind reading is her persistent wish to be held high in Orville's esteem. But acting in line with the perceived perceptions of others only induces a fuzzy, elusive method of deductive reasoning that accounts for the inconsistency of Evelina's actions.[36]

The letter ends with another anxiety: "But what will poor Mr. Macartney think of me?" (253). Subscribing to the authority of another, whether it be Villars or Orville, exposes the problem of dependent, or unenlightened, thinking. What happens when the thoughts and perceptions of others are in conflict with one another? How is Evelina to please more than one man or mentor in this society? The pressures of patriarchy demand that Evelina make a choice. Villars's response to Evelina's problematic attempt to resolve her own feelings of self-consciousness (as worldly embarrassments) may read like a tirade against the passions (infused with the hurt, perhaps, of being supplanted by another man). But it also delivers the rhetoric of Burney's alternative to the patriarchal problem:

> Young, animated, entirely off your guard, and thoughtless of consequences, *Imagination* took the reins, and *Reason*, slow-paced, though sure-footed, was unequal to a race with so eccentric and flighty a companion. How rapid was then my Evelina's progress through those regions of fancy and passion whither her new guide conducted her!— She saw Lord Orville at a ball,—and he was *the most amiable of men!*— She met him again at another,—and *he had every virtue under heaven!*
>
> I mean not to depreciate the merit of Lord Orville, who, one mysterious instance alone excepted, seems to have deserved the idea you formed of his character; but it was not time, it was not the knowledge of his worth, obtained your regard ... [fancy] ... painted to you, at the moment of your first acquaintance, all the excellencies, all the good and rare qualities, which a great length of time, and intimacy, could alone have really discovered. (254)

Villars's allegorical depiction of the imagination exposes the trappings of a kind of thinking, or judgment formation, that exists only in the context of a present time frame; imagination takes flight in the immediate space of our instinctual, affective reactions to our environment. This fallacious "guide" allows the mind to leap from sight to judgment, connoting the forceful power of spectacles on a mental process that confuses impressions for ideas. "Knowledge," however, in the Lockean sense, occurs along the trajectory of duration, from a "great length of time" that "discovers," or reveals, the mind to itself. The appositive "it was not time, it was not the knowledge" thus equates knowledge with time. What Villars dubs imaginative thinking is akin to a kind of self-consciousness ruled by one's immediate environment; the only cure to such thinking, Villars asserts, is "the assistance of time and absence" (255). Only as the mind abstracts itself from a merely spatial understanding of persons and events into a temporally inflected type of contemplation can it attain a higher form of judgment.

On another level, however, Villars's teachings here take the shape of a transacted memory. Having no first-hand impressions of Evelina's interactions with Orville, his information comes entirely from Evelina's letters. What he "sees" is a biographical, epistolary account. He then replays this partially transcribed narrative back to Evelina in the new context of his own words and embellishments, altering the transacted memory of Evelina's original experience as he goes. The intent, it seems, is to supplant Evelina's felt memory of an original experience with a more rational history. For Villars, the new memory has a more ethical claim to reason because it implies that memories should alter our original impressions over time. The moral gist of the letter may be true for Burney, but transacted memories have darker implications in her novel about the powers of self-conscious thinking and acting.

Ironically, Villars's letter has the opposite effect from its intentions. Immediately before reading it, Evelina is, on her own, beginning to learn the wonders of conscious reflection. "Is not this a strange event?" she comments on the discovery that Macartney is her brother. "How little did I think that the visits I so unwillingly paid at Mr. Branghton's would have introduced me to so near a relation! I will never again regret the time I spent in town this summer; a circumstance so fortunate will always make me think of it with pleasure" (265). Novelistic coincidence, a narrative trope that continues well into the Victorian era, illumines how time recasts events in the mind. We, like Evelina, perceive and reperceive events by contemplating circumstances in and through time. What was once a mere occasion for social embarrassment, an authorial commentary on Evelina's excessive sympathy, now becomes an object of contemplative pleasure. In this manner, Evelina's autobiographical narrative encourages a type of self-consciousness that is dependent on time and slow cognition and that solicits the work of the long-term, conscious memory. Time allows thoughts to unfold and fold back upon themselves. In doing so, memory changes the felt nature of the experience. Juxtaposing what was thought then with what is known now, memory alters the account and changes history. What was once a "regret" is "never again" recalled, as it transforms into a feeling of "fortunate pleasure."

Reading Villars's letter, however, only causes Evelina to revert into a kind of self-consciousness that falters under feelings of disapproval; anxiously she bends to the imagined perceptions of another (i.e., her surrogate father). Repeating and absorbing the parts of Villars's letter which are indeed heavy-handed in their language against the passions—"*His sight is baneful to my repose,—his society is death to my future tranquillity!*" (266)—Evelina relinquishes the kind of independent thought that arises from self-contemplation across time in favor of a strained effort to repress passion in accordance with doctrinal duty. "*I will* quit him," she asserts, missing the thrust of Villars's advice (266). Evelina's sudden awareness of her own feelings comes by way of Villars's perceptions and thus creates a crippling, embarrassed form of self-consciousness that rashly leads to taking on the perceived "*will*" of another: "I will run away," "I will set off," "I am going," "implicitly will I follow your advice" (266). All of Evelina's intentions and actions are governed by another's judgments and memories, her thoughts swayed in a moment with the same kind of immediacy that Villars warns against.

Again, Evelina cannot please more than one agent, and when Mrs. Selwyn forms a new plan for Evelina's fate, she readily complies, writing to Villars, "I hope you will not be displeased at my compliance, though it is rather against my own judgment" (267). Psychological conflict arises for Evelina as she internalizes the thoughts and perceptions of more than one person. Her chaotic mind acts like a sponge or container for a collective consciousness that absorbs the warring opinions of her elders. Thus when she fails to act in accordance with her own judgment, we hear Burney's underlying irony; this is a kind of thinking as "compliance," a thinking that lacks self-authority and agency. As long as Evelina complies with external judgments, her consciousness and her self are at constant risk. Is it passion that threatens Evelina's peace of mind? Or is it rather the sensory risks of sympathy, patriarchal pressure, and a nagging habit of self-objectification that continue to thwart Evelina's mental development?

Pages later, still processing the contents of Villars's letter, Evelina turns the text over in her mind as she wonders whether Villars approves of her change of conduct. She effusively exclaims in the same apostrophic style of Villars's moralizing that her "mind was unequal to sustaining [her passion] without danger" (277). Unable to compose her mind, Evelina expresses the problem that patriarchal duty places on feminine enlightenment: "The wish of doing well governs every other, as far as concerns my conduct,—for am I not *your* child?—the creature of your own forming?—Yet, Oh Sir, friend, parent of my heart!—my feelings are all at war with my duties; and, while I must struggle to acquire self-approbation, my peace, my happiness, my hopes,—are lost!" (277). The letter sounds something like Burney's prefatory appeal at the novel's commencement to her father as "muse," which might be read as a poetic resolution to write and act independently despite one's filial ties, affections, and duties. Self-approbation, Burney suggests, must come from within. The rhetorical question, "for am I not *your* child?—the creature of your own forming?," equates childhood with a rudimentary form of consciousness that sees the self as a mere extension of its genetic (or adopted) origin. If sustained, the struggle between duty and feeling leads only to the loss of one's future self. In order to attain selfhood, one must abstract the mind from its parentage. Evelina's path to independence relies notably on a feeling, and thereby feeling cannot be extricated from the process that is Evelina's development of self-consciousness. However, Evelina's feelings can only become self-authorized by activating her conscious memory, by reflecting on her own experience. As long as Evelina seeks approval, as long as her actions require external sanction, she does not know her own mind.

Eighty-two letters into the narrative, with an abundance of writing as reportage, we still do not fully know Evelina's mind. Within the context of an epistolary fiction, this is something we might expect to have access to. As one commentator in the pump room says of Macartney's poetic description of Evelina, "But then . . . her *mind*,—now the difficulty is, to find out the truth of *that*" (269). The irony here is that textual representation fails to reveal true thinking. As poem or letter, Evelina is an unformed truth, words without meaning. The question is whether she will extricate herself from the status of mere text—of the aesthetic object that everybody reads and feels for but nobody truly knows—to a self-authorized thinking subject. Reading and writing only lead to true thinking, Burney suggests, when they reveal a self-consciousness born out of the operations of time and reflection.[37] Memory is the elusive faculty that will allow Evelina to *make up* her *own* mind. Only then, can she remain in the public sphere as more than something *seen*.

Willoughby in the Garden

As Evelina learns that thinking takes time, we, her readers, also begin to see another kind of self-consciousness emerge in the novel—one that rises above the dangerous consequences of self-consciousness as a feeling of how others are wont to perceive us. Not only is thinking a time-consuming activity, but time is what shapes self-understanding, conscious memory, and decision-making. Once Evelina considers herself a product of her past, present, and future awareness, the notion of herself in time gives way to a kind of enlightened consciousness that leads to independent action:

> I begin to think, my dear Sir, that the sudden alteration in my behavior was ill-judged and improper; for, as I had received no offence, as the cause of the change was upon *my* account, not *his*, I should not have assumed, so abruptly, a reserve for which I dared assign no reason,— nor have shunned his presence so obviously, without considering the strange appearance of such a conduct.
>
> Alas, my dearest Sir, that my reflections should always be too late to serve me! dearly, indeed, do I purchase experience! and much I fear I shall suffer yet more severely, from the heedless indiscretion of my temper, ere I attain that prudence and consideration, which, by foreseeing distant consequences, may rule and direct in present exigencies. (282)

The phrase "I begin to think" has crept up into Evelina's epistolary narrative disrupting its signature style of reportage. The tag reveals an increasing tendency to place thought within the passage of time; time shapes thought and causes our thoughts to change. First impressions, as Burney (and subsequently Jane Austen) would have it, change; they change because they are affected by events in time. In this manner, Burney warns us against "sudden" versus gradual transformation. Evelina deems her own "sudden alteration" of behavior "ill-judged"; this is the novel's first definitively self-authorized self-judgment. She characterizes her actions as "improper" not because they fail to conform to Villars's advice (for she still believes Villars would have her disengage from Orville's attentions). Rather, this assertion arises out of a process of mental reasoning that attempts to organize memory, impression, and event in and through time.

To be sure, this assessment follows a moment of mind reading; Orville neglects Evelina, and she perceives how he must perceive her (finally, an accurate form of sympathetic judgment!). However, Evelina's ability to remember feeling in this instance intimates the crucial role that memory plays for agency and survival: reflection allows Evelina to "foresee distant consequences." As Evelina meditates on her actions, she relives the past through an imagined logic of would-be behavior, revealing the fact that reason is ever tied to a process of reflection: "As I had received no offense, as the cause... was upon *my* account... I should not have assumed." Duty no longer conforms to patriarchal indoctrination. Rather, Evelina's moral sense arises from an "if-then" system of inferences that attempts to match cause and effect in a rational manner. Notably, Evelina writes one "should not assume," as though duty cannot ever arise from the absence of knowledge. In accounting for her actions, Evelina essentially holds herself accountable ("upon my account"). Accountability, evidence of one's will and autonomy, is tied to something other than the excuses of mechanism, shame, or mere transient feeling. Actions uphold not only a situational logic but also a temporal one; they *should* arise from causes, and they *should*, or rather do, have future consequences. "Reflection" and "consideration" assist feeling and the urgent need for action, as the self foresees its "distant consequences" through the avenues of memory. In this manner, actions derived from self-reflection are preceded by our past and indicative of our futurity; moreover, the mental faculties of memory and imagination are not at war (as per Villars's implications), but they work in concert so as to achieve agency and independent subjectivity. By considering herself in time, Evelina gains a more sophisticated, reflective and reflexive, kind of self-consciousness. She learns to shape future actions and events from memories of the past.

Evelina's thought processes in this case involve a temporary abstraction of the self from her social environment in order to allow one kind of self-consciousness (determined by the overwhelming immediacy of sympathetic feeling) to give way to another: this latter, more durable form of cognition reveals Evelina's ability to situate and contemplate the self in time. In the following paragraph, Evelina's thoughts are inflected by a more contemplative mood as she "saunter[s]" into "the garden" to take time to think: "Here I believe I spent an hour by myself; when, hearing the garden gate open, I went into an arbour at the end of a long walk, where, ruminating, very unpleasantly, upon my future prospects, I remained quietly seated but a few minutes, before I was interrupted by the appearance of Sir Clement Willoughby" (282). Suddenly, Evelina becomes something like the Romantic solitary walker, or *saunterer*. Having finally learned the exercise of contemplation, she enters the temporal structures of self-consciousness as a meditation on the self in time. Her thoughts are no longer momentary. Rather, they take on the qualities of "ruminating," indicating a self-sufficiency that depends on slow cognition. Evelina is careful to account for the passage of time, marking her solitary experience with temporal tags such as "a few minutes" and "an hour." Notably, the time spent alone is ambiguously tagged, "I believe I spent an hour by myself," suggesting that this kind of pondering is absorptive—but not necessarily prone to the risks of self-loss (as in enthusiasm or sympathy). Evelina is at once in the present and the future, able now to distance herself from her immediate environment as she considers her "future prospects"; however, she is easily wrenched back into the present moment by way of sensory experience, the sound of the garden gate opening.

The few minutes that pull her back into a present state of awareness are definitively accounted for, or timed, standing in contrast to the long absorptive hour of meditation. This quick shift in temporal experience, of course, indicates an urgent need for action. Prepared for the kind of scandalous attacks on female virtue that eighteenth-century garden scenes so often occasion, the reader here expects something worse than a mere interruption of Evelina's contemplative mood. Yet this new kind of thinking seems to arm Evelina against the dangers of the seductions that follow. In his usual manner, Willoughby calls on Evelina's sympathy to assist his aims: "look upon me with pity" . . . "say, then, that you pity me" . . . "O . . . pity me!" (284). (Why not? It has worked before!) But the libertine's enthusiastic language, his urgent call for sympathy, even his seductive promises of reform ("you shall new-form, new-model me," 284) fall on deaf ears. Evelina's reproaches are decisive, formed out of a kind of self-consciousness as memory. Defiant and armed against embarrassment, this time Evelina does not allow an overly acute concern for the thoughts of others to intercede, and she urgently cries for help. To be sure, Evelina cannot disentangle herself from Willoughby without some physical assistance, but her voice is heard here, her opinions are pronounced, her truths declared.

This is not to say that Evelina loses the human tendency toward self-conscious feeling as embarrassment in the final pages of the novel simply because she achieves a more mature type of self-consciousness as self-reflection and autonomous action. Evelina still experiences the pains of a sentimental constitution; we see her describe herself as "all consciousness," as feeling "awkward and distress[ed]" in meeting Lord Orville (287), but accompanying these moments of distress are a decisive ability to rise to her social obligations. Feeling does not so easily overwhelm. "Turning" from the gaze of the other, Evelina allows herself to regain control over her actions, if not entirely her feelings (287). This shift into a less risky form of social consciousness registers the necessity of memory in acts of mind reading and sympathetic exchange.

When Evelina is reintroduced to Louisa, this time as Miss Belmont, she feels "an involuntary motion of contempt" but does not act wholly in accordance with her immediate feelings (315). Rather, mechanism soon gives way to reflection: "observing that she [Louisa] blushed extremely at my refusal, and recollecting she was sister to Lord Orville, my indignation subsided" (315). Evelina's ability to read others, now coupled with the powers of memory, begin to influence her actions. As feelings are remembered in time, the recollection of emotion provides both catharsis and self-consciousness. The challenging scene wherein Evelina finally meets her father provides a potential foil to Evelina's newly formed strength of mind. But even in a scene of such sentimental excess that it rivals the Mr. Macartney meeting in volume 2, Evelina resorts to the powers of time and memory to protect herself from self-dissolution. She recollects her father's "afflicting words, *I can see her no more*" with emotion; they "were never a moment absent from my mind" (309). But this seemingly indelible impression finds alleviation in a kind of consciousness capable of existing in simultaneous temporalities. Evelina tempers a painful memory by remembering the consoling relief of her present. Memories, spliced and rescaled across time, evolve and change with subjective circumstances. This allows Evelina to forge onward into a future wherein her father indeed does see her again. In the face of potentially overwhelming emotions, the birth of a kind of self-consciousness as an awareness of the self in time arms Evelina against the dangers of sensibility and excessive sympathetic feeling.[38]

Finally, when Evelina expresses a hope for Villars's sanction of her marriage to Orville—"Perhaps the time is not very distant when your Evelina's choice may receive the sanction of her best friend's judgment and approbation" (294)—we must note that her wish, or desire, for Villars's approval has become disentangled from her actions; she has already made her choice. Situated somewhere in between the patriarchal transactions of one adopted father and another biological one, Evelina experiences a momentary freedom from patriarchal structure. She takes advantage of that moment to execute a self-authorized decision. Certainly, it could be argued, as critics have before, that Orville is yet another substitute father figure in the novel who guides Evelina's thoughts and actions.[39] It is tempting to read the novel this way. However, an examination of the various operations of Evelina's self-consciousness in the text offers a nuanced complication to such a reading, and even as she upholds the marital conventions of patriarchy, Burney seems implicitly to subvert a gendered concept of Enlightenment.

Evelina's choice to marry does not bar her from independent thinking and acting. Take, for example, the thoughts and actions that occur in the wake of Evelina's reception of a final letter from Willoughby (one that attempts to explain his misconduct in drafting the false letter from "Orville"):

> What a strange letter! how proud and how piqued does its writer appear! To what alternate *meanness* and *rashness* do the passions lead, when reason and self-denial do not oppose them! Sir Clement is conscious he has acted dishonourably, yet the same unbridled vehemence which urged him to gratify a blameable curiosity, will sooner prompt him to risk his life, than confess his misconduct. The rudeness of his manner of writing to me springs from the same cause: the proof he has received of my indifference to him, has stung him to the soul, and he has neither delicacy nor forbearance to disguise his displeasure.
> I determined not to shew this letter to Lord Orville. . . . (321–22)

This contemplative response to Willoughby's letter reveals the multiple lessons Evelina has learned on her way to attaining a higher form of self-conscious thinking. Among them is the same age-old warning against unbridled passion and enthusiasm. This warning never discards feeling from moral action but rather assumes the need for reason as a curbing limitation to passionate excess. Evelina's mind-reading skills have achieved a higher level of sophistication through her reflection on her own experiences: she recognizes this letter as the product of a kind of self-consciousness as shame, one that leads to self-disavowal as opposed to self-accountability. Such lower-level consciousness deprives subjects of their responsibility; as Evelina states, Willoughby's letter lacks true confession. Although it exhibits "consciousness," it reveals a mind that fails to hold itself accountable for its actions. Willoughby's writing mechanically "springs" from passion, from quick conduct, and from the feelings of the moment. It disowns action and fails to judge the self in and across time. Evelina deems such writing fatal, which indeed it is, since the letter ends in a suggested proposal for a duel.

The failure to account fully for the self and one's motives in time poses a direct and obvious threat to subjectivity.

Evelina's commentary might be considered an astutely accurate form of textual analysis, one that reveals the completeness of Evelina's mental development in the novel. Most strikingly, her thinking ends in an act that can be read as definitive evidence of such independence of mind and action. In withholding the letter from Orville's sight, Evelina acts of her own accord. She writes to Willoughby, "THE letter you have been pleased to address to me, is so little calculated to afford Lord Orville any satisfaction, that you may depend upon my carefully keeping it from his sight" (322). Rerouting the discourse of libertine pleasure into a feminist voicing of her own independence of mind, Evelina protects her husband to be—not the other way around.

Marriage here does not require a subsumption of the self but rather, as the closing lines of the novel indicate, a "unit[ing]" of the "self" with the "object" of one's "eternal affection" (336). This concept of matrimony within the context of a burgeoning Enlightenment wishes to extend the independence of thought and action to feminine self-consciousness.[40] Marriage is possible because Evelina has achieved selfhood, and Evelina gets what she desires because the growth of her conscious memory has made her into a subject capable of independent agency and action.

Monkey Say, Monkey Do

Such a reading, furthermore, explains Burney's inclusion of one last foray into satire at the novel's end. Throughout this chapter, I have been arguing for the necessary role of memory in developmental self-consciousness, all the while suggesting that autobiographical memory in its link to intentionality is important for the survival of the subject in the context of a social Enlightenment. I want now to return to the issue of genre and how Burney plays with archetypes in her novel. For it is at the level of the archetype that Burney impacts the reader's social memory: moving from a personal account of memory development to the question of how remembered fictions affect a social network of English readers, she drives home a feminist message. Already Burney has overturned gender stereotypes that reach back to the chivalric romance when Evelina's triumphant use of memory saves both herself and her lover, Orville. However, Burney's inclusion of the monkey scene at the novel's end takes a more pointed stab at the eighteenth-century archetype of the she-tragedy. In doing so, it underscores the novel's aim to rewire our historical memory of fiction, suggesting that fiction is the place to change the social status quo so that women may be re-membered from bodies raped and seen into thinking, speaking subjects.

Critics have suggested that the monkey scene calls into question figures of satire, performance, and the distinction between the human and animal.[41] I believe we can also read this scene as an allegory for the novel's argument about self-consciousness, one that affirms the subtle changes in Evelina's developmental rise to the work of conscious memory in volume 3. The monkey episode is precipitated by an important conversation that takes place in the bath houses, where Evelina remarks in her letter: "At the pump-room, I was amazed at the public exhibition of the ladies in the bath: it is true, their heads are covered with bonnets, but the very idea of being seen, in such a situation, by whoever pleases to look, is indelicate" (325). The closing exchange between the Captain and Lovel recalls the theatrical themes of volume 1 in its emphasis on spectacle and the problem of "being seen."

At this point in the text, Evelina seems to have triumphed over her perpetual status of objecthood. The emphasis on Lovel in the monkey episode, however, reminds us of the alternative to Evelina's newfound agency. Lovel embodies the satirical figure of the fop, or man of fashion, one who devotes himself to the exercise of performance, to being a spectacle, or aesthetic object.[42] As the novel returns to the topic of aesthetic modes of taste foregrounded in volume 1, Lovel responds to Louisa's request for fashion assistance in swimming attire:

> "Who, me!—O dear Ma'am," said he, simpering, "I can't pretend to assist a person of your Ladyship's taste; besides, I have not the least head for fashions.—I really don't think I ever invented above three in my life! but I never had the least turn for dress,—never any notion of fancy or elegance."
>
> "O fie, Mr. Lovel! how can you talk so?—don't we all know that you lead the *ton* in the *beau monde*? I declare, I think you dress better than any body."
>
> "O dear Ma'am, you confuse me to the last degree! *I* dress well!—I protest I don't think I'm ever fit to be seen! I'm often shocked to death

to think what I figure I go. If your Ladyship will believe me, I was full half an hour this morning thinking what I should put on!"

"Odds my life," cried the Captain, "I wish I'd been near you! I warrant I'd have quickened your motions a little! Half an hour thinking what you'd put on? and who the deuce do you think cares a snuff of a candle whether you've any thing on or not?"

"O pray, Captain," cried Mrs. Selwyn, "don't be angry with the gentleman for *thinking,* whatever be the cause, for I assure you he makes no common practice of offending in that way." (326)

As the epitome of the fop, Lovel has a penchant for fashion, which he thinly disavows in the false humility he expresses to Louisa. He is performative, described as a theatrical combination of narcissism and imitation. (Hence the monkey and the mirror become his monikers.) Looking at the passage cited above, we realize that this dialogue is not only an aesthetic commentary on tastes and modes, or even on the nagging social tendency (mocked in volume 1) to *perform* taste. Strikingly, the passage examines the topic of thinking, and how the operations of consciousness are to be defined. Embedded in Lovel's seemingly narcissistic self-view is a troubling confession that tells the truth about his character: Lovel does not think; he "puts on." "I really don't think," Lovel begins to say. The word "invention," which Lovel applies to the world of fashion, is ironic. Invention does not connote creation or discovery (as its modern usage typically implies). Rather, in this context, "invention" is reduced to a matter of mere performance, of dressing and ornamentation. Thinking, or not thinking as the case may be for the beau monde, is "put on." An exercise akin to wearing, dressing, and performing, it entails an obsessive preoccupation with being seen.

This is what Julie Park has called "abjection" in Burney's fiction, which extends, I would suggest, well beyond the female characters of her texts: "While it works as a powerful figure for the overlapping structures of the body and society, abjection also accounts in grammatical terms for what happens to a psyche striving to become a subject while cultural forces (itself included) insist on its objecthood."[43] By implicitly confessing his status as aesthetic object, Lovel disavows his own subjectivity. He is a self-proclaimed "figure," or metaphor, in this case not merely of the man of mode but of a kind of thinking as thoughtless self-exposure. It is no surprise that the Captain uses the monkey to reveal to the crowd what Lovel truly is. This method of satirical exposure is referenced in the Captain's allusion to our human nakedness in his comment, "Who do you think cares a snuff... whether you've any thing on or not?" As Mrs. Selwyn satirically suggests, Lovel does not think, he is simply seen. Like the women in the novel who fail to attain independence through self-conscious development, Lovel succumbs to the status of the spectacle, or the aesthetic object, by allowing himself to pass "for a figure." The concept that it takes a full half an hour for Lovel to think about what he will put on parodically reveals a kind of self-reflection that, although it is reliant on the conditions of slow time, is invested merely in the perceptions of others. Lovel *spends time* perceiving himself as others would perceive him; thus time here is wasted, not used, as it fails to influence and shape thought to achieve independent action. Lovel shows others what they want to see; he is a mirror to the world, but never an autonomous self. In this sense, he is unenlightened.

Most significantly, his status as a mere form reminds us of the she-tragedy's silent commentary on the importance of intentions—how they provide a counterforce to the attendant risks of being seen. Like Monimia, Lovel opens himself up to possibilities of harm when he forsakes his own mentality for the love of the beau monde. His mind is made up, as it were, by extrinsic laws of fashion and societal approval. Albeit satirical, the episode of the monkey is, after all, a story of assault. As such, it asks its readers to reminisce on an alternative ending to Burney's narrative—one that we may have all along anticipated, given the history of female rape and subjection that plagued the novels and plays of Burney's time.

As a mere figure,[44] the fop also serves as a metaphorical reminder of Evelina's own journey toward the conditions of selfhood; the allegory warns that consciousness is more than the objective quality of being seen. If thinking takes time, then time must also influence the development of our ever-unfolding self-conscious awareness. Remembered experience is necessary to the degree that it allows subjects to reshape their histories. Ruminating on the past opens new pathways into the future. Burney heralds memory as a boon to the sociohistorical conditions of an inhumane crisis: the epidemic of rape in the rise of modernity. Such memory requires self-conscious development and exercise. Yet the exercise of thinking is so rare in this world of would-be subjects that when seeking self-consciousness, we so often end up with a handful of empty figures.

Lovel is not alone in the novel in this regard. He is, in fact, one of many. The Captain-versus-Lovel scene might be read as two brutes mutually outing one another. In this manner, society can be viewed as a kaleidoscopic prism of subject mirroring,[45] one wherein mimetic substitution causes us to mistake performance for thoughtful action. Yet the novel's characteristic insistence on combining sentiment with comedy asks us to take a hard look at its compositional strategy.[46] The satirical portions of the text disclose the remnants of an old order, a disappearing genre of thinking as performing. These passages recall the Restoration tradition of satirical "character" wherein readership takes on a semiotic structure, asking us to "mind read" our way into a kind of consciousness that promotes empirical structures of thought.[47] Burney's closing social satire floats above the text like a passing buoy atop an intricate *Bildungsroman* narrative that seriously attempts to resolve the aesthetic complications of human consciousness.

Beneath the figure of the man-as-monkey, we read the hopeful message that this is a story about one woman's psychological development, a complex but successful mental *Bildung*. With her excessively sympathetic constitution in tow, Evelina triumphs over one kind of empirically driven existence to arrive at a more phenomenological understanding of self and world. This transition relies on the privileging of time over a strictly spatial tendency to place thought within the context of our immediate environment and surroundings. Reading *Evelina* in this way forces us to consider the relationship between memory, time, and self-consciousness. This relationship demonstrates a movement away from a representation of character as pure figurative play; the monkey, like Lovel, is a trope, a concept of character as sign left over from the theatrical genre of Restoration comedy.[48] He sits awkwardly atop a new understanding of self-consciousness that forces him, in the end, to exit the scene. This new literary practice is one invested in novelistic *Bildung*—in the sense of a dialectic that ultimately encourages us to transcend the historical ideology of our own self-objectification.

Novels, Burney suggests, force us to take time; they encourage a reflective type of thinking that moves aesthetic feeling and sympathy into a new register of temporally driven contemplation. A knowledge of the self emerges as novels attempt to put the distance of time between people and things, or between people and other people. Thereby novels explore the force of memory as an agent that brings about self-conscious experience.

This moves self-consciousness away from a mere sense that one is feeling and perceiving to a more enduring notion of agency.

Memories grow in social contexts, only to allow for a sense of self-possession, ownership, and authorship. For Burney, memories are the key to reclaiming women's bodies, to infusing feelings with the powers of consent. Remembering her experiences over time frees Evelina from a Monimian crisis. With this narrative of self-conscious reflection, and developmental memory, Burney rewrites the history of rape that haunted her generation. It is a fiction that begs realization—urging its readers to believe in memory's power to heal history, to change social trauma and the cultural status quo.

Read together, novels such as *Robinson Crusoe*, *Tristram Shandy*, and *Evelina* begin to expose the complex implications of socially networked memory. On the one hand, transacted memories have the power to revise personal circumstances for the better; on the other, individuals can have an impact on collective memory structures as they become conscious of themselves within the context of a larger cultural activity of history-making. Memories thus evolve dialectically and continuously as they are reassimilated. Drifting between persons, they prompt us to make creative adjustments to our feelings, environments, and things. The next chapter focuses on Charlotte Smith's innovative approach to literary composition in her novel, *Celestina*. For Smith, literary citation is not an activity of borrowing or repeating. Rather, like the other transacted memories we have observed in this book, Smith's quotations become vehicles for easing psychic distress when they are used to rearrange form and revise its meaning.

❖ CHAPTER 4 ❖

Strange Concussions of Nature

Celestina's Mindscapes

> Anne's object was, not to be in the way of any body.... Her *pleasure* in the walk must arise from the exercise and the day, from the view of the last smiles of the year upon the tawny leaves and withered hedges, and from repeating to herself some few of the thousand poetical descriptions extant of autumn.... She occupied her mind as much as possible in such like musings and quotations; but it was not possible, that when within reach of Captain Wentworth's conversation with either of the Miss Musgroves, she should not try to hear it; ... Anne could not immediately fall into a quotation again. The sweet scenes of autumn were for a while put by—unless some tender sonnet, fraught with the apt analogy of the declining year, with declining happiness, and the images of youth and hope, and spring, all gone together, blessed her memory.
> —JANE AUSTEN, *Persuasion*

On what might be called a literary ramble to the neighboring town of Winthrop, Jane Austen's nineteenth-century heroine, Anne Elliot, reveals how thinking walks the line between fact and fiction, experience and memory. By prefiguring wandering as a mental and physical exercise, the passage sets both mind and body on parallel paths in a shared geography. At its start, the matter of pleasure seems tied to physiological touch, physical motion, and sight (the ability to "view" and examine one's surroundings). For the avid reader, the tactile nature of experience comes under scrutiny, however, when she arrives at a handful of clichés embedded within the landscape. The hackneyed descriptions of the year's "last smiles," its "tawny leaves" and "withered hedges," seem out of place, making Anne's experience appear less her own and more like a representation. Indeed, the free indirect style soon reveals its delightful trickery: with the phrase "repeating to herself some few of the thousand poetical descriptions extant of autumn," the reader's eyes are opened. What passes for nature is, in fact, art.

The passage parodies the empirical concept of the eighteenth-century memory storehouse. Alluding to a feminized practice of reading as collecting quotations, Austen refers to a style of mental occupation as a retreat into fiction.[1] What is collected here is not personal sensation but Anne's experience of reading. Representations are recycled, recalled, and reborn, coloring her view of nature. Quotation seemingly provides Anne with an escape route from emotionally painful realities. And yet Austen suggests that reading, unlike minds or bodies, is something that we "fall" into and out of. The "sweet scenes" of fiction flicker across the mind in a temporal way. They are put by and taken up again like a book on the shelf—interrupted by the penetrating sounds of Anne's natural and social environment. Quotation, after all, is by nature metonymic; it reduces the artistic body to a representative piece that stands in for the whole. In quoting, we slice up fiction so as to reconfront, reengage with, and represent the world. In its relationship to representation, quotation demonstrates how memory borrows feelings so as to alter personal reality.

Adela Pinch has read this scene from *Persuasion* as an example of "the limits of literature as consolation." For Pinch, literature's limits tell the story of an "autonomous" mind: Austen "warns that mental space is always impinged upon." In her argument about the role of quotation in *Persuasion*, Pinch figures reading as a mode of mental "resistance" because the notion of an enclosed psyche threatens the tenets of empiricism and its historical reliance on sensation: "If one of the things people read for is . . . absorption . . . reading also conditions people's reception of the outside world, not only of melancholy landscapes but of overheard voices and of other people."[2] As Pinch reads it, quotation drums out experience with repetition. As I show in this chapter, quotation does this, and more: it adopts a complex role in the mind's continual interface with forms in the world. Like memory, quotation never merely re-presents or repeats experience; rather, it becomes an indexical marker for forms remapped by the mental processes of creation and transformation.

Anne's walk to Winthrop ends with a reference to quotation as the "blessing" of "memory." The episode closes with a mental and emotional transaction between feeling and its fictional analogue. Anne "puts by" quotation only to take it up again as a comparison to the natural reality of her present "decline," of time passing and forms decaying. And yet, as a revitalized form, the "analogy" itself underscores not form's decline but its endurance. Like Austen's characteristic usage of the em dash that punctuates time's passage, the "tender sonnet" that intrudes into experience marks how literary form remains and also changes in new literary and mental contexts. Purportedly, the sonnet brings consolation. But how could a poem about the "decline of happiness" "bless . . . memory"? According to Pinch, the passage may evoke Charlotte Smith's *Elegiac Sonnets*, whose popularity caused them to be "widely imitated" in early nineteenth-century literature.[3] Indeed, the paradoxical approach to pain as pleasure savors of Smith's literary exploits—and also of her approach to quotation. For Smith, quotation was memory's way of "taking up" what was seemingly "all gone" and recycling it, not to repeat the form but to recontextualize it, thereby creating new things out of old proverbs. Collecting quotations may be more than a matter of storing up. For Charlotte Smith, it is the author's way of transfiguring form, of altering the face of fiction so as to reinhabit reality in new and worldly ways.

Stuart Curran writes of Charlotte Smith, "I know of no other writers in the later eighteenth century, whether in prose or verse, who so continually and so extensively incorporate other voices within their texts."[4] In his work on intertextuality, Curran has attributed Smith's excessive use of quotation to an effort to insert herself into literary history, especially the canon of English poetry. For Adela Pinch, the use of quotation in Smith's *Elegiac Sonnets* has darker implications. Blaming quotation as the cause and effect of distress throughout Smith's poems, Pinch avers "asserting that writing makes one miserable takes the form of quoting someone else. If quotation involves incorporation of someone else's expression, perhaps writing makes one miserable because writing always involves taking in, reproducing, other people's expressions of feelings."[5] As in her work on Jane Austen, Pinch assumes a relationship between quotation and repetition in Smith's sonnets that renders the anxiety of influence a felt reality.[6] In contrast to critics such as Kerri Andrews and Stephen Behrendt, who consider Smith's approach to both reading and writing as part and parcel of a social system of sympathy and consolation,[7] Pinch's epistemological inquiry into borrowed and quoted feeling causes her to underscore the affective risks of Smith's verse: "From the first sonnet onward, [the poems] seem to argue that their melancholy may indeed be caused by the strange effects of reading and writing."[8] Pinch is not alone in her anxieties about the feelings that writing and reading produce for Charlotte Smith and her readers. Mark Sandy argues not only are loss and grief the sources of Smith's poems, but her works also suggest "the limitations of art to compensate for that loss"; they intimate "the artifice and the fragility of art to wrest consolation from loss."[9]

Indeed, reading Smith can feel a bit like flatlining into misery, and it is no surprise that many critics have read her work as the progeny of a life of distress. Louise Duckling notes that Charlotte Smith became a cultural icon of misery both posthumously and for her contemporaries.[10] The readers who have found "succour" in turning to Smith's writing attribute this consolation merely to the boons of a late eighteenth-century cult of sympathy.[11] In what follows, I take up the rather difficult task of salvaging Smith from the depths of her "miserable" reputation. Reducing Smith to an iconography of distress causes us to overlook the subtle ways in which distress is overcome in her novels.

Smith's 1791 novel, *Celestina*, is a particularly curious object of inquiry in Smith's oeuvre, for in it she makes a habit not simply of citing other writers from the literary canon but also of engaging in a practice of literary self-reference. The novel is riddled with Smith's own excerpted poems, mostly taken from the *Elegiac Sonnets*. These pass not as self-quotations but as her protagonist's own compositions. In this manner, the line between quotation and self-authorized production becomes blurred throughout the text. Although one of the major focal points in Smith criticism has been the author's self-allusive habit of inserting thinly veiled autobiographical references into her novels, I do not approach self-quotation in *Celestina* in this way (however tempting it may be).[12] Rather, I highlight a difference between how these quotations operate in the novel versus how they operate in the sonnets themselves. Once these works are transported to and recontextualized in the body of a new fiction, they become part of a larger, more complex system of referentiality—one that gives new meaning to the eighteenth-century association between remembering and collecting.

Dahlia Porter notes in her analysis of *Beachy Head* and Smith's *Conversation* poems that poetic composition for Smith was something like the scientific habit of collecting as a mode of empirical inquiry. While demonstrating how Smith's poems become "meditations on the work of collecting," Porter places Smith's work in an Enlightenment tradition of memory and epistemology.[13] Nevertheless, (re)collection, as an operation of quotation in *Celestina*, functions very differently from the material and empirical notion of collection that Porter evokes in her reading of Smith's late verse. The manner in which Smith collects and rearranges quotations in *Celestina* astutely lines up maxims quoted from her literary forefathers with her own self-referenced poetic works, causing us to reread her poetry in a tradition of philosophical revision. In this, Smith demonstrates how the activities of writing, reading, and remembrance recycle form only to alter and reshape it. By considering the metonymic function of quotation, Smith forces us to note the importance of forms in context. Literature too has an environment of its own, and, like nature, *Celestina* offers a glimpse of that environment in an ever-unfolding process of evolution.

In *Celestina*, quotation leads to (re)production, altering form and changing the status quo of feeling. As minds take up and put by the "declining" forms of the past, they insert themselves into nature's organic processes of transformation. But the novel's use of quotation also calls attention to the writer's talents of playing with the boundaries between art and nature, fiction and reality. Much like Anne Elliot on her walk to Winthrop, Celestina wanders through liminal territories; her thoughts walk the line between fact and fiction, memory and imagination, mind and matter. Quotation's context also occupies a multidimensional mental space in the novel. In addition to inciting activities of literary production (for quoting other authors seemingly inspires Celestina to write sonnets of her own), quotation activates the reader's memory. It asks us to participate in heuristic processes of memory and rearrangement. As textual snippet and analogue, quotation revises the meaning of form—taking minds, through memory, into new contexts. These indexical markers also highlight the interstitial and contingent relationships between minds and worlds, between minds and other minds. They relativize sensation and reroute it along new pathways. Analogues in *Celestina* have a way of desensitizing feeling or of changing its direction. Much like Uncle Toby on the bowling green, who finds a virtual playground in the recompensatory forms of metaphor, quotations for Celestina are the stuff of mental play. They incite the pleasures of composition, and they historicize feeling so as to dampen its sting. For Celestina, distress is just an analogy.

In and Around Alvestone

Celestina is particularly concerned with the mind's engagement with physical processes and with how this interaction influences the experience of feeling. The author takes care to distinguish physical sensation from emotional, and yet, in moving feelings from the realm of the world into the mind, Smith also gives them hope. As a state of mind, distress can be altered or fluid, unlike a persistent handicap or disability. Once a feeling like distress becomes a mental state and not just a sensation of the body, it finds a temporary escape route. In the mind, feelings change. This Romantic mental capacity for creating new and "companionable forms"[14] out of old stuff alters not just form but the feeling form produces.

In *Celestina*, Smith takes a vested interest in what minds do in their wandering states: they re-collect and rearrange, cut and reframe, remembering fiction and reality so as to create new things out of the mix. Minds are always in a state of play, but like the forms they alter, they are themselves pliable and plastic, subject to natural law and the passage of time. Smith sees the mind as part of a natural environment; it is of the world, and so it works both with and within that world. For Smith, the mind, like all organic things, functions in time. Like Anne Elliot, we must always come back to the world. With a latent vitalism, the novel thus continually puts feeling into motion by sending bodies and minds on parallel journeys. Most compelling is what happens at the intersections between these two vectors of motion, when feelings cross over from the body into the mind.

Critics have often turned to the motif of wandering in Smith's novels as an archetype for border crossing. In their readings, scholars such as Amy Garnai, Katherine Astbury, and William Brewer note how Smith's characters traverse boundaries in physical and geopolitical ways, a motif that speaks to the historical contexts of Smith's novels in the time of Romanticism and the French Revolution, when questions of cosmopolitanism and nationhood were on the rise.[15] Looking at borders in a geographic sense, we note how very recursive and futile the impulse toward wandering in Smith's prose can be. As Garnai observes, "The act of wandering that [Smith] represents cannot be ameliorated, or lead to transcendence, either by privileging of nature or introspective solitude."[16] Although wandering in Smith's *Celestina* may never provide the kind of transcendence that Romantic readers (Smith's characters included) were looking for, the novel does intimate emotionally recompensing transactions of feeling as they wander across the borders of body and mind. Crossing over from embodied to mental and environmental states, sentiments are recycled as they are read in the world and finally rewritten.

What happens to feelings as they become resituated? In *Celestina*, feelings change, in quality and meaning, as they find, and inhere within, new forms. This chapter travels to several sites in the fictional world of *Celestina*. There I look at five of Celestina's poetic compositions, taken from Charlotte Smith's own late eighteenth-century verse. Each of these self-quotations follows similar, evolving patterns of production. Born out of practices of reading (and quotation), they recycle literary form to re-member and reshape it. Moreover, their compositions follow the physical activities of wandering that stage poetic composition on the borders of natural and mental landscapes. Here the uncanny echoes between mind and world serve to put geography in its place, as nature becomes a map of indexical markers that reference memory's power to alter form and feeling.

Celestina's first scene of writing sets up a pattern for the process of composition throughout the text:

> Celestina, to avoid being seen from the windows of the house, which commanded the garden and the meadows near it, took her way down this lane. Her thoughts ran over the strange events of the preceding years, in which she had experienced so much anguish, aguish embittered by the transient promise of supreme happiness. As she reviewed her whole life, it seemed to have been productive only of regret. . . .
>
> These melancholy reflections led her on, till a turn out of the road brought her to the style of the church yard. She leant pensively over it, and read the rustic inscriptions on the tomb stones. One was that of a young woman of nineteen: it was her age; and Celestina felt an emotion of envy towards the village girl, whose early death the rural poet lamented in the inscription.
>
> "Merciful heaven!" cried she, "is early death ever really to be lamented? and should I not be happier to die now than to live; as perhaps I shall not be forgotten?" Insensibly this idea took possession of her fancy; and with her pencil she wrote the following lines in her pocket book, not without some recollection of Edwards' thirty seventh and forty fourth sonnets. (188)

The passage begins with a curiously casual alignment between emotion and motion, between the "running" thoughts that wander across time and Celestina's wandering body. As if to suggest that motion activates memory, Smith depicts a mind that scales time in tandem with the geographic relocations of her subject in space. These parallel motions extend to the literary forms themselves, for as Celestina takes a "turn out of the road," so does the passage reflexively scramble the mind-body relationship.

Just as motion seems to activate thought in matter, so too thinking changes the direction of Celestina's movements: "these melancholy reflections led her on," Smith writes, to the edge of the churchyard. For Smith, the dialectical relationship between mind and body is less an investigation into the hard problem of consciousness than it is about the nebulous origin of feeling.[17] The "anguish" that is purportedly associated with memory is contingent and relative. Celestina's "whole life in review . . . produces only . . . regret" because, as the appositive suggests, anguish comes from the "embittered transient promise" of a would-be future. What is lost here is no real thing but a fictional circumstance, a promised and wished-for possibility. It is not memory that brings pain but imagination.

Celestina's melancholy comes from a "seeming" reality, a once believed to be true fiction or fantasy. The fact that this fantasy remains unrealized at this moment in the text is the actual source of her anguish—not her claims to experience. In this sense, expectation, not sensation, brings pain. As though pitting John Locke's theory of recollection against David Hume's theory of the causal mind, Smith's subtle distinction between emotional and sensational pain posits a new universe of thought that inverts the traditional empiricist dichotomy: one in which imagination collects while memory transforms. The two categories of memory and imagination flip-flop and converge throughout the narrative of Celestina's mental wanderings, but for a moment here Smith questions our assumptions about the felt experience of mental faculties in eighteenth-century philosophies of mind. The word "seemed" is significant. Like the narrator's need to qualify her use of the term "anguish"—"she had experienced so much anguish, anguish embittered by the transient promise of supreme happiness"—it relocates what might be assumed as the pains of memory into the pains of imagination, of fiction itself. Issues of mind and matter become strangely entangled in a nebulous history of emotion grounded in the fictional stories we tell ourselves and appropriate as truth.

Fittingly, Celestina's review of her life story leads her not only to an existential setting but to a moment of existential reading. Reading the "rural poetry" inscribed on the tombstone of a girl her own age, Celestina makes a mental transaction in which she imagines herself, like this stranger whose story remains unknown, underground—in a state of unfeeling immobility. Smith overwrites the archetype of reading as an activity of sensibility in the tradition of the graveyard poets when she assigns not sympathy but envy to Celestina's emotional state. As she looks at the gravestone, Celestina is prompted to color a would-be scene of mourning into pleasing fantasy by the enticements of her imagination. Importantly, Celestina's wish for death is not merely a drive for "insensibility" but a drive toward posterity. The same woman who has just fled beyond the windows of the house so as not to be seen in fact desires only to be seen: she longs to become an object of remembrance to others. Poetic posterity is the ruling passion that incites Celestina to write her first poem.[18] Writing promises consolation not from the sympathy it may bring but in its capacity to activate the surviving memory of one's readers and loved ones.

To add to the strange emotional circumstances that inspire Celestina to write, we might note that the sonnet is written as a product of memory, a recollection of reading Edwards's sonnets. This calls the sonnet's own authenticity into question. Is it a product of Celestina's feeling, a reproduction of feeling, or a fictional projection? This is something like what Adela Pinch has characterized as the dubious epistemology, or etiology, of feminine feeling in Charlotte Smith's poetry.[19] Whether feelings are personal or derived from literary form can never be determined. Rather, Smith asks us to locate feeling on the margins of fiction and experience.

For my purposes, I am less interested in the genuine nature of the feeling than in how fiction and memory come into play in transactions between pleasure and pain. The memory of a fiction that never comes to be triggers Celestina's impulse to wander and the "anguish" of melancholia. But the remembered fiction also produces its own re-membered fiction: a sonnet that is a mélange of literary quotation, fantasy, emotional projection, and transaction. Celestina imagines a future in which she will be re-membered, transformed from a mere sensitive body into an ideal imprinted on the minds of others.

When Smith writes, "insensibly this idea took possession" of Celestina's "fancy," I suggest that she does not indicate that writing is an unconscious practice but rather that it is an unfeeling one. Celestina wishes for, imagines herself as, the desensitized body; she writes to be remembered and to become "insensible." The sonnet that follows transforms sensation into remembered form while redefining experience as the fantasies of fictionalized memory:

> SONNET
> Oh thou! who sleep'st where hazle bands entwine
> The vernal grass, with paler violets drest;
> I would, sweet maid! thy humble bed were mine,
> And mine, thy calm and enviable rest.
> For never more, by human ills opprest
> Shall thy soft spirit fruitlessly repine:
> Thou cans't not now thy fondest hopes resign
> Even in the hour that should have made thee blest.
> Light lies the turf upon thy virgin breast;
> And lingering here, to love and sorrow true,
> The youth, who once thy simple heart possess'd,
> Shall mingle tears with April's early dew;
> While still for him, shall faithful Memory save,
> Thy form and virtues from the silent grave! (189–90)

The poem imagines insensibility as a blotting out of our awareness of the future; the "enviable rest" of death, its pleasures, lie in the fact that the youth no longer can entertain her "fondest hopes." She must "resign" herself to a radically material state. Much like Wordsworth's Lucy, Smith's graveyard girl is "entwined" and entangled in earth's material processes.[20] Celestina's mind-over-matter fantasy of time and nature arrests the mind, subjecting it to matter's potential immobility. The wished-for moment is one that paralyzes the pathological motions of matter and mind. And yet vitalism lives on as a property not of nature or of materialism but of minds, and mental transactions. For "form" survives in the final couplet, "save[d]" from the "grave" (a state of utter finitude) by "Memory."

Although the sonnet's allegory of memory figures it as a "faithful" entity, something that preserves and records form, the scene and the sonnet tell us otherwise. In context, the dead girl is not remembered for her life that was, or even her death that is, but as a product of her viewer's—of Celestina's—own imagination. Moreover, the sonnet itself is both a self-authorized production and a quotation that echoes Edwards's sonnets. As we imagine Celestina jumping the "style" that gates the churchyard, so too we can see the poem as a restylized fiction. Smith's avowed use of quotation highlights the strange crossover between fact and fiction as a problem of affective property: how to disentangle the feelings of others from those we call our own.

Celestina's first endeavor at authorship is one that speaks to the sentiment of being read and to the affinities between reading and remembering. To corroborate this notion that writing forces the self as an object into the purview of another's memory, the first sentence of prose that follows the sonnet tells us: "Celestina, who had a natural turn to poetry, had very rarely indulged it; but since she had passed so many hours with Willoughby, his passionate fondness for it, and his desire that she should not neglect the talent she had received from nature, had turned her thoughts to its cultivation" (190). In short, Celestina writes because Willoughby wants her to—or rather because she remembers Willoughby's desire. To write is to recall, to revivify Willougby's great wishes. Moreover, the sentence's repeated emphasis on nature as the derivative for writing also speaks to a dialectical turn between mind and matter throughout the novel. There's a hint of Neoplatonic theories of art and nature in this phrase. Smith tells us that Celestina writes because it is her "natural gift," and yet, like a natural form, the gift must be "cultivated." Itself an organic form, the mind's job is to form, and re-form nature, to "cultivate" it, as it were.

Yet there is also something strange about the manner in which Smith frames Celestina's first literary production and how it calls attention to the embedded use of poetry in Smith's prose. It is as though Smith must give us a reason for the sonnet's existence as a more than quoted form in the context of the novel at large. The elegy is Smith's own self-quotation reattributed to Celestina in the fiction, and it is the first of many to come in the novel. Clothing the text in autobiographical elements is also a way of calling attention to the very process of writing as a self-conscious habit of literary reattribution and revision. It is thereby important to note that the raison d'être of Celestina's first sonnet is memory. Remembering Willoughby, Celestina's poem also inscribes the author's self onto the minds of others, operating much like the epitaph on the young girl's grave.

Celestina's second literary production is staged much in the manner of her first. The impulse to write follows on the heels of wandering feelings, forms, and memories. As Celestina's travels take her directly in the way of

Alvestone Park, she is seized with a desire to revisit the old remembered spot, and Cathcart, her traveling companion, indulges her in this wish:

> She then went into the park over the stepping stile, and walking about half a quarter of a mile, reached the group of beech trees which shaded a high knoll in the park; from whence the house, half concealed by intervening wood, appeared to great advantage. It was now the beginning of May, and the trees under which she stood were just coming into leaf.... One of the trees of this clump was marked by Willoughby with her name, his own, and his sister's, and the date. It was five years since; and the bark had grown rough and knotted round the scars, but the letters still remained. It was to revisit this well known memorial that Celestina had been anxious; and now she could hardly bear the thoughts of leaving it. She recollected every trifling circumstance that happened when Willoughby cut those letters: the cloaths he wore, and his very look, were again present to her; while in the breeze that sighed among the trees she fancied she heard the sound of his voice, and that he pronounced the name of Celestina. In this state of mind she had almost forgotten that Cathcart waited for her. (240)

The excursion bears an almost uncanny resemblance to the first scene at the graveyard. Again, contemplation and composition spiral forth from a whimsical impulse to wander. As Celestina moves across the landscape, she transgresses another border by hopping another stepping stile. As in the graveyard scene, what lies on the other side depicts the act of reading as remembering. Like the epitaph, the markings on the tree are natural ephemera that signal the passage of time, even as they gesture toward what is preserved and saved "five years" hence. The way the bark naturally metamorphoses and becomes entangled with other parts of the tree only serves to underscore a contrast between the natural form and its literary ornament. For the scrawling "letters" still "remain." In this most of all, the visit to the beech tree memorial shares a kinship with the gravestone sighting. Both are contemplations of remains. The markings mark what lies beyond the waste; as memorials, they attest to writing as a promise of longevity, posterity, and remembrance.

Celestina's "recollections" here are purportedly acute and specific, implying that her powers of retention are highly sentimental. Remembrance operates in the passage in the Proustian sense, as a kind of relived experience, for images become present again, invoked and revitalized by the powers of the mind. In this manner, Smith evokes a concept of associative memory, but Celestina's conscious reconjuring of past details and events leaves something to be desired. What is strange about this passage is not what is remembered but what is left unsaid in Smith's representation of the mental landscape. Most striking are the absent details of Celestina's "sensitive" recollection. We are told she remembers Willoughby's clothes and looks, but such specifics are invoked never to be described. Smith thereby gestures toward a conceptual stereotype of memory that would be well known to her Romantic reader. We are meant to read the sign and fill in the gaps, all the while recognizing the insufficiency of the reference.[21] By never actually presenting her reader with memory's acute records, Smith leaves us to imagine the exact inner workings of another's recollection. She thus exposes empirical association for what it is: a mechanical reduction that cannot fully account for the strange overlaps between memory and imagination, or the intersubjective nature of feeling.

Celestina's vaguely detailed memories give way to an act of "fancy" that is at once delusional and archetypal. The Romantic "breeze" of inspiration that wafts through the scene, in yoking memory to imagination, causes us to question the sound nature of Celestina's "state of mind." Paradoxically, by invoking the very "memory" we have come to know as that storehouse of perfectly recorded events, Smith questions its efficacy. In what sense does memory forget and create at will? We are left to ponder memory's abstracting nature, its capacity to take us away from present distress, for the scene ends with a gesture toward what is almost forgotten by the reader—namely, that Cathcart's and Celestina's journey stems from the heroine's own self-imposed exile.

The sudden shift back into the present is what triggers a sensation of pain. And Celestina finds "herself too much affected" by "the contrast between what she now was, and what, hardly a month since, she expected to be" (241). Notably, it is not memory that brings pain here but unfulfilled desire. The memory recalls not feeling or experience but "expectation." Again, Smith foregrounds the power of time as it operates on form: a mere month can effect so much change. Yet the allusion considers time not as a force of nature but of the mind. No formal change has occurred but the loss of an expectation, a shift in the imagination's point of view. As Celestina remembers what she once imagined, Smith compels us to reconsider the notion of memory not as that great record-keeper of events and things but as a marker of the mind's own evolutionary and transpositional nature.

It is worth noting that this is not the first time that the novel mentions the knoll and the clump of trees that Celestina visits in this scene. In fact, the author has been slowly zooming in on this particular spot. In volume 1, when Celestina first travels from London back into the countryside with Jessy, she "indulges" herself in walking to another knoll at the outskirts of a neighboring estate to watch "by the help of a telescope . . . a clump of firs in Alvestone Park" (135). At this point in the text, the meaning of the clump of firs has not come fully into view for the reader. It is only until much later that the telescopic perspective takes on microscopic meaning. Sightlines are mapped both materially and mentally throughout the novel's multiple frames. At first we were outside looking in, but now, as Celestina looks back at the house of Alvestone from inside its grounds, we find our perceptions turned around and inside out. Smith's reversal of the point of view only foreshadows Austen's later usage of the knoll in the Sotherton episodes of *Mansfield Park*. In both novels the spatial shift in perspective is a metaphor for the mind in time. Cognition is mapped and marked by external sites in the landscape. Smith gives thought an indexical form of reference so as to lend it meaning, all the while insisting that the affective vicissitudes of her protagonist are not a matter of sensation but of the mind.

In Celestina's mourned-for expectation, Smith demonstrates just how powerful a mental state can be. It is "in this state of mind," in the illusions and abstractions of memory, that Celestina briefly "forgets" her painful reality, only to eventually transfigure it by acts of arrangement and composition:

> . . . while Celestina, as her thoughts went back to past pleasures, and as her heart felt all the bitterness of disappointed hope, indulged herself without restraint in the sad luxury of sorrow. She no longer saw the objects she passed, or thought of whither she was going: but Alvestone was still present to her eyes, and she saw Willoughby wandering among its shades as if looking for lost happiness. . . . She heard him sigh forth too late his regret, and lament that for advantages he could not enjoy, he had relinquished the competence he might have possessed. . . . Tears fell slowly down her cheeks as these distressing images presented themselves, and insensibly the tender adieu she had taken of the place, the tender wishes she had formed for the lamented

friend and lover to whom it belonged, arranged themselves into verse, and produced the following. (242)

The return to the memory that sparks Celestina's sonnet assigns surprisingly affective characters to remembrance and imagination. It is memory, the "thoughts" that go "back," that revitalizes "past pleasures," whereas "hope," the flights of imagination now "disappointed," brings "bitterness." Nevertheless, Smith does not wish for us to think of these two faculties of mind as strict binaries. The rhetoric of paradoxical feelings reminds us of memory's brush with imagination. "Sorrow" is a "luxury" that Celestina willfully returns to again and again throughout the novel. Phrases such as "soothing melancholy" (482), "melancholy pleasure" (175, 490), and "melancholy satisfaction" (539) abound within the text. For Smith, the notion of a happy melancholia perfectly describes the unified work of memory and/as imagination.

The next thought epitomizes this sentiment and highlights the pleasures of remembrance alongside its ability to dampen distress. Celestina's memory abstracts her from her present, physical state. "She no longer" sees the objects in front of her or the direction she takes, but as the point of view shifts with the erasure of the present, it re-presents the past in fictionalized form. "Alvestone . . . still present to her eyes" is no photographic record or data point but a mental vision that jump-starts the imagination. Delusively, Celestina *sees* Willoughby "wandering" in search of "lost happiness." The psychic projection of her own mental state onto the imagined memories of her lost love object divests memory of its personal qualities. Celestina extracts an imagined memory from her own mind only to reinscribe it onto another's.

This second sonnet marks another effort at poetic posterity. The distress of fancy's "images," the memory of what never was but might have been, all amount to a sentimental good-bye that links memory to imagination. The parallel structure of the final sentence levels the "tender" adieu of the past with the "tender" wishes for the future. Together, memory and imagination "arrange themselves" into "verse," spawning a "production" of the mind that "insensibly" finds new form. Again, I read this term not simply as an unconscious transaction, for memory and imagination are "luxuries" that Celestina, it seems, consciously "indulges herself" in. Rather, as the mind re-members so as to fictionalize experience, translating it into text, the consolation of the composition lies in its numbing effects. By writing, Celestina becomes "insensible" both to her present reality and the road that lies ahead.

The sonnet itself figures the "blessings" of "remembrance" as the relived experience of an all-too-perfect past:

> SONNET
>
> Farewel ye lawns! by fond remembrance blest,
> As witnesses of gay unclouded hours,
> Where, to maternal friendship's bosom prest,
> My happy childhood past amid your bowers.
> Ye Wood-walks wild! where leaves and fairy flowers
> By Spring's luxuriant hand, are strewn anew:
> Rocks, whence with shadowy grace rude Nature lours
> O'er glens and haunted streams!—a long adieu!
> —And you!—oh! promis'd *Happiness!* whose voice
> Deluded fancy heard in every grove,
> Biding this tender, trusting heart rejoice
> In the bright prospect of unfailing love:
> Tho' lost to me—still may *thy* smile serene
> Bless the dear Lord of this regretted scene. (242)

Nature here bears "witness" to a past that the mind perhaps sees differently, for the flowers' "fairy" powers frame Celestina's recollections as rosy-colored remembrances. To remember in the first half of the sonnet is to reexperience a childlike point of view, to see elements and forms "strewn anew." In this manner, Smith seems to invoke a lived stereotype of Romanticism as the idealization of nature and reflection. Yet the sonnet turns, only to figure imagination in a bad light. "Fancy," "deluded," promises what never comes to be, and the trappings of a perverse sentimentalism turn out to be the mind's attachment to its own fictions. As though wrenched out of a Wordsworthian dream, we seemingly find ourselves within one of Jonathan Swift's boudoir poems.[22] What is mourned here is the lost "prospect," and yet, like the opium addict, the sonnet returns to the very drug it renounces, concluding with a vision of imagined happiness. Fancying her lover happy in the environs of the "regretted scene," the speaker's sonnet weds memory to imagination, retrospect to prospect, environment to a projected mental fiction. The final lines thereby reveal the composition for what it is, a rearrangement of memory and imagination's forms, a rewriting of the fictionalized "scene" that sets the stage of consolation.

"Serenity" is the real feeling, in the actualized form of the sonnet, that recompenses the speaker for her lost fictions. Fiction, like form, is something recycled, remembered, and rearranged. So Smith describes the effects of the sonnet in the very next sentence of the novel: "This disposition of mind, mournful as it was, afforded Celestina so much melancholy indulgence, that it was very reluctantly she was roused from it by their reaching Honiton" (242–43). The pleasure of regret signals a difference between mind and world. The mind travels of its own accord in worlds apart from the body's own motions and travails, yet this time something remains as the protagonist is jolted back to reality, "roused" from the tumbles of her indulgent memory. The mental "disposition" that pleases and seduces the mind away from reality has become a real thing, a new form unto itself, a composition that can be revisited, reread, and even rearranged. In this manner, Smith's *Elegiac Sonnets*, self-quoted and rewoven into the framework of her prose fiction, are more than just an authorial reference, an indexical marker of the author's own autobiography of pain. Rather, the forms displaced reveal the power of recollection as re-collection—of writing's capacity to remember and transform pain until, transplanted into the framework of a novel fiction, it takes on a pleasing logic all its own.

The Hebrides

I have been emphasizing the curious arrangement of poetry and prose in Charlotte Smith's *Celestina* as an effect of the heroine's various affective and cognitive faculties. In doing so, I have tried to shed light on the thin thread that unites mind and body in this text in a barely metaphorical way. All of the poems that Celestina produces are couched in a similar setting: all stem from acts of wandering that both parallel and distinguish mental from physical travel. By setting the mind in motion, and likewise figuring the body in settings of travel and evolving natural landscapes, Smith does more than allude to a parallelism between the two. Rather, her text adopts the rhetoric of vitalism, all the while distinguishing mind wandering from what we might call the travel bug.[23]

Characters in *Celestina* are continuously trying to shake off feelings of grief and woe by relocating, and yet travel itself proves to be an ineffectual cure-all for emotional upset. In this manner, Smith disturbs the eighteenth-century symbiosis between somatic and mental motion—claiming that although the body may move, the mind exists in a world apart. In other words, nature and mind may run in parallel directions throughout the novel, and at times the two even intersect or collide. But still they are distinct entities for Smith: their relationship may be dialectical, but they possess geographies of their own.

In Celestina's travels to the Hebrides, the forces of mind and body are sent on a sublime journey that asks the reader to consider nature as a reference to the mind's own great power to rupture, repair, and transfigure form. Smith depicts nature as an analogue to the mind with a canny anatomical figure:

> The party now put off from shore . . . landed them safely on the ilk. It did not contain more than three acres of land, and the sole inhabitant of it was a solitary herdsman, whose temporary dwelling, composed of loose stones, turf, and heath, he had raised under the protection of a large cliff of grey slate, that seemed to have started away, in some strange concussion of nature, from some other island, and to have fixed itself as a sea mark amidst the perpendicular and abrupt rocks that fenced this on every side. (291)

Traveling at sea, Celestina's bark briefly anchors itself on shore, only to encounter a "temporary dwelling." The reference to the hermit's island "inhabitan[ce]" exerts a standard parallel between thinking and living in the verb "to dwell." Meaning both to ruminate on and to occupy one's environment, the word here also implies an attempt to seek out "protection." As the double entendre is carried through the whole scene, the reader is compelled to think of dwelling's double meaning as both a protective environment and a protective mechanism of the mind. There is relief and shelter in thought, and Celestina's thoughts take her to places far-off and sublime.

The most striking metaphor, however, comes in the sentence's final clause, when we find that by seeking refuge in nature, the solitary man has opted for thin insurance. For his protection comes from nature's own terrifying capacity to rupture form. The cliff that "seemed to have started away" is evidence of vitalism in the most unexpected places. Rocks, like minds and lovers, can break away. Smith describes the geological formation as "a strange concussion of nature," as though rocks, once conscious, have become stupefied. As a conscious-esque force, nature shares a relationship to human thought: it is both transfigured by the forms in its surroundings and has the power to transform those forms. Breaking away from companion cliffs, the rock re-fixes itself into a newly enclosed system. The allegory alludes to Celestina's travels, but it also asks us to consider what conscious memory can and will do to transform situational realities. Solitary and fenced in, like Celestina or the hermit herdsman, the cliff's new structure becomes a marked and markable sign to be read by sailors lost at sea. In Smith's sublime geology, minds and bodies move, re-form, and are read in a landscape that everywhere indicates the inherent energies of form itself.

Both mind and nature share a special power of self-transformation. As a geological and indexical form, Smith's "strange concussion of nature" more clearly becomes a metonym for mind once the passage transitions from the subject of natural form to literary form. Moving seamlessly from the landscape into Celestina's consciousness, Smith returns to the novel's favored topic of memory:

> The sea birds, in swarming myriads, were returning to their nests among the ragged precipices beneath her; and Celestina, recalling to her mind the "green delights" of Alvestone,
> "Its deepening woods, gay lawns, and airy summits,"
> compared it, in pensive contemplation, with the scene before her; yet different as they were, she thought that with Willoughby any place would be to her a paradize; and that even in such a remote spot as this she should be happy if it gave only a subsistence with him.
> This train of thought a little indulged, made her have recourse to her pencil, and produced an address to him in the following. (291–92)

Typically, in late eighteenth-century literature, narrative descriptions of lookouts and prospects quickly transport the reader from the landscape into a character's personal memories of past places and times. Such a pattern denotes a Romantic version of associative memory that links natural forms in the world to the personal history of character consciousness. Invoking this tradition, the "ragged precipices" and swarming birds that Charlotte Smith places before Celestina feel as though they are prospects straight out of Edmund Burke's sublime or a novel by Ann Radcliffe; yet such Gothic scenes share nothing in common with pastoral Alvestone. The mismatch is key to understanding Smith's revision of late eighteenth-century memory archetypes. Celestina's mind, ever fixed on one object, insists on a parallel that is not natural. Perched on a physical overlook, she participates in a mental practice of overlooking;[24] the forms she perceives are drawn together despite their dissimilarity through the dislocating properties of Celestina's mind. In fact, what she sees in her mental rear view mirror is neither Burke nor Alvestone itself but poems from the mid eighteenth-century sensibility canon.[25] Quotations, the stories of others, substitute for remembrance as a record of *personal experience*. Memory's job here is to supplant reality with literary fiction. When Celestina insists that "any place" with Willoughby "would be to her a paradize," we are meant to take this not as mere melodramatic fancy but as evidence of memory's fanciful powers to transfigure reality.

Celestina's wandering mind transplants Alvestone to the sublime Hebrides, but her memory of Alvestone is fashioned out of a snippet of eighteenth-century sensibility poetry. The "green delights" borrow from line 956 of *Summer* in James Thomson's *The Seasons*. Out of context, the citation seemingly denotes an idealized setting. In Thomson's poem, however, it takes on a very different meaning. Smith's pithy literary landmark triggers our memory of a verse paragraph that famously laments the woes of solitude: "UNHAPPY he! who from the first of Joys, / Society, cut off, is left alone" (939–40).[26] The scene from *The Seasons* depicts a traveler at sea who longingly yearns for mainland life: "Yet here, even here, in these black Abodes... Disdainful of *Campania's* gentle Plains, / And all the green Delights *Ausonia* pours" (951–56).

Counter to what critics have inferred about Smith's abundant use of quotation in her writing, here the author does more than merely invoke her readings so as to elevate her own work to the status of the sensibility canon. Like the seemingly misaligned landmarks of the Hebrides and Alvestone in Celestina's sightline, the foreign landscapes of Italy in Thomson's poem share very little in common with rural England. In the lines from *The Seasons*, the subject's memory works so as to recycle past ideal landscapes while his body is assaulted by the distress of a wilder, more remote environment. Mind and body here exist, for a moment, apart. To illustrate this fact, Thomson's poem (like Smith's novel) is rife with classical allusion. Yet in this particular verse paragraph from *The Seasons*, memory's reinvocation of a pastoral ideal has a different affective effect; the sailor feels only "disdain" for a past that haunts him. Smith transplants a snippet of

Thomson's verse, borrowing just enough of the poem to be identifiable to her eighteenth-century reader's memory, only to change Thomson's tune. The subtle nature of the transaction speaks to the significance of a quotation out of context: it demonstrates memory's capacity to rearrange, and thereby transform, form.

For Celestina, the memory of Alvestone alters the feel and meaning of the Hebrides. In quoting Thompson, she finds not the distress of the lines she references but rather the power of her own mind. Her remembrance of Alvestone and Thomson combined does not scar her with pathologic yearning but triggers the pleasures of fancy when she wishfully imagines Willoughby with her in this exact scene: an airy wasteland becomes a virtual "paradize," a "happy" site of "subsistence."

Moreover, the quotation "indulges" new "thought," causing Celestina to "have recourse to her pencil":

SONNET
On this lone island, whose unfruitful breast
Feeds but the summer-shepherd's little flock,
With scanty herbage from the half cloath'd rock,
Where osprays, cormorants, and sea mews rest;
Even in a scene so desolate and rude
I could with *thee* for months and years be blest;
And, of thy tenderness and love possest,
Find all *my* world in this lone solitude!
When the bright sun these northern seas illume,
With thee admire the light's reflected charms;
And when drear Winter spreads his cheerless gloom,
Still find Elysium in thy sheltering arms;
For thou to me canst sovereign bliss impart,
Thy mind my empire, and my throne thy heart.

The broad orb of the sun was now only half seen above the horizon; and Celestina, who had little marked the progress of time, rose, and hastened to join her companions; as she turned for this purpose towards that part of the island where she had left them, she saw the highlander . . . who was in a complete highland dress, which is now not often seen, and which made him, as he walked very quickly on before her, seem exactly the figure a painter would have chosen to have placed in a landscape, representing the heathy summits and romantic rocks of the Hebrides. (292–93)

The sonnet reconfigures Thomson's allegory of solitude when it conceives of an "Elysium" "found" within "a scene so desolate and rude." The use of the word "scene" emphasizes how mental perceptions artistically embellish natural forms. By imagining a new point of view, the mind operates both like the "sea mark" of the cliff and like the fiery sun, "illuming" so as to "reflect" back unto itself its greatest desires. Repeated twice, the word "find" imparts a very specific relationship between mind and world that recalls the survival tactics of Daniel Defoe's Robinson Crusoe. Stranded on a desert island, the wanderer finds what she desires only when memory informs and urges on imagination. Moreover, the poem recalls the concept of dwelling that reminds us of the setting in which it has been conceived. The "sheltering" arms that protect Celestina in a "desolate and rude" landscape are figments of the imagination. And yet like the "empire" of her lover's "mind," or the "throne" of his heart, these figments provide a necessary and consoling manner of "temporary dwelling." Akin to the hermit's home or the "scanty herbage from the half cloath'd rock," they are creations that shelter the speaker from distress. The double emphasis (both metrical and italicized) on the word *my* hints at the mind's tendency to make a world of its own. Read and rewritten, quotation evinces memory's creative capacities. Through "a strange concussion of nature," the mind reorders literary historical experience and transposes it into new forms and feelings.

At the sonnet's end, Smith's reader anticipates a return from Celestina's dreamscape to the reality of the novel's fictional plot. But this is not what we get. As the sun sets in the novelistic setting, the "broad orb" echoes its poetic counterpart with its "charming" brightness. Even as Celestina returns to her companions, time stands still within her consciousness. She "fails to mark its progress," but we do not fail to mark its lyrical function. Nature's timepiece only serves as a recurrent figure, much like the other natural and geographic sites in the novel that lyrically refer us backward from one fiction to another.

The reciprocal line between art and nature punctuates Celestina's return from her "temporary dwelling" with illusion and artifice, and like the referential play of the sun, mirrored in life and sonnet, we cannot find the frame that closes the artwork in. Celestina returns to the same spot to seek her companions, as though they might stand immobilized in time and space. Magically, she finds them there no worse for the wear (293). But what she encounters first is a strange highlander whose dress makes him appear unnatural, like a work of art. (As we later find out, this *is* an unnatural habit for the "highlander," who turns out to be her fervent stalker, Montague Thorold, in disguise. Nevertheless, at this moment in the narrative, the highlander remains an unrecognizable form in the landscape to both Celestina and the reader.) Celestina fancies him "placed" in the scene as if part of the landscape's own wild and "romantic . . . summits." In fact, the thought is more romantic than the scene. Celestina's mindscape turns reality into artistic form, rendering it "figural" and "representational." Although the sonnet loses its frame in the context of the narrative, Celestina draws a frame around the highlander, marking him out as a picturesque device of the author or "painter." Cutting and framing forms at will, the mind transforms nature into art, art into nature.

The Hebrides scenes in the novel are apt to fall into such recursive, repetitive structures of description, quotation, and composition. Another sonnet, "The Laplander," is couched in a mirror setting to that of the above:

> In one of these walks, along the edge of the very steep rocks, where the scene presented only desolation: the dark and turbulent sea on one side, and on the other a succession of mountains, which seemed to have been thrown upon each other in some tremendous convulsion of nature, she turned towards the yet more dreary North, and reflected on the condition of those whom the poet describes as "the last of men," the inhabitants of Siberia, of Lapland, and those extreme regions where "Life at last goes out."(308)

In another meditation on solitude, Smith sets the wandering scene in the same sublime geology. Again the magnificent rocks, divested of their characteristic inertia, take on a magical and metaphorical force all their own. Now, Smith exchanges her queer phrase "strange concussions of nature" for a more neurological one. The "tremendous convulsion of nature" rewrites the figure to reveal a mind losing its grip on agency. "Thrown together" by an unidentified source, the mountains in motion seize as though subjected to a cruel materialism of nervous energy. We know to read this scene as the darker twin to Smith's sonnet above, for it quotes again from Thomson—this time not from *Summer* but from that season's polar opposite, *Winter*.[27]

Displaced, the quotation again makes a slippery play of meaning. Thomson's phrase, "Life at last goes out," seems to speak of death and extinction. In context, however, it references not the bitter end, but survival and the fruits of human perseverance:

> Still pressing on, beyond *Tornéa's* Lake,
> And *Hecla* flaming thro' a Waste of Snow,
> And farthest *Greenland*, to the Pole itself,
> Where failing gradual Life at length goes out,
> The Muse expands her solitary Flight. (887–91)

Although the environment is one of frozen "waste," immobility and decay, the "Muse" in Thomson's lines pushes on with an energy all her own. This allegorical reference to literature's own creative vitality tells us something about Celestina in this new landscape. Here she is a force counter to nature. "Turning on towards the yet more dreary North," she seems to float apart from the terrors and "convulsions" of her natural landscape. Smith's commentary on mind and world subtly draws attention to the issue of agency. In poetic history, Celestina or Smith, like Milton or Thomson, "expands her solitary flight," flaming and flickering in a landscape of wasted life.

The allusion in this passage to the Laplander from line 937 of Thomson's poem evokes a similar motif for the eighteenth-century reader. As a symbol of resilience, the Laplander lives in a land on the margins of frost and light. These natives in Thomson's *Winter* "waste the tedious Gloom" (943) by night, only to rise in daylight with a resiliency characteristic of Smith's greatest heroines: "Till Morn at length, her Roses drooping all, / Sheds a long Twilight brightening o'er their Fields, / And calls the quiver'd Savage to the Chace" (*Winter*, ll. 947–49). Smith's chosen lines from Thomson's *Winter*, set against the previous quotation from *Summer*, provide an exceptional pairing. As Thomson reminds us, *Summer* and *Winter* are not what they seem—for mental inscapes need not match their outer landscapes.

Just as Celestina rewrites Thomsonian despair in the first composition, she transfigures his allegory of mental tenacity in her poem, "The Laplander." Once again, quotation inspires self-authorized composition:

"Alas!" cried she, "if they have not our enjoyments, they suffer not from those sensibilities which embitter our days."

... A deep sigh closed this short soliloquy; and after indulging a little longer this train of thought, it produced the following sonnet:

THE LAPLANDER.
The shivering native, who by Tenglio' side
Beholds with fond regret the parting light
Sink far away, beneath the darkening tide,
And leave him to long months of dreary night,
Yet knows, that springing from the eastern wave,
The sun's glad beams shall re-illumine his way,
And, from the snows secur'd within his cave,
He waits in patient hope—returning day.
Not so the sufferer feels, who, o'er the waste
Of joyless life, is destin'd to deplore
Fond love forgotten, tender friendship past,
Which, once extinguish'd, can revive no more:
O'er the blank void he looks with hopeless pain;
For him those beams of heaven shall never shine again.

A few days after this, an interval of calm weather gave to Mrs. Elphinstone courage to determine on embarking: but the evening before ... they should go, she told Celestina, ... that she could not be satisfied to leave the island without visiting the spot where lay the remains of her husband. (308–9)

Recycling the word "waste" from Thomson, the sonnet is a meditation on lifelessness—on what, like snow or love, is "extinguished" and cannot be "revived"—except, of course, through literary form. Alone, the poem seems a marker of memory's pains—its "hopeless" pathology in eighteenth-century theories of nostalgia. But as a revised quotation, it reveals Smith's complex take on mind and matter. The first two quatrains summarize the verse paragraph from Thomson. They tell the story of the Laplander waiting out the night for the return of warmth and daylight. However, Celestina's less painterly approach lends omniscience to an otherwise static scene of representation. What was once a reference to the materiality of nature is recast through the vital energies of the mind. In her mental pre-draft of the poem, Celestina imagines what the men must *think* while waiting. Minds have motion while bodies stand still. It is one thing to persevere physically, another to do so mentally. Pain, Smith implies, is a state of mind.

Without mentality, the iconic Laplander feels atavistic. Celestina humanizes him, showing how consciousness ignites feelings (either of pain or solace). Yet she also implies that the Laplander cannot "suffer" because he lacks "sensibility," and sensibility comes from *knowing pleasures lost:* "If they have not our enjoyments, they suffer not." Unlike the Laplander, the subject in the third quatrain "suffers" due to her loss of pleasure. *Knowing* arises as a transaction between feelings that shift from pleasure to pain, from one mental state to another. On the other hand, the Laplander, aware of the recursive cycles of nature only, illustrates the mental repetitiveness of expectation that reminds us of David Hume's model of cyclical memory. In Smith's recontextualization of waste, we are asked to read consciousness relatively.

This comparative technology of feeling is key to our reading of the poem and its placement in the text. Most important, it concurs with the gap between the reader's knowledge and Celestina's at this juncture of the narrative. Unlike the icy North or Mrs. Elphinstone's husband, Willoughby and his memory are anything but dead. All along, the reader knows that Willoughby still loves her, even as Celestina considers herself a "forgotten" form. In this, we also note that suffering, and writing, come from a *feeling* that one is *forgotten*—from a yearning to participate in processes of social recollection. In fact, Celestina's tendency to "deplore" that she is "forgotten" is an imaginative projection, not a mental record of events.

As an exposition of Celestina's mind, "The Laplander" forces us to parse out fact from fiction, mental life from material life, through a manner of relative reading. What is laid to waste at the poem's conclusion is Mr. Elphinstone. And his wife, a subject of true suffering, perseveres like the Laplander. "Called to the chase" by nature and subject to its vicissitudes, Mrs. Elphinstone re-embarks on her voyage as soon as the first "interval of calm weather" comes her way.

Thus we may consider Celestina a little too self-pitying. In this, we would join the majority of Smith's historical readers. (Anna Laetitia Barbauld and Mary Wollstonecraft maligned Charlotte Smith for what they saw as an odious species of self-pity in her writing that her readers could have done without.[28]) Yet it is important not to take Celestina's self-indulgent pain at face value, as so many critics have done, or even simply to equate it with the author's own distress (despite the novel's many autobiographical resonances). Unlike the anticipation of the Laplander, the sufferer in the third quatrain "suffers" because of the relative nature of emotion. Feeling is described as a temporal transaction, not just from pleasure to pain but from one form, and one state of mind, to another.

In scaling sensation through a matrix of subjective and citational reference points, Smith asks us to consider the potential role of the mind in all this matter. Celestina's emotional embellishment, her rewriting of another's literary form and story, causes her to imagine the Laplander's "insensibility." In doing so, she becomes momentarily insensible to the pain of her companion, but this in itself should be excusable in a heroine who possesses an abundance of sympathy and sentimental feeling. The activity of composition here and elsewhere in the novel shares with memory the powers of abstraction and transfiguration. As poetic and natural figures are recycled and transformed, collected and rearranged, Smith speaks to the capacity of memory to change the status quo of feeling. Nature's "concussions" and "convulsions" are violent reformations that index the energies of conscious matter. Together, these figures play on each other like the convex mirrors once used by travelers to frame the picturesque. Depending on the point of view, the force that alters the form may come from within or without, but both are subject to laws of change and relativity. Geographically and geologically, Smith's heady mountains of the Hebrides are "sea markers" for students of mind and brain at the turn of the century. Adopting a latent rhetoric of vitalism, these godlike forms ask us to consider a force behind matter that is both neural and natural. With the secular powers of her mind, Celestina makes a mountain of a molehill, but then again, she moves mountains too.

The Avalanche

Celestina's last poetic composition in the novel is a perfect testament to the fictions that come from memory. This "little" work (460) is sourced from the entangled energies of remembrance, imagination, and reading. With her inclusion of "The Peasant of the Alps" in the final volume of her novel, Smith defies the notion of realism as mimesis, and the concept of art as an exact record of life. Unlike Celestina's encounters in the Hebrides with sublime forms of nature, the Cheltenham episodes are where Celestina spends "many hours every day in reading travels though France, Italy, and Switzerland" (459).[29]

"The Peasant of the Alps" is Celestina's only lyric poem in the novel, and unlike the sonnets, it delineates a closed system that severs fanciful memories from the purview of their immediate environment. Yet Smith intimates the potential consequences of this dangerous lyrical autonomy as a "turning away" from natural form.[30] Celestina ignores one kind of pleasure in searching for another. Blind to her pleasing environment, she sets aside the pastoral forms of nature to create, as it were, a natural catastrophe. Celestina's turn away from nature into art is an exploration into the mind's interface with fiction: one that warns against an absorptive style of reading and remembering. Rather, Smith argues for a kind of mediational memory, one that revises fiction and reality through their playful interplay. Only as a dialectical force and a conscious faculty can memory provide succor and soothe distress.

Steadfast to a motif of writing and wandering, the final poem of the novel has peripatetic roots:

> The whole world was her country; and with that restlessness to which the unhappy are subject, she fancied that in any part of it she should find more satisfaction than in her present situation.
>
> By her wandering continually alone in the pleasant country that surrounded the town where she resided, at a season too when the face of nature was every day growing more lovely, her talent for poetry, which sometimes remained for whole months unexercised, was again called forth; but whatever were the objects really before her, whatever were presented to her mind by books, Willoughby was ever the principal figure in the landscape. If she sat on the green hill, as she often did for hours together, lost in mournful yet not unpleasing reverie, it was only to recollect scenes that were passed; which the same sounds she had then heard, the simple sheep-bell, the early song of birds; the same scents of fresh turf and wild flowers, brought again most forcibly to her recollection.
>
> If in her reading, she was by the traveller's lively description of the countries he had passed through, to fancy herself there, she reverted instantly to the delight she should have felt could she in a progress

through such romantic scenes have been the companion of Willoughby; and it was in this disposition of mind, that after perusing an account of a cottage and its inhabitants overwhelmed by the fall of an avalanche, a great body of snow from the mountain above, she composed the following little lyric poem. (460)

Critics have read the first line of the passage quoted above as evidence of Smith's attitude toward cosmopolitanism.[31] But the emphasis that rests on the verb "fancied" suggests less of a geopolitical statement than one about the powers of the imagination. To be sure, the "restlessness" of the castaway is the result of the promise of "satisfaction" in other lands and situations, but what use is emigration when Celestina fails to experience, or see, the new territories through which she actually travels? The source of her restlessness lies not in external oppressors but in "fancy's" conceptual tendency. Her grass-is-always-greener mentality is gently satirized in the following paragraph when we realize that imagination dominates with equal ardor over both reality and fiction: "Whatever were the objects really before her, whatever were presented to her mind by books, Willoughby was ever the principal figure in the landscape."

From the first, Smith emphasizes that Celestina's "wandering" has been "continual"—not just an excessive habit, but one that creates continuity in a world of perpetual change. Paradoxically, Celestina incessantly "wanders" in the very place, or town, where she "resides." The contradiction suggests that although the body is in one place, the mind is in another. The landscape that Smith describes, seen by the reader but not Celestina, functions for us, if not for her, as a reference to the importance of the mind-body continuum. Like the little town, utterly "surrounded" by pleasing things, Celestina's mind resembles the fashions of enclosure. By seeking pleasure in the avenues of her mind, she has effectively sealed herself off from palpable gratification. The irony underscores what may happen to the mind's protective mechanisms if subject to overuse.

Smith's next sentence endows nature with a countenance, "a face" that can be read as it transitions into loveliness. Again, the sign is legible only to the reader, for Celestina, we soon realize, sees nothing of the "objects really before her." Despite Celestina's unawareness, the setup is key, for in it, Smith reverses our assumptions about poetry's origins. At first, when we see that nature "again call[s] forth" Celestina's poetic "talent," we are apt to

read this as a reference to Romantic inspiration and the creative properties of the genius loci. The notion that nature itself has a legible countenance likewise alludes to the secular principles of Neoplatonism. Both traditions place the literary maker within, and in dialogue with, an environmental context.

Rather abruptly, however, Smith's historical lexicon takes a sudden grammatical turn ("; but"). The semicolon and ensuing conjunction dash out the history of poetic conception with a single blow. How can Celestina be inspired by what she never sees? How can she infer meaning from signs left unread? The entire passage disavows the very traditions it invokes. In tricking the reader, it also calls attention to itself as a form apt to revise literary tradition. The inspiring source of Celestina's poetic composition lies within a fiction; it stems from her readings not of nature but of literature. The poem remembers, as it were, the travels and experiences of another author.

But this is not an exact literary plagiarism or mimetic replication. Rather, it appropriates forms from literature only to embellish them with personal memory fantasies. For Celestina, both nature, "the objects before her," and reading "whatever were presented to her mind by books" are pushed aside by one sovereign image of the mind. Willoughby is everywhere. She sees him in the landscape even when she fails to see the landscape: "Willoughby was ever the principal figure in the landscape. If she sat on the green hill, as she often did for hours together, lost in mournful yet not unpleasing reverie, it was only to recollect scenes that were passed." The sentence avers that although Celestina sits on a "green hill," she sees not her environment but "only . . . scenes . . . passed." The word "only" signals a radical state of mental abstraction and may draw an important distinction between distractive versus dissociative memory. Yet this mental exposition is not described in pathological terms. The paragraph rolls on, much like the would-be landscape that Celestina never sees, into the "not unpleasing" realms of past sensory experience. Now, we get all the delicious details: the sounds and scents of bells and flowers, birds and grass, are offered up to the reader on a platter of "recollection." The idea that reconverts itself into an impression, much as David Hume would have it, is more forceful than the original.

We might note this entire paragraph amounts to a single sentence. Punctuated as the syntax of cognitive flow, it barely stops, rolling on into new objects and sensations like the mind's own evolving thoughts. Uniting form and feeling in a vitally seamless way, it almost fools us. We are apt to take it for that absorptive experience that artistic representation seductively offers. We almost forget that this is a memory, not a descriptive scene. What passes for a landscape is a mindscape. But yet again, it is hard to parse memory from fiction. The next paragraph stages Celestina in the act of reading much as the first paragraph sets her in a geographic setting. All along, Smith tells us that Celestina fails to register the images of reading and nature, as her memory of Willoughby overshadows her point of view. Thus we begin to wonder why nature and reading even figure here at all as heuristic devices.

Again, the use of the word "fancy" in this paragraph is telling. The book Celestina is reading is one of a traveler and his voyages. Significantly, Smith fails to provide us with any details or a reference—a coy move from an author who revels in referentiality. As Celestina "fancies" herself in the fictional scenes she reads, we note that she is not at all reading them. Distracted, her mind "reverts instantly" to Willoughby. Imagining herself in the barely read scene, she embellishes a fiction with fiction. Imagining Willoughby with her, she does it again! The verbs in the sentence are all notably subjunctive. The "progress" the syntax entertains is never read or seen, but imagined. And yet the use of the word "reverted," coupled with the previous passage's exposition and the perpetual citation of Willoughy—and (oh!) Willoughby there again—conflates memory with imagination. The "romantic scenes" that Celestina finds in her novel, through a method of what might be called deconstructive reading, have nebulous origins. Are they wrested from creative fancy, from "scenes . . . passed"—or both? If we see memory and imagination as entangled faculties, then the picture becomes clear. The repetitious eruption of Willoughby tells us one thing for sure: creative memory colors the whole.

At the end, the passage takes a purported turn from distraction to attention when Celestina "peruses" an "account" in her book of an avalanche. Although Smith's language implies a process of hermeneutic reading, she is careful to overlay Celestina's sudden attentiveness with a mental state. It is "in this disposition of mind" (what I later describe in Austen's *Mansfield Park* as a type of wistful and wishful thinking) that Celestina takes up her book again, reading in such a way as to blur reality with fiction. The "account" of the avalanche parenthetically described as "a great body of snow from the mountain above" seems to leap off the page and find a literal, geographic location in Celestina's world. Is the "mountain above" *that* mountain, in the text, or *this* mountain, within Celestina's natural grasp? The lack of quotation is destabilizing. With no marks to frame the account, we question the origins of the avalanche as a form in the world; it seems to slip from text into nature, from imagination and memory into the atmosphere. As Celestina's nostalgic mental state influences her reading, a once representational literary form begins to lack any direct indexical relationship to the world.

Artificial in its origin, the avalanche slides between text and context so as to rerender and rearrange its "great body" into a "little lyric":

> THE PEASANT OF THE ALPS
> Where cliffs arise by Winter crown'd,
> And through dark groves of pine around,
> Down the deep chasms, the snow-fed torrents foam,
> Within some hollow, shelter'd from the storms,
> The Peasant of the Alps his cottage forms,
> And builds his humble, happy home. (460)

The first stanza substantiates the poem's true place in Charlotte Smith's *Celestina*, for it brings us back to the novel's own thoughts on "dwelling forms." The coupling of "forms" with "storms" in the rhyme scheme reveals the work of both Celestina and Smith as writers: to form new dwellings in the midst of catastrophe or distress. Though "humble," the home that the peasant builds brings "happiness" and "shelter." Like Celestina's creative composition, it reminds us of the mind's own protective mechanisms.

The following stanza discovers the affective value of the humble "hut"; the form itself provides an oasis of feeling in an otherwise harsh environment. As a sentimental object, to which the peasant's "heart" becomes "attach'd," the hut, in such an atmosphere, represents emotional pleasure in a landscape rife with potential, sensory suffering (l. 11, p. 461). What lies within is most significant. Since the man's wife "dwells" inside (l.13), he "Finds all he wishes, all he loves" (l. 12) in the form itself. Smith indicates a philosophy of aesthetic feeling that hints at those energies of mind that lurk within form, the mental origins of created things. As a "dwelling," the hut becomes a metaphor for the mind, most noteworthy for its capacity to dampen physical sensation by remembering emotional pleasure.

On the other hand, when "absent from the calm abode," the peasant is immediately susceptible to the harsh forces of nature. The poetic allegory likewise warns against an overreliance on mind, for the story goes on to tell what happens to the peasant on leaving his home, how he gets caught in an avalanche. On the one hand, we might read nature as a cruel force here, but the latent message lies in the poem's larger position within the framework of the novel. Reminding us of our materiality, it gestures toward the necessary dialectic between mind and matter as reciprocal forming forms.

As we transition from poem back to prose, Smith's third-person narrative reflects on the poem in context: "While Celestina was thus, with more tenderness than discretion, cherishing the memory of the friend she had lost, Willoughby was very differently occupied from what her imagination suggested" (462). The stark contrast between imagination and reality comes suddenly into view, as though the work of art is reframed by a narrative intervention. By "cherishing . . . memory," Celestina has lost herself in it. No longer "temporary," her dwellings have become more "tender" than discrete. For Smith, memory is a device of mind—one that eludes pain by developing illusions so as to alter form and feeling. Yet the "temporariness" of the device is key for a mind in flux and flow: minds, like forms, evolve. As Celestina turns away from nature in her final composition, she loses grasp of one system of reference only to create her own, newly self-enclosed system. In the novel at large, the avalanche is just another metaphor of mind, like the cliffs of the Hebrides that "concuss" and "convulse" with vital energy. Nevertheless, the avalanche is a matter not of nature but of fiction. Subjected to a lyrical enclosure, it locks itself in. Static and apart, it is a figment of fancy that brings not pleasure but reiterative pain.

The final lines of the poem warn of what happens when memories become "fixed":

> A fate too similar is mine,
> But I—in lingering pain repine,
> And still my lost felicity deplore;
> Cold, cold to me is that dear breast become,
> Where this poor heart had fondly fix'd its home,
> And love and happiness are mine no more. (462)

At first glance, the sentiment of these last lines may ring true to the reader of the novel who feels that Celestina's gift for melancholy has propelled her into perpetual misery—into a distress so one-dimensional that it resembles that of poor Mrs. Elphinstone. Nevertheless, if we read the poetry in and across the novel as part of a careful system of reference, there appears more to Celestina's bemoaning. Temperature-wise, the tautological "cold, cold" harks back to the quoted environments of the Laplander in *Winter*. Images echo and reverberate; they are recycled and requoted. Unlike the sonnets, however, the lyric "fixes" form and dwelling in a self-conceived "home." Thoughts "re-pine," and thus pain "lingers," extinguishing "love and happiness" with a terrifying finality. Falling in love with a fictional form can be like a landslide.

Nevertheless, the lyric's allusion to the relativity of feeling speaks alternative possibilities. In comparing herself to the peasant in his frozen grave, Celestina, once again, erroneously compares physical to emotional distress. The transaction, like the very first self-composed sonnet of the novel, envies the dead with its odd sympathetic reversal and a perverse desire for insensibility. What lingers in Celestina's malingering pain is what the reader has come to know over the course of the novel: that mental and physical sensations must not become one and the same. In the house of the mind, pain finds other dwelling forms—less distressing though equally poignant feelings. The poem's melodramatic turn, "But I—," hints at a different story—at something like the novel's actual ending. Here, Willoughby and Celestina together finally and miraculously "fix" their home at Alvestone—just as they have wanted to for the past 542 pages. And yet, after all this time, they wander again into France. In the context of fiction, form evolves according to mental transformation: fixed only in time, it may be refixed again. Wandering between world and mind, feelings undergo endless transactions and translocations.

Smith's work practices a literary environmentalism, one that reuses and recycles form so as to reduce sensation, thereby altering it and making it mean anew. This formal practice is a credo that extends itself to her novelistic theory of mind. Losing sight of one's surroundings, fixing the mind on an absent home, is not the kind of radical interiority (or nostalgia) that Smith's novel wishes to entertain, and it is here exposed as her heroine's one authorial foible. Rather, Smith's novel places mind and matter in a dialectical system, one that distinguishes between fixation and the fluid mental processes of transformation. In a delicately balanced economy, materiality and mentality delimit one another. On the edge of too much sensation, memory swoops in. On the other side of memory is a "whole world" of matter just waiting to be seen. For Smith, creative memory, vital and in motion, savors of Romantic nature's great sublime.

❖ CHAPTER 5 ❖

Wistful Thinking

Fanny's Absent Forms

Three years ago, this was nothing but a rough hedgerow along the upper side of the field, never thought of as any thing, or capable of becoming any thing; and now it is converted into a walk, and it would be difficult to say whether most valuable as a convenience or an ornament; and perhaps in another three years we may be forgetting—almost forgetting what it was before. How wonderful, how very wonderful the operations of time, and the changes of the human mind!
—JANE AUSTEN, *Mansfield Park*

> Once again I see
> These hedge-rows, hardly hedge-rows, little lines
> Of sportive wood run wild; these pastoral farms
> Green to the very door; and wreaths of smoke
> Sent up, in silence, from among the trees,
> With some uncertain notice, as might seem,
> Of vagrant dwellers in the houseless woods,
> Or of some hermit's cave, where by his fire
> The hermit sits alone.
> Though absent long,
> These forms of beauty have not been to me,
> As in a landscape to a blind man's eye.
> —WILLIAM WORDSWORTH, "Lines Written a Few Miles above Tintern Abbey"

Fanny's famous musing on the hedgerow in volume 2 of Jane Austen's *Mansfield Park* brings to mind a line from William Wordsworth's "Tintern Abbey." Like his emphatic use of poetic enjambment, Wordsworth's "hedgerows, hardly hedgerows" evokes an aesthetics of unboundedness. The "little lines" of poetic shrubbery "run wild" through a verse paragraph that considers forms as things at once perceived, and erased, by the mind's eye. The poem's meditation on memory is a testament to its evolutionary qualities. The mind does not merely store up the ghosts of "absent forms," but it *transforms* them. Images are subject to the "vagrant dwellings" of a memory that, like the grammatical suggestiveness of Wordsworth's favorite semicolon, never perfectly inscribes or circumscribes form in time.

To readers of Wordsworth's lyric, what is so very memorable about the figure of the hedgerow is its momentariness. The commas that enclose also repaint and revise the fuzzy image. The punctuation that is meant to contain the form in fact frees it from its strictures. Austen's later use of the same figure likewise makes a subtle allusion to the "wonderful" capacity of human consciousness to "convert" things and create forms by way of memory. Fanny's hedgerow has often been read as a self-conscious allegory, or as a sign of late eighteenth-century landscaping practices of enclosure.[1] Yet the hedgerow is more than a symbolic allusion to Fanny's self. As an emblem of memory, it echoes Wordsworth's restylization of empiricism's famous "storehouse": it speaks to a wandering, form-freeing style of cognition as "vagrant dwelling." Memory in *Mansfield Park* does not contain form, it alters it.

Like Wordsworth's hedgerow, Fanny's hedge-now-walkway signals the organic process of evolution as a phenomenon enacted not by nature but by the mind. The form is there or not there depending on whether or not it is "thought of," "forgotten," or remembered; it changes with "the changes of the human mind." Austen's symbolism is unmistakable: the new image of the *pathway* reforms any strictly empirical divisions between persons and their environments, minds and things, places and time. The conduit becomes a perfectly apt metaphor for the way that *Mansfield Park* treats the dialecticism of mind and world, and Fanny's description of how we get there provides anecdotal evidence for Austen's investigation into the possibilities of what memory can do.

What is striking about Fanny's philosophy of mind is how thought projects itself into and through time. Fanny imagines a future moment when we "may... almost" be forgetting. In other words, thinking is both visionary and revisionary, and the prospect of what will be is ever tied to a fuzzy memory of what once was.[2] Through the filters of mental perception, external objects are transformed. Austen's theory of remembrance shares a kinship with the Romantic imagination, or what neuroscience calls "confabulation."[3] Memory is a reconstructive process that tears the boundaries between fact and fiction; it is the force that dissolves form and creates it anew.

In *Mansfield Park*, memory creatively transforms characters' and readers' experiences within natural and social environments. In what follows, I show how Austen's novel colors memory with the fantastic and transformational qualities that Romantics typically associated with the imagination.[4] My approach to memory in *Mansfield Park* shares a kinship with Nicholas Dames's attempt to reclaim what we might consider to be the pains of nostalgia in Austen's narratives by suggesting that memory's untruths, its distortionary tendencies, have the potential to heal distress and trauma.[5] My work differs, however, from Dames's account of Austen's nostalgics in *Amnesiac Selves*. Dames focuses on the blissful nature of forgetting, or memory's absence, as the defining character of modern nostalgia; it is a "winnowing of the specificity" of memories into a "diluted, vague, comfortable retrospect."[6] Accordingly, Dames reads *Mansfield Park* as a story of Fanny's "biographical amnesia" wherein the origins of her "individual experience" are progressively erased.[7] In my account of Austen's novel, I am less interested in associations that die out and more in those that evolve so as to charter new pathways and ultimately change future narrative outcomes. My emphasis on the healing power of altered, as opposed to forgotten, memories in Austen's writing hinges on the concept of transacted experience.

For Austen, memories often do not derive from individual sense experience, as empirical accounts of recollection suggest. This facet of empiricism sits uneasily within Austen's novels, which have been heralded by such critics as Deidre Lynch, Lisa Zunshine, and Adela Pinch as exemplary of the social nature of cognition.[8] In my reading of the novel, acts of forgetfulness have the potential to produce pain. On the other hand, memories that become tinged by imaginative and interpersonal encounters have a greater curative potential. Throughout the novel, as thoughts are "smuggled in,"[9] borrowed and made up from the opinions, desires, and stories of other persons, they change the course of actions and events. For the most imaginative and willing characters in Austen's novel, conscious awareness, combined with memory's plasticity, can result in the positive work of actualizing personal desire. Memory, for Austen, is the essence of fiction-making.

In their work on nostalgia, Kevis Goodman and Nicholas Dames remind us of the term's somatic history.[10] In the eighteenth century, nostalgia was a medical term, divorced from its later association with memory. As a "pathos" of "motion,"[11] Goodman describes it as the willful severing of mind from world when she equates the term with extasis: "[Nostalgics] are exstatic in a precise sense: they have been 'put out of place' . . . and seem to occupy another place, preoccupied by *absent things* as if they were present. Forced to move, their minds resist and stand still."[12] Curiously, this notion of nostalgia dangerously subverts eighteenth-century scientific beliefs about embodied minds: the mind, in a world apart, no longer mirrors the body but abstracts itself from the somatic pains of motion. It is perhaps no surprise that when Goodman details the cure for medical nostalgia, she hints at that externalist stronghold of eighteenth-century science: the "travel cure" recommended "change of scene and air for the debilitated, as if external mobility could jumpstart internal fixation."[13]

Whereas Goodman's work shows how medical nostalgia lingers on into the nineteenth century as an aesthetic form, Nicholas Dames presumes a shift from pathology to pleasure in Jane Austen's turn-of-the-century novels. For Dames, what was once a "mental and physical disability" becomes a "more pleasurable, a vaguer, form of recollection in Austen's works."[14] Like Goodman, however, Dames describes the cure for eighteenth-century nostalgia in terms that recall the source of the disease: medics fought the ills of forced motion with, well, enforced motion. In short, the scientific problem with Enlightenment nostalgia was that it gave unto the mind a world of its own. Nostalgics resisted the movement of space and time. In carrying the past with them, they were "vagrant dwellers" on "absent forms."

The Enlightenment pathology of nostalgia also tells us something about how late eighteenth-century thinkers, scientific and philosophical alike, grappled with memory. Was it a force, a point of view, a collection of things? As I indicate in the introduction to this book, Enlightenment memory did not share with the imagination that starry-eyed reputation of pleasure. This is true of critical accounts of memory in Austen studies as well.[15] Margaret Doody says of memory in Austen's novels that it "apparently is—or can be—a great handicap to human freedom."[16] In her essay "Jane Austen and the Old," Claire Lamont categorizes "things that are old" in Austen's novels as "boring, irrelevant, and restrictive."[17] As a repository of the past and the old, does memory, like Fanny Price, suffer from a bad reputation in Austen criticism?[18]

What William Galperin has labeled the "uncanny" in Austen's novels, and what Sonia Hofkosh has described as Austen's "enchantment," are perhaps the best way of accounting for her revolutionary philosophy of mind in *Mansfield Park*.[19] As both critics note, Austen has a unique way of both deploying and subverting realist principles, encroaching on the improbable while all the while making it appear to be the most likely thing in the world.[20] In *Mansfield Park*, Austen sees the enticing power of fiction writing as a practice of wish fulfillment, and yet wishes come true, I argue, by way of their perpetual entanglement with memory. Memory is what makes "illusion" possible,[21] what renders fiction real.

In what follows, I look at affective transactions in this novel, wherein misery is alleviated by pleasure as a function of imaginative memory and as an endorsement of what medical definitions of nostalgia most feared: the notion of a mind that might operate differently from its contextual world or environment. Austen's mind-world dialectic emphasizes those moments wherein the *mind moves the world*, altering and reordering it irrevocably. The way that memories and desires are acquired in *Mansfield Park*, however, can be as elusive as Austen's allegory of the ever-evolving hedgerow. In addition to considering how Austen's characters reshape their fates through the fictions of memory, this chapter addresses how activities of reading and conversation infiltrate our remembering faculties. Memory and imagination collide in the novel in a manner that reminds us of that slim cognitive space between author and reader in a work of fiction: like the hedgerow or the ha-ha, the line that divides these mental frontiers is thin and hard to see. The ha-ha is as much an allegory for cognition as it is for the novel at large. From it, we learn that memory can be tantamount to a perceptual illusion; looking back, we jump over the gaps, we piece together the whole, and, in the genre of fiction, we create only the pleasing landscape we wish to see.

Minding the Gap: The Ha-Ha Re-membered

In an essay on memory and desire, Annette Baier reminds us of the following: "Memory is of times, while knowledge is of facts."[22] Similarly, Austen depicts memory in *Mansfield Park* as the province of time and the antithesis of fact. In the opening pages of the novel, Austen decouples the Lockean equation of memory with knowledge in a bit of satirical wisdom from Mrs. Norris:

> "Very true, indeed, my dears, but you are blessed with wonderful memories, and your poor cousin has probably none at all. There is a vast deal of difference in memories, as well as in every thing else, and therefore you must make allowance for your cousin, and pity her deficiency. And *remember* that, if you are ever so forward and clever yourselves, you should always be modest; for, much as you know already, there is a great deal more for you to learn...."
>
> ... In the country, therefore, the Miss Bertrams *continued to exercise their memories*, practice their duets, and grow tall and womanly.
> (16–17, my emphasis)

Irony lies in what is yet to become apparent to the reader—that is, the novel's increasing impulse to equate Fanny herself with memory, with a kind of remembering that defies the exercise of memorization as a practice of storing up information. Mrs. Norris's comment on the subjective quality of memories in fact corroborates Fanny's later philosophical claim about its marvelous "inequalities"; as Fanny notes, memory is the most pliable faculty of the human mind. Memory's plasticity and its subjective nature resonate with Mrs. Norris's futile but significant injunction to remember modesty. From a rereader's perspective, Mrs. Norris's prescriptive morality foreshadows what is to come, but it also serves a narrative double function, for with it, Austen ironically mocks the notion of knowledge as finite, or even educational. The parody attacks a rote style of education as an "exercise" or "practice" of memorization. The narrator's use of parallelism, which likens the "exercise" of retentive memory to the "practice of a duet," also satirizes materialist concepts of the mind as an organic thing—as something that can swell and grow like the womanly forms of the Miss Bertrams. If memory is plastic and subjective, then it is no accountant, no factual record-keeper; it cannot quantify experience, nor does it collect it. Rather, memory is more akin to those "wonderful operations of time" that Fanny describes in her musings on the walkway-once-hedgerow. For Annette Baier, memory is nothing but time, and it approaches time not as a quantity but as a subjective register of experience. As a marker of the "wonderful operations of time," memory does not record information but evolves with the "*changes of the human mind,*" its experiential vicissitudes.

How do we get from memorization to memories, from memory as knowledge (to evoke Mrs. Norris's latent empiricism) to memory fiction, at the turn of the century? Austen gives us an apt history lesson through her use of allegory. Take, for example, the implications of the following satirical debate between characters on the banks of Sotherton. When Mary Crawford casually remarks on her sense of their walking pace, Edmund's retort foregrounds memory's shifting relationship to empirical data-keeping at the turn of the nineteenth century:

> "I am really not tired, which I almost wonder at; for we must have walked at least a mile in this wood. Do not you think we have?"
>
> "Not half a mile," was his sturdy answer; for he was not yet so much in love as to measure distance, or reckon time, with feminine lawlessness.
>
> "Oh! you do not consider how much we have wound about. We have taken such a very serpentine course; and the wood itself must be half a mile long in a straight line, for we have never seen the end of it yet, since we left the first great path."
>
> "But if you remember, before we left that first great path, we saw directly to the end of it. We looked down the whole vista, and saw it closed by iron gates, and it could not have been more than a furlong in length."
>
> "Oh! I know nothing of your furlongs, but I am sure it is a very long wood; and that we have been winding in and out ever since we came into it; and therefore when I say that we have walked a mile in it, I must speak within compass."
>
> "We have been exactly a quarter of an hour here," said Edmund, taking out his watch. "Do you think we are walking four miles an hour?"
>
> "Oh! do not attack me with your watch. A watch is always too fast or too slow. I cannot be dictated to by a watch." (67–68)

Edmund's insignificant watch is an item that reminds us of the cultural constructions of an eighteenth-century concept of time measured through the diurnal, calendrical sounds of Stuart Sherman's *tick tick tick*.[23] Such "attacks" (as Mary Crawford would have them) pose an assault on a Romantic consciousness that wishes to recall time through the sublime experience of memory tinged with imagination. Edmund's time is rife with "dictates" and boundaries. His exact reckoning of minutes past insists on time's material qualities, on a notion of time that maps so much space.

In his call for Mary to remember the furlong, Edmund's allegory of time represents a finite perception of space that encloses the entire "vista" of human experience within a set of iron gates. The parody of empiricism here laughs at the notion of time as a thing calculated and seen. Mary's refusal to think in this way accounts for a post-Enlightenment concept of time that is radically subjective: "I know nothing of your furlongs!" she retorts. What is at stake here is a shift in the way that memory is characterized in early novelistic representations of consciousness. Mary's Romantic refusal of the watch disposes of a Lockean notion of memory as spatial retention, of a kind of time that maps and measures thought in distances.[24] In its place, we encounter a new time that fails accurately to align itself with space. What Edmund dubs the "lawlessness of feminine consciousness" lies at the heart of Austen's concept of fiction and underscores the powerful forces of a memory that both subjectivizes and revises experience.

My investigation into memory in *Mansfield Park* considers the strange temporal structures of the novel's fictional consciousness. Since this is a text that relies heavily on the literary device of allegory and the rhetoric of the late eighteenth-century picturesque, it is no surprise that critics have typically categorized consciousness, like aesthetics, in *Mansfield Park* as spatially constructed and inflected.[25] Instead, my focus will be on a "point of view" much like Mary's—one that creates a Romantic fissure between the mental perceptions of time and space. In this manner, I go against the grain of another critical pastime of separating memory in this novel from the forward, prospective work of imaginative or intentional thinking. Until recently, these two cognitive frames, past and future, had been torn asunder in our readings of the novel for the simple fact that we so often associate Fanny with sentimental attachment or reflection, whereas Henry Crawford has become synonymous with the "evils" of "improvement."[26] Reading the novel through this kind of dualism entraps us in the very kind of thinking that Austen warns against, one in which wishing and remembering become disjointed faculties of mind. Rather, Austen makes a case in *Mansfield Park* for a kind of memory that forms intention and actualizes desire. When memory aligns with imagination, our greatest fantasies are realized; *wist*ful thinking, like *wish*ful thinking, has the power to alter history. Remembrance, as Mary would have it, represents the pleasurable "lawlessness" of fiction itself.

To return to Sotherton, where Mary and Edmund are still struggling to resolve their debate about time and space, they choose to do so in a supposed "endeavour to determine the dimensions of the wood" by approaching the ha-ha, now famous in critical debates as a ditch rife with metaphorical readings.[27] Fanny, of course, is left behind. This transgression of the garden's limits and into the imagined vista of Romantic experience is also a transcendence that in a narrative sense leaves behind Edmund's precious eighteenth-century timepiece. The ha-ha scene begins with a narrative moment wherein time and space become misaligned as the reader crosses over from one chapter to another:

> At last it was agreed, that they should endeavour to determine the dimensions of the wood by walking a little more about it. They would go to one end of it, in the line they were then in (for there was a straight green walk along the bottom by the side of the ha-ha,) and perhaps turn a little way in some other direction, if it seemed likely to assist them, and be back in a few minutes. Fanny said she was rested, and would have moved too, but this was not suffered. Edmund urged her remaining where she was with an earnestness which she could not resist, and she was left on the bench to think with pleasure of her cousin's care, but with great regret that she was not stronger. She watched them till they had turned the corner, and listened till all sound of them had ceased.
>
> CHAPTER X
> A quarter of an hour, twenty minutes, passed away, and Fanny was still thinking of Edmund, Miss Crawford, and herself. (69)

Mary and Edmund choose to resolve their debate Edmund style, by way of empirical data and experience—an approach to knowledge that takes on another ironic metaphor of the "straight" path green and ripe with opportunities for discovery. But this is a mode of accounting that cannot be kept up in the context of Austen's fiction. The lovers declare their intentions, by way of the free indirect style, as an activity that will be circumscribed by a small interval of time—just "a few minutes." Yet the reader knows better. Indeed, what Yoon Sun Lee has called Austen's signature tempo of "small-scale synchronization" becomes quickly protracted: several minutes turn into a quarter of an hour, become twenty minutes—and eventually dissolve into that unaccountable concept of time as experience, into thought itself.[28] Lost in Fanny's mind, we begin to lose our grasp of any clear understanding of just how much time has passed. We also fail to imagine the parameters of space and Fanny's environment—exactly in what direction did Mary and Edmund go, and how far off are they? Only the reader can be blamed for the possibilities.

As the passage moves from the landscape into the inscape of Fanny's mind, it takes on a metaphysical life of its own. Chapter 9 ends with Fanny's regretful, backward-looking consciousness: she "watched them till they had turned the corner, and listened till all sound of them had ceased" (69). Her thoughts are both reflective and imaginative in remembering what might have been had she felt less tired in body; her placement at the height of a prospect, unmentioned by the narrator but imagined by the reader, is of course ironic, since the chapter closes with what Fanny can no longer see or hear, with the limits of sensory experience.

This notion of remembrance as a prospect of retrospective yearning—as a place that exists more or less in the mind—is definitively nostalgic, in both the current and the eighteenth-century sense of the term. First, the passage, in its use of allegory, attempts to fuse external landscape with mental cognition much in the manner of the eighteenth-century medical prognosticator of nostalgia; in this case, the literal, material world becomes a reference point for the mind to the reader.[29] Moreover, the pain of Fanny's prospective retrospections is a consequence of "suffering" to abide by Edmund's recommendation that she cease moving. Just as Fanny's body remains in one place, so too does her mind. The next chapter begins with Fanny in the same place: on the prospect dreaming of Edmund. Fanny's somatic immobility becomes a sign of her mental cleaving to a now absent image of Edmund. Chapter 10 begins, "A quarter of an hour, twenty minutes, passed away, and Fanny was still thinking of Edmund. . . . She began to be surprised at being left so long, and to listen with an anxious desire of hearing their steps and their voices again" (69). The chapter breaks, but Fanny's mind does not.[30] Lost in a desire to replicate events, to defy any progressive movement of time and space, Fanny's mind looks to the wished-for past as a reparative for her present discomfort and her anxiety about the future. Her mind imagines a return of the wished-for companions; it overrides space and attempts to disorder time. Although time has passed, although the chapter has suffered a break, on the edge of the estate, on the perimeter of the ha-ha, the narrator asks her reader to suture the gap. Moreover, even as Fanny's anxiety causes us to defy Edmund's empirical logics of time by making the narrative leap, or elision, we are unconscious of the move. Our mind, distracted, is in two places at once.[31] The reader's imagination is caught up not in space or time, or even in Fanny's feelings, but in the potentially illicit actions of the text's absent characters. Like Fanny, we are apt to *dwell* on *absent things*.

At this point in the novel, Austen's "sorcery,"[32] as it were, has not come to the fore, and Fanny's desires remain unrealized. In lieu of Mary's and Edmund's arrival, we thus get another scene and a second love triangle. The transition continues with the metaphor of the ha-ha to deliver a related argument about memory as a force of wish fulfillment. As Henry suggests on the following page, the passage is meant to be read both literally and figuratively; thus critics have often interpreted it as a metaphorical foreshadowing of the novel's amorous plots.[33] Embedded in the language, however, we also find an allegory of mind that depicts memory as a fiction capable of literalizing our greatest fantasies:

> After some minutes spent in this way, Miss Bertram observing the iron gate, *expressed a wish* of passing through it into the park, that their views and their plans might be more comprehensive. *It was the very thing of all others to be wished*, it was the best, it was the only way of proceeding with any advantage, in Henry Crawford's opinion; and he directly saw a knoll not half a mile off, which would give them exactly the requisite command of the house. Go therefore they must to that knoll; and through that gate; but the gate was locked. *Mr. Rushworth wished* he had brought the key; *he had been very near thinking whether he should not bring the key*; he was determined he would never come without the key again; but still this did not remove the present evil. They could not get through; and as Miss Bertram's inclination for so doing did by no means lessen, it ended in Mr. Rushworth's declaring outright that he would go and fetch the key. (70, my emphasis)

The characters' collective, fervent desire to get beyond the bounds of the landscape into the far tracks of their point of view highlights imagination as the dominant cognitive frame. But more than one boundary is crossed here, as the ha-ha scene comes to remind us of Wordsworth's hedgerow—a line or limit that sportively runs wild, not simply like the figures in the landscape but like the thoughts that run between minds in Austen's early novelistic example of stream of consciousness.

The narrative begins simply and openly enough with Maria's clearly expressed wish to trespass beyond the gates. These are the very same iron gates that Edmund has recently described as the imposing and closing limit to Sotherton's whole "vista." Even here, the character's imagination triggers the reader's memory, for we quickly associate the two Marys in remembering Edmund and Miss Crawford's debate. Much like Mary Crawford, Maria's cognition is quick to form mental views of the beyond, or so we think at first. A synchronic reading of the very next sentence unveils Austen's trickery in a deft use of syntax and free indirect style: "the very thing of all others to be wished," "the only way of proceeding" turns out to be none other than Henry Crawford's "opinion." The novel immediately asks us to read forward and backward at the same time. We imaginatively remember now what we never knew before: that Maria's wish is, in fact, Henry's, because Henry has communicated it to her. Moreover, rereading also causes us to footnote the fact that Henry's way of thinking is not only catchy but is something like his sister's.

The semicolon now asks us to visualize the landscape according to Maria and Henry's point of view, and to imagine what is beyond the bounds of the scene by the knoll less than half a mile away. This is nothing more than a "comprehensive," a newer and better, point of view that promises the characters a fuller "command of the house." The prospect, in other words, causes the characters to imagine a moment when they will be remembering, or looking back. Imagination and memory collide through Austen's allegorical system of figures, which conjointly value the future only insofar as it evokes, both cognitively and aesthetically, memories of the past. Like the novel itself, the Crawfords' boundless version of consciousness imagines a moment when "we may be forgetting—*almost* forgetting."

What is most striking about this passage, however, is Mr. Rushworth's "wish" to gratify Maria's "wish," for it is articulated as an act of remembering what has been forgotten, or almost remembered: "he had been very near thinking whether he should not bring the key." His regret is described not as a *near action*, "I thought about bringing the key but then forgot to do so," or even "I intended to bring the key, but didn't," but rather as an indistinct reflection that cannot be categorized as thought, a "near thinking," as it were. If we are at odds to understand exactly what "near thinking" means, Austen's sly, syntactic way of representing cognition gives us a few clues. At first the passage tries to pass off Mr. Rushworth's wishes as his own: "Mr. Rushworth wished he had brought the key." The declaration comes on the heels of the discovery that the gate is locked, and so we presume that Austen's narration merely echoes Mr. Rushworth's own direct statement of his wishes. Like the clause "he was determined he would never come without the key again," Rushworth's claim implies that his thoughts, his intentions, are his own: they are statements of his voluntary will. They imagine a future when he will no longer be forgetting. Like the ha-ha, they invoke memory as the key to wish fulfillment. This all seems congruent with the philosophy of memory that Austen has all along been feeding us.

Yet the next phrase throws the whole story of internal consciousness off balance. On the one hand, the sentence proposes that a complete thought, like a complete memory, might remove "present evil." On the other hand, it asks us to read "present evil" in multiple ways: as a reference to the locked gates, as a reference to the possibility of the sexual transgression that toys with the reader's imagination, and finally as a reference to poor Mr. Rushworth's lousy memory.[34] Most important, it threatens the very idea that consciousness, or memory, is *one's own*—that thoughts are things that can be personally possessed.[35] For how can one ever "near think" anything? Or how can we forget what we never remembered? We either have a thought, just as we remember the thought, or we don't.

The next sentence tells us exactly what kind of game Austen is playing: "They could not get through; and as Miss Bertram's inclination for so doing did by no means lessen, it ended in Mr. Rushworth's declaring outright that he would go and fetch the key." Not only is Maria's "inclination" the determinant of Rushworth's actions, but her wish suspiciously aligns with Rushworth's "near thinking." Mr. Rushworth's memory is, I would argue, a fiction—it is Maria's wish working its way into Rushworth's consciousness and presenting it to himself as his own memory. Much in the way that we believe we have early childhood memories that turn out to be borrowed from our parents' stories of past events, Maria's intention slips and slides into her fiancé's mind as a fiction that he accepts as true.[36] In this manner, Austen redefines the very parameters of memory as something beyond the notion of retention and beyond even the individual. Maria's wish, which is really Henry's wish, which looks a lot like Mary Crawford's wish, becomes Rushworth's wished-for memory.

Rushworth is absentminded in the most literal sense of the term, and yet we cannot fault him for this, for he is part of a cognitive landscape bent on the creation of absent form. Thus, when Rushworth remembers a moment when he was forgetting, or near remembering, we read the remembered thought not as fact but as a factlike fiction. Since cognition, unlike action, cannot be proven, we are left suspecting the true nature of Rushworth's remembered mentality. Thinking back on what he was thinking then, Rushworth produces a memory that never was. Rather, the "near thought" is a fiction so perfectly aligned with Maria's wishes that it touches on the various ways in which imagination and memory collide in the text. Austen herein dissolves the limits between minds. The allegory stands in support of the notion that collective fictions, and imagined memories, alter reality. For Rushworth literally (not just cognitively) turns back to fetch the key, and this turning back (an archetype for memory throughout the novel) is what allows Maria and Henry to pass beyond the limits of the ha-ha into Maria's realized fantasy.

It is likewise important to remember that what lies at the base of Rushworth's absentmindedness is not even Henry Crawford's true wish. In a moment that smacks of feigned nostalgia, Henry states, "I do not think that I shall ever see Sotherton again with so much pleasure as I do now. Another summer will hardly improve it to me" (70). Crawford not only performs feeling,[37] he performs imagined memory, implanting a sentiment into Maria's mind that causes her to envision a future that looks just like this very moment, their soon-to-be past. The notion that the pleasures of Sotherton cannot be improved by time mocks the very idea of nostalgia as a pathological symptom of the mind's static revolutions. For memory is something invented here, a *made-up* illusion that does the work of *making up* by reifying new realities, futures, and things. Thoughts are borrowed, implanted, implied, and performed in a manner that tells the truth about Austen's consciousness: whether real or imagined, whether pronounced or free and indirect, it is always an operation of fiction.

As the reader's imagination dips below the ha-ha to compare the two transgressions that happen there, the passage ends with Fanny's "no increase of pleasant feelings" (71). She remains "without sight or sound" in sensory oblivion "for some minutes longer" to imagine impossibilities: "She seemed to have the little wood all to herself. She could *almost have thought,* that Edmund and Miss Crawford had left it, but that it was impossible for Edmund to forget her so entirely" (71, my emphasis). In a sensory abstraction, wherein time is at best ambiguously reckoned and the location of the novel's characters can no longer be accounted for, we are left with Fanny's conscious musings. This is a memory, charged with a regretful feeling for the missing Edmund, that presumably causes Fanny to imagine Edmund's whereabouts. But imagination is rendered impossible here with what the narrator or Fanny cannot admit to—what is yet again beyond Fanny's sightline but still projected, on some level, through the narrative point of view. The reader may imagine the illicit, unmentionable flirtations, but the notion that Edmund has forgotten her is a conscious disavowal on Fanny's part vaguely described as "disagreeable musings" (71).

This is not the first instance of Edmund's forgetfulness; all characters in the text are charged with lapses in memory and intention. Fanny's "almost thought" of Edmund's departure is a conscious elision that operates like our contemporary notion of nostalgia in its selective remembering and imagining. But it also shares something with Rushworth's near thinking. What cannot be accounted for is part of a revisionary fiction writing wherein memories evolve so as to adapt to our desires. When Edmund returns to Fanny's prospect, he admits to forgetting time, and Fanny's "best consolation" is derived from an assurance in his "history" that "Edmund had wished for her very much" (74). The term "history" here might be read by way of its eighteenth-century meaning, as a mere story, one that may or may not be a fictional account of past events and thoughts. And yet the willful suspension of disbelief, the *wish to buy into Edmund's wish* as true simply because it concurs with Fanny's own wishful thinking, is the "best consolation" to the pains of Fanny's nostalgia.

On the banks of Sotherton, we find a peculiar metaphor of mind wherein desires and memories all convene at a sociocognitive intersection of mental traffic. The ha-ha disorders our notion of time as progressive or regressive; it sutures past to present, fiction to real, memory to imagination, so as to grant wishes and make what was only a thought come true. The allegory of the ha-ha begins and ends in the same way, with the wished-for memory that transforms what we see from the fuzzy heights of the fictional prospect, irrevocably altering through its changes of mind and perception—what is, will be, and once was.

Uncertain Things: Reading in the East Room

Fanny has often been accused of hypocrisy when it comes to her notions about memory in *Mansfield Park*. Critics note a disjuncture between theory and practice in consistently pairing Fanny's contemplations on the hedgerow to her own faulty memory in the Portsmouth episodes.[38] Of course, the two novelistic scenes are of a piece; they speak to memory's inaccuracies. Its "wonderful ... inequalities," I have been suggesting, share a special relationship to fiction itself, one that bears both on how we think about human cognition and on our understanding of fictional (auto)biography. As memory in *Mansfield Park* becomes synonymous with fiction-making, it destabilizes our association of memory with knowledge in the empirical discourse and begins to look a bit more like the facets of mind we have always attributed to the Romantic imagination—its creative qualities, its affinity with illusion, and its powerful use of perception as a device of transformation. Of course, fictions are both made and read in *Mansfield Park*. In various ways, we, like Fanny, buy into the fictions of a world that exchanges painful realities for pleasurable creations so as to gratify our greatest wishes. It is no surprise, therefore, that the novel figures the act of reading this way in its signature metaphor for the mind.

The East room has been repeatedly interpreted as a Lockean archetype of the memory storehouse, a conservatory of sentimental objects.[39] Like the collector's cabinet, it houses feeling in things through the associative aspects of the mind. In this manner, it seems to stand apart from the kind of memory I have been discussing in this chapter, and yet I will attempt to show that Fanny's visit to her metaphorical memory storehouse transforms our notions about memory at the turn of the nineteenth century.

Fanny visits the East room to make a decision as to whether or not she should "act" in the domestic theatricals. The room, of course, like its own little theater of objects, is the space where Fanny can and does act, in the sense that it is here that she acts out her own private fantasies.[40] Her escape route to the East room, however, is an unpleasant journey that savors of emotional distress. On her way upstairs, Fanny's mind harbors something akin to the eighteenth-century nostalgia disease, or what writers would later come to call trauma. Apt to dwell on absent things, Fanny's thinking takes a tyrannical turn: "When the evening was over, she went to bed full of it, her nerves still agitated by the shock of such an attack from her cousin

Tom. . . . To be called into notice in such a manner . . . to be told that she must do what was so impossible as to act . . . had been too distressing at the time, to make the remembrance when she was alone much less so,—especially with the superadded dread of what the morrow might produce" (105). Time operates here in a static way, much like the pathological model of nostalgia in the eighteenth century. Although time passes, Fanny's emotional experience of the past does not; her mind remains in past events, albeit recent ones, and she carries them with her on her trip upstairs. This is all to say that although her body moves, her mind stands still. It carries events with it—filled like a vessel with the pains of the evening. To take the rhetoric of nostalgia one step further, Fanny's plagued consciousness is a physiological symptom. Holding on to the past only "agitates" her "nerves," and her "distress" sparks a "superadded dread" of tomorrow. The passage begs the question of the degree to which our past may or may not color and control our future. What is the role of the will in all this mess of time? Will fate or Fanny win the day?

In his essay "Time and Her Aunt," Michael Wood characterizes "the world of time" in Jane Austen's novels as "the world of chance meetings" and "the world of aging and healing": "Time is the enemy of marriage for women in Austen, which is why its supposed healing powers are so often treated with skepticism."[41] To be sure, this is not the approach to time that I have been taking in this chapter. However, in the above passage, memory looks more like an embodied thing, embedded, as Wood might say, in time's strictures and passage. It is not the kind of memory that the novel elsewhere heralds—one that uses time to its advantage by reconstructing experience. Fanny's distracted walk upstairs leads her to adopt the nostalgic's cure, a change of place, as her only hope. Much like her predecessor Evelina, Fanny removes herself from the scene of her distress.

Thus it is here in the East room that Austen overturns our expectations about memories and minds. No longer the puppet of her relatives, nor subject to the progressive dread of time as fate, Fanny finds "immediate consolation" in her own "willing mind":

> The aspect [of the room] was so favourable, that even without a fire it was habitable in many an early spring, and late autumn morning, to such a willing mind as Fanny's, and while there was a gleam of sunshine, she hoped not to be driven from it entirely, even when winter

came. The comfort of it in her hours of leisure was extreme. She could go there after any thing unpleasant below, and find immediate consolation in some pursuit, or some train of thought at hand . . .—or if indisposed for employment, if nothing but musing would do, she could scarcely see an object in that room which had not an interesting remembrance connected with it.—Every thing was a friend, or bore her thoughts to a friend; and though there had been sometimes much of suffering to her—though her motives had been often misunderstood, her feelings disregarded, and her comprehension undervalued; though she had known the pains of tyranny, of ridicule, and neglect, yet almost every recurrence of either had led to something consolatory; . . .—and the whole was now so blended together, so harmonized by distance, that every former affliction had its charm. (106)

The scene opens in a rather melancholy strain, with Austen's signature use of irony and parataxis.[42] The room was "favourable," she tells us, because it was freezing cold (that is to say, merely "habitable" in select shoulder seasons). The contradiction makes itself clear, of course, in the next clause, which avows the artful use of free indirect style. These are Fanny's thoughts, or better yet imaginings; they belong to her "willing mind." This is not merely a joke at Fanny's expense (for to be sure, her hope for sunshine may smack of satirical pathos). It is also part and parcel of Austen's philosophy of memory error. Fanny's willful mind makes a heaven out of hell. Although the passage begins by relapsing into a rhetoric of eighteenth-century medicine and the Johnsonian work ethic—"pursuit" and "employment" as the cure-all for nostalgic nerves—thought continuously wins out over bodily exercise.[43] The "train of thought at hand," the "nothing but musing," is the basis of Fanny's perceptual illusions, her "willing" attempt to transform not only things as they are but memories as they were.

The manner in which cognition flows through the paragraph is worth noting, for it transcends even the strictures of Austen's own brilliant, grammatical structures. As D. A. Miller has noted, Austen has a tendency to "*overorganize*" her sentences "as if Style were secretly prey to a fear of losing itself in a linguistic fluidity that endangered the very possibility of controlling it."[44] But here the passage's economic attempt to register affect into organic structure feels like an intentional spiraling out of a once precise control. The passage is anything but Socratic in its philosophy, anything but balanced in its form. The listlike clauses demonstrate an accretion of suffering, and the heap of distress—"misunderstood . . . motives," "disregarded . . . feelings," "under-valued . . . comprehension," the pains of "tyranny," "neglect," and "ridicule"—far outweighs the notion that, when combined as a "whole," these emotional assaults might "lead" to anything consolatory. Most troubling is the notion that "consolation" stems from a "recurrence" of these awful events. To today's reader, Fanny's history screams "trauma," and yet much like her predecessor Uncle Toby, Fanny makes of experience what she *will*. The arrival at "consolation" at the end of the passage defies all logic—both grammatical and philosophical. Still, it marks the scene's crowning moment.

The final lines substitute what looked like eighteenth-century pathological nostalgia at the start with a definition of its contemporary counterpart, that rosy-hued remembrance[45]: "the whole was now so blended together, so harmonized by distance, that every former affliction had its charm." "Charm" is the key word here.[46] It tempts us. And we accept it as truth, despite its utter improbability. As Hannah Arendt writes, "What the public realm considers irrelevant can have such an extraordinary and infectious *charm*."[47] This, for Arendt, is the ethos of "modern enchantment," and it is perhaps why we accept Fanny in all her irrelevance, surrounded by her tattered things, as a monument to the triumphs of a mind-over-matter mentality.

The desire to override the heaping stuff of pain, to remember it as pleasure and reconstruct personal history, wins. In the end, the room is less a curiosity cabinet than a curious commentary on the transformational powers of memory. If we choose to accept something of Fanny's philosophy, then the passage privileges narrative *sequence,* a kind of fictional time, over narrative vocabulary—that quantity of words as things that signal past suffering. Things that should be associated with pain become objects of pleasure through memory's powerful and willful capacity to play with time.

Memory's ability to alter and relativize the shades of feeling participates in a practice of emotional reading, for Austen divests things of any inherent power. It is not the things themselves but their role as subjective, legible signs that moves Fanny to reorder, remember, and rewire experience. Is it then such a surprise that the last few things mentioned in the room have archetypal significance in the history of memory and Romanticism? The "three transparencies, made in a rage for transparencies" (106), in their glittering luminousness remind today's readers of M. H. Abrams's famous

Romantic metaphor for the mind as that "radiant projector which makes a contribution to the objects it perceives."[48] There is, of course, Wordsworth's iconic Tintern Abbey, holding its "station" between an Italian cave and Cumberland (the English seat of Romantic poetry). And finally the sketch of a ship, which recalls the naval history of the eighteenth-century nostalgia disease (107). As though seeking to insert Fanny's East room into a history of archetypal signs, Austen implicitly asks us to read her memory metaphor as a newly instated image in the history of mind.

Among these now seemingly significant cultural referents, we also find a mundane collection of family portraits "thought unworthy of being anywhere else" (107). It is this collection of neglected portraits that drives the metaphor home:

> To this nest of comforts Fanny now walked down to try its influence on an agitated, doubting spirit—to see if by looking at Edmund's profile she could catch any of his counsel, or by giving air to her geraniums she might inhale a breeze of mental strength herself. But she had more than fears of her own perseverance to remove; she had begun to feel undecided as to what she *ought to do*; and as she walked round the room her doubts were increasing. Was she *right* in refusing what was so warmly asked, so strongly wished for? What might be so essential to a scheme on which some of those to whom she owed the greatest complaisance, had set their hearts? . . . and as she looked around her, the claims of her cousins to being obliged, were strengthened by the sight of present upon present that she had received from them. . . . and she grew bewildered as to the amount of the debt which all these kind remembrances produced. A tap at the door roused her in the midst of this attempt to find her way to duty, and her gentle "come in," was answered by the appearance of one, before whom all her doubts were wont to be laid. Her eyes brightened at the sight of Edmund. (107)

The passage begins deep in the Romantic discourse of inspiration. In coming to the East Room, Fanny has rushed to what might be read as an architectural metaphor for her own memory as a cure for her nostalgia.[49] Austen implies that Fanny seeks out memory, and that this conscious return to a room of one's own indeed has the power to "influence . . . an agitated, doubting spirit." Not knowing what to do, Fanny begs inspiration from memory and its symbolic consorts. Her secular-Romantic belief in the powers of representation and inspiration send her running to an altar of aesthetic and natural idols. Like the great enthusiast, she expects to "catch ... counsel" from Edmund's profile; like the Romantic, she imagines herself akin to the geranium that "inhales" a "correspondent breeze,"[50] the influx of inspirational air pummeling through an open window.

The whole Romantic plot goes south when she arrives, however. Why? Because Austen insists that things are incapable of feeling or action.[51] Again, Austen aligns memory with reading. Things in *Mansfield Park* are always there as referential and indexical markers of the forces of the mind: they must be interpreted so as to mean.[52] As it turns out, like memory itself, the room's capacity to inspire or harm depends entirely on the subject's mental state, and in this moment, Fanny's feelings are in no way courageous. Fearful, doubtful, undecided—these are the emotional filters Fanny must contend with. Thanks to Fanny's sudden "revolution of mind," the East room loses all its historical charm and becomes a mnemonic device that issues forth a "debt" of "remembrances," remembrances that trouble Fanny with moral problems of action, intention, and will, causing her to reconsider what she *"ought to do."*[53] Fanny's pedantic monologue is an economy of oughts. But just when we are about to slip into the ethics of duty and self-sacrifice, fiction sweeps all of those painful feelings under the rug. Austen offers up a bit of that enchanting magic.

In the end, Fanny actually gets what she desires from her walk down memory lane. Just as she is looking to his portrait for inspiration, Fanny's keen remembrance suddenly produces Edmund himself, in real, not representational, form. If the reader is paying close attention to Austen's improbable probabilism, then she might feel as though she is suddenly reading a fairy tale similar to *The Velveteen Rabbit*, for in the enchanted kingdom of the East room, old retired things, those repositories of memory and make believe, become real.

Nina Auerbach and Karen Valihora have categorized the "oughts" of *Mansfield Park* as lacking in authoritative value, but this is often the case when memory and intention become misaligned or disrupted by the novel's fantastical impulse toward wish fulfillment.[54] Edmund's tap at the door "rouses" Fanny from mind into body; this arousal converts inspirational musings into real, desired forms as Fanny is suddenly accosted with Edmund's physical presence. As Adela Pinch has argued of *Persuasion*, the numerous "rousals" in *Mansfield Park* function like mental shocks—whether pleasing or painful—that wrench Fanny back into the conversational world of the present and away from her more abstracted turn of mind.[55] In this case, the knock disrupts an "attempt to find her way to her duty" when Fanny loses the thread of consciousness. The lost thoughts themselves are a series of moral conjectures about how, and if, to act, based on remembered debts—suggesting that the moral "ought" of action might arise from intentions ballasted by memories. The desire not to act comes true—Fanny gets what she wants if not exactly in the way that she imagined it, when Edmund arrives only to announce his own decision that he will himself perform in the domestic theatricals. The result may sound something like "be careful what you wish for," but it also hints at the powers of memory fiction: as memory reifies and changes our experiences, feelings, and things, it alters their meaning.

Moreover, Edmund supplies Fanny with a telling bit of advice at the end of their tête-à-tête. (After all, this is presumably why she invoked his image in the first place—to conjure up some friendly advice.) On departing from the East room, he suggests: "You want to be reading" (109). Recommending various texts from the canon of verse, travel, and essay writing, Edmund assures us that reading alone will "empty [Fanny's] head of all this nonsense of acting" (109). But in her distress about Edmund's own intentions, Fanny becomes debarred from any course of individual action, and there is no reading of any kind at the close of the chapter: "He went; but there was no reading, no China, no composure for Fanny. He had told her the most extraordinary, the most inconceivable, the most unwelcome news; and she could think of nothing else" (110). Austen's use of the appositive tells us that reading may be synonymous with composure, and thus Fanny's inability to read in a state of heightened feeling has consequences. It speaks to the rather problematic source of her recurrent pain at the close of the East room chapter.

Fanny's inability to retrack her train of thought speaks not to her nature but to the nature of desire. It is singular; it is absorptive; it dangerously overthrows the power of suggestion. There can be no reading when Edmund is by, or when Edmund is cavorting with her rival. What ensues from Fanny's not-reading reminds us of the protagonist's discourse on the wondrous inequalities of memory: "The doubts and alarms as to her own conduct, which had previously distressed her, and which had all slept while she listened to him, were become of little consequence now. This deeper anxiety swallowed them up. Things should take their course; she cared not how it ended; ... and if at last obliged to yield—no matter—it was all misery *now*" (110). We move here from long-term memory to short-term memory; the older "alarm," the "previous distress" wherein she was remembering the events of the evening, becomes "swallowed up" by a new misery. Austen subjects memory not just to the scales of time but to the shades of feeling. If feeling is relative, then so is memory. What is attended to in the annals of memory is the remembrance most *felt*. Feeling and wishing reorder and rewire experience in time.

I want to emphasize at this moment not what or how Fanny remembers but how she forgets, and the consequences of those forgotten feelings and intentions. According to the passage, Fanny's memory suddenly dissipates when Edmund is before her.[56] But as the memory momentarily sleeps, charmed into a subconscious state while Edmund is speaking, it is not fully erased by the mind's eye. Indeed, it can be reawakened. The sentence sends the subjects of "doubts and alarms" on a rather tumultuous journey. They begin as agents of distress, and in a single, momentary clause are lulled to sleep; then they are partially revivified. Distress "become[s] of little consequence." Like a vague memory, it becomes a near-forgotten mental state against the urgent backdrop of Fanny's desire for Edmund under threat. In short, memory bends to Fanny's feelings and wishes, and thereby it must be consciously framed or contextualized. But as Fanny refuses consolation in the distraction of reading, as she chooses forgetfulness over memory and indifference over desire ("she cared not how it ended"), she becomes a mere mindless thing, awash in an environment wherein minds and memories are submerged, repressed, forgotten.

Fanny's sleeping intentions ironically result in the amoral, if not immoral, act of acting without thinking. The passage returns to the triumph of an eighteenth-century materialism that reduces action, like acting, to an automatic function, which, though material in nature, does not "matter." Wishing, remembering, intending are all erased, and so is the significance of "actions" better described here as temporal "events."[57] In a mechanical rendering of time passing, "things ... take their course"; personhood, like moral feeling, gives way to externalism. Handing herself over to the controls of time's diurnal mechanics, Fanny describes the sentiment of automatism as an enduring and palpable pain: "*it* was *all* misery" (my emphasis). Her acceptance of the it-ness of things, her failure to alter her circumstances, to create or change her environment, owes to the misalignment of memory and intention, of memory and desire. Not surprisingly, the theatrical episodes begin with Locke's rhetoric of habitual thinking and duration: "Every thing was now in a regular train; theatre, actors, actresses, and dresses, were all getting forward" (114). As thinglike subjects move in mechanical progression, time issues forth an environment of distress: "Every body began to have their vexation . . .—*nobody* would attend as they ought, nobody would remember on which side they were to come in—" (115, my emphasis). Like Denis Diderot's players on a stage, these various "no bodies" are void of memory, attention, and intention; thus acting is described as vexatious motion without an "ought" (115).

In her voyage back from the East room, Fanny slips on an empirical trap. It is a case of no reading. In it, Austen warns against an alternative type of memory that is something like the automatic practice of duets. Caught up in the knowledge of Edmund's actions, Fanny forgets just what memory can do. Keeping time with Edmund means relinquishing a bit of that "feminine lawlessness," and it is much better to read and re-member than to submit to the status of a forgotten thing. In its most thoughtful moments, the text is less concerned with oughtful action than with the creative powers of reflective consciousness. Again and again, Fanny's thinking seeks to realize desire by way of her subjective memories. And so she finds consolation from the distresses of worldly "deception" (181) in the pleasantries of fantasy.

The kinship between reading and remembering fiction resurfaces in the novel's second volume:

> Till she had shed many tears over this deception, Fanny could not subdue her agitation; and the dejection which followed could only be relieved by the influence of fervent prayers for his happiness.
>
> It was her *intention,* as she felt it to be her *duty,* to try to overcome all that was excessive, all that bordered on selfishness in her affection for Edmund. . . . To think of him as Miss Crawford might be justified in thinking, would in her be insanity. To her, he could be nothing under any circumstances—nothing dearer than a friend. Why did such an idea occur to her even enough to be reprobated and forbidden? *It ought not to have touched on the confines of her imagination.* She would endeavor to be rational, and to deserve the right of judging of

> Miss Crawford's character and the privilege of true solicitude for him by a sound intellect and an honest heart.
>
> She had all the heroism of principle, and was determined to do her duty; but having also many of the feelings of youth and nature, *let her not be much wondered at if*, after making all these good resolutions on the side of self-government, she seized the scrap of paper on which Edmund had begun to write to her, as a treasure beyond all her hopes, and *reading with the tenderest emotion* these words, "My dear Fanny, you must do me the favour to accept"—locked it up with the chain, as the dearest part of the gift. (181–82, my emphasis)

On the heels of Edmund's avowed affections for Mary Crawford, a painful event—painful because it runs counter to Fanny's innermost desire to be Edmund's lover—becomes rehistoricized through the filter of Fanny's mind. We may read the passage differently from Fanny, as her self-deception, and not as a worldly "deception" in which Edmund is fooled by Mary's character. Nevertheless, the word "deception" in Austen's hands describes the very business of literature: to render the greatest "insanity" real, to un*confine* and unleash the imagination, to rearrange the borderlines of truth through practices of remembering and rereading.

Fanny's imagination is "touched" and released from a guilty *conscience*, only to embrace a *conscious* practice of deconstructive, or radically subjective, reading. In reattributing the language of Edmund's brief letter to another scenario, easily imagined by the reader as a marriage proposal, Fanny's preservation of the note tells us something about the alignment of wishful with wistful thinking. Reading herein demonstrates how imagination and memory collide. For Austen describes the text, not its companionate object, the necklace, as the "dearest part of the gift." It becomes the sentimental remembrancer of a fictional event of willful misreading. Foregrounding this notion of interpretative reading as the gifting of intentions, Austen then transfers the "ought" of the passage from Fanny's mind onto the reader's, asking us to read and imagine in a certain way: "let her not be much wondered at." In a wonderful exchange, Austen makes her plug for a forgiving reader who *ought* to see nothing but what is natural in a mind that finds consolation in *a memory of what never happened*. This, after all, is the gift the fiction gives.

The Fiction's Fiction

The peculiar reifying powers of Fanny's mind suggest that there are physical effects brought about by the mental work of memory, but what is emphasized is a temporal concept of remembrance that gives way to the work of imagination. Take, for example, the following sentences: "As she walked slowly up stairs she thought of yesterday; it had been about the same hour that she had returned from the Parsonage, and found Edmund in the east room.—'Suppose I were to find him there again to-day!' she said to herself in a fond indulgence of fancy" (183). The whimsical thought begins with a recollection of former times, "she thought of yesterday." It then imagines, through the logic of Humean causation, the repetition of a desired event: "it had been about the same hour. . . . Suppose I were to find him there again to-day!" What immediately occurs is an uncanny embellishment on David Hume's cause-and-effect theory of expectations. Fanny does find Edmund, whose voice startles her again, rousing her from a state of pensive fantasy into bodily shock: "'Fanny,' said a voice *at that moment* near her. Starting and looking up, she saw across the lobby she had just reached Edmund himself, standing at the head of a different staircase. He came towards her" (183, my emphasis). The occasion instantaneously spins a world out of a mind. Of course, Edmund is in a different place; time and situation do not line up, and after all, you might say, the two do live together in the same house. Still, Fanny's body becomes a sign to the reader of just how she is reading the very same situation.[58] Her start affectively reverberates through the text so as to entertain the possibility that this is more than a coincidence.[59] Fanny's fanciful memory represents a wistful-as-wishful thinking, wherein retrospect and prospect collide to produce the shockingly physical effect of bringing Edmund to her literal doorstep. What Edmund calls the "lawlessness of feminine imagination" is the essence of fiction-making because it seemingly turns mental fantasies into real events and actual substances. Of course, nothing ever occurs exactly as planned, and so Fanny must adapt to her own realized fantasies. She is both writer and reader of her own text.

What might at first be considered the pains of nostalgia or the shocks of nervous anxiety has its comforts, for on the flip side of Fanny's heightened sensations and mind-body reactions, her somatic sentiment as it were, is the pleasure of a mental fiction making that can and will be realized. The effect across Austen's narrative is a pattern that only seems to get stronger as the text proceeds toward a fantasy ending that the reader anticipates if only because it is Fanny's own culminating wish. One is tempted to read the novel *as* Fanny's, for the fiction, like Austen's later *Persuasion*, narrates a realization of the heroine's most impossible desires.⁶⁰ Yet *Mansfield Park* carries with it an extra sense of improbability. Although *Persuasion* might be the better example in Austen's oeuvre of memory as a re-membered, fictionalized, and realized account, the famous passivity of *Mansfield Park*'s protagonist begs pause. Fanny gets what she wants not because of her actions but because of her unacted-on intentions, her secret wishes and desires.⁶¹ Thinking alone does the trick or—insofar as Austen's readers are concerned—the trickery.

Take, for example, the following passage from early on in volume 3, in which Fanny's wishes are announced to the reader. At this point in the novel, we do not yet know whether Fanny will succumb to Sir Thomas's pressures and Henry's wishes. For all we know, Austen might change her mind . . . unless, that is, we lend credence to *Fanny's* thoughts as the absolute sovereigns of the novel: "So thought Fanny in good truth and sober sadness, as she sat musing over that too great indulgence and luxury of a fire upstairs—wondering at the past and present, wondering at what was yet to come, and in a nervous agitation which made nothing clear to her but the persuasion of her being never under any circumstances able to love Mr. Crawford, and the felicity of having a fire to sit over and think of it" (223). Austen gives away her entire plotline here in a single sentence, one that synthesizes mental plotting with narrative plotting. Once again, Fanny's willful intention is derived from a state of reflection: her wish for the future is a remembrance of the past crystallized in time. Thinking across the temporal landscape of past, present, and future, her clarity of mind comes from a resistance to "circumstance," from a mind-over-matter determination that demonstrates thought as something temporal, nonlinear, unconfined—and "felicitous." By now, it should come as no surprise that in the avenues of memory and reflection, "sober sadness" becomes "felicity"— or even that Fanny's painful "good truth" morphs into an imagined, pleasing fiction. The pleasure of remembering what will never be is Fanny's greatest consolation, a most reassuring prospect that soothes nervous distress and the "sober sadness" typically associated with nostalgia. Such memories alter the reader's expectations, rendering true the story that Fanny chooses to tell herself about herself.

Fanny's meditation on an imagined possibility renounced by her own mind is in some sense a memory, a self-reminder, of her will and what will never be. The passage represents the pleasure that can be found in remembering fiction, in contemplating what William Galperin calls the "missed opportunities" of *Mansfield Park*.[62] It also emphasizes that what matters in the text is not the plot itself, that is to say what happens to its characters, but in what we as readers of fiction *think* has happened—our memories of what we have imagined, and what we imagine we remember.

This strange manner of narrative accounting defines the peculiar consciousness of *Mansfield Park,* and it perhaps speaks to Nicholas Dames's assertion that Jane Austen's works are evidence of nostalgia's etymological shift over the course of the nineteenth century—even though, as Dames points out, Austen never uses the word "nostalgia" itself.[63] For her novels do reconsider the troublesome question of the mind's relationship to absent forms, a mystery that haunted eighteenth-century medical theories of nostalgia, empirical philosophies of memory, and Romantic lyric poetry.

Above all, *Mansfield Park* considers the value of the fictions that we carry with us. In its main travel scene, during Fanny's retransplantation to Portsmouth, the novel remarks on fictionalized memory as a buoy that serves the heroine in a time of mental distress:

> It was sad to Fanny to lose all the pleasures of spring. She had not known before what pleasures she *had* to lose in passing March and April in a town. She had not known before, how much the beginnings and progress of vegetation had delighted her.—What animation both of body and mind she had derived from watching the advance of that season which cannot, in spite of its capriciousness, be unlovely, and seeing its increasing beauties, from the earliest flowers, in the warmest divisions of her aunt's garden, to the opening of leaves of her uncle's plantations, and the glory of his woods. (293)

The passage begins in Fanny's mental state of disconsolate distress, which Austen notably links not to memory but to knowledge. The sense of loss here stems from learning; the word "known," repeated twice, is a comparative device that contrasts what is felt now against what was felt before. In early empirical discourses, knowledge and memory are practically synonymous.

To know, as John Locke would have it, is to organize sensations stored up in the mind. Only through the lens of knowledge can the antithesis of pleasure come from its "passing," its loss. But a different kind of memory emerges in the interjection that lies between Austen's two characteristic em dashes. First, it revitalizes an image that is notably pleasing, as though the "animation both of body and mind" is "derived" from the absent form.

But as the reader rolls through the accretion of pleasant clauses and images, held together by commas and dashes in the punctuated confines of Fanny's mind, we come to find that the absent forms are anything but a perfect record of events. This is not merely to say that Fanny's memory is faulty. Rather, Austen cultivates a difference here between the reader's memory and Fanny's. Unsurprisingly, as Austen's privileged readers of free indirect style, we are wont to consider our own the truer version of the two. For our memories of Sir Thomas's plantations, our memories of those dubious woods of Northamptonshire, are anything but pleasing—they are darkened by suspicions about what the novel has all along implied but never said. Yet it is important to remember that the political and racial implications of injustice that haunt the image of Sir Thomas's "plantations," that the scandalous, perhaps sexual, events hidden in the county's "glorious" woods, are indeed never described, always just hidden from the reader's point of view in the actual text of the novel. Simply put, these are things we have all along *imagined to be there.*

Just as Fanny resorts to idealism in memory, so do we remember what we never saw, the figments of our own imagination. All along, Austen's narrative dances on the border between fiction and reality, between memory and imagination, suggesting perhaps that they are one and the same. The line that divides mind from world, that purports to contain form, is slippery and in constant motion. As David Hume might suggest, the whole exists entirely in the mind's eye; everything is a matter of perception. Like Fanny sitting atop her prospect, when it comes to memory and imagination, we gloss over the distinctions, buying into the narrative's sublime point of view.

Such is the phenomenon of reading a text that ends as Fanny would have it, which is why the opening lines to the final chapter of the novel have had such a discomfiting effect on its readers.[64] When the narrator breaks the fourth wall, "Let other pens dwell on guilt and misery. I quit such odious subjects as soon as I can, impatient to restore every body, not greatly in fault themselves, to tolerable comfort, and to have done with all the rest," the reader, suddenly denied illusion's greatest comfort—its absorptive mode of consolation—finds herself lumped in with "all the rest" (312). Austen is done with us, as she is with her fiction. The simulated, virtual consciousnesses that we have taken on as real deflate into mimetic representations. Austen's jarring trompe l'oeil marks the illusion as such, erecting a frame not previously registered by the viewer's eye. As though we are suddenly standing at the bottom of the ha-ha, we see the gap for what it is.

Nevertheless, the final chapter of *Mansfield Park* in some sense has nothing to do with the rest of the novel, for it is the place, as William Galperin says of "missed opportunities," of imagined would-be worlds.[65] Just like Lady Bertram's brief suggestion at the start of the novel that Fanny exchange places from Mansfield to White House, a transference that never happens, the novel ends with a nostalgic whiff of "what if"—one that asks us to imagine the entire story from a different point of view, to project on the novel a memory of what never was. If we take William Warner's notion of fiction as real, as an object of mediation, then Austen's decision to frame her novel in this way in fact reifies the very project of memory's kinship with imagination.[66] In this case, the representation becomes real thanks to the new and uncomfortable situation of the reader.

In order to explore the very real consequences of this rather brilliant transition from the characters' consciousness to the reader's consciousness,[67] I want to look at one of the chapter's most ethically curious "missed opportunities." The novel concludes with Henry's inevitable error, with another "ought" that sits awkwardly atop the narrative's aesthetic framework, and in the end only points to the subjunctive nature of its finale. But the morality of Henry's regret is not registered in the same slippery way as, say, that of his predecessor Willoughby (another of Austen's libertines, equally versed in the art of acting). Rather, in asking us to consider Henry's point of view, Austen's narrator speaks to the instrumental role that memory plays in realizing our desires. In Henry's irrevocable error, the reader is above all forced to consider fiction's fantasies as realized only through intentional memory or remembered intentions:

> Had he done as he intended, and as he knew he ought, by going down to Everingham after his return from Portsmouth, he might have been deciding his own happy destiny. But he was pressed to stay for Mrs. Fraser's party; his staying was made of flattering consequence,

and he was to meet Mrs. Rushworth there. Curiosity and vanity were both engaged, and the temptation of immediate pleasure was too strong for a mind unused to make any sacrifice to right; he resolved to defer his Norfolk journey, resolved that writing should answer the purpose of it, or that its purpose was unimportant—and staid. He saw Mrs. Rushworth, was received by her with a coldness which ought to have been repulsive, and have established apparent indifference between them for ever; but he was mortified, he could not bear to be thrown off by the woman whose smiles had been so wholly at his command; he must exert himself to subdue so proud a display of resentment; it was anger on Fanny's account; he must get the better of it, and make Mrs. Rushworth Maria Bertram again. (317)

Henry shares the "vanity" of his Austenian predecessors (Willoughby, Frank). But this is not the causative agent of his lost "happy destiny." We may even feel differently about Henry than we do about Austen's other libertines. This is because of the strategies of our narrator, who delivers the final footnote to his story by continually evoking alternative circumstances and endings: had he "gone down to Everingham," had he felt the repulsion as he "ought," had an "indifference" separated the two "for ever." Austen sets the stage for our expectations only to tear down the curtain. And if the guilty reader is touched by these disappointments, then it is not because she is unethical. Rather, it is because Austen exerts herself as puppeteer over both the sentimental machinery of her characters and readers, implanting imagined memories not otherwise seen or read.

What Henry so dangerously desires, more even than Fanny as his wife and lover, is "command"—but only the author of the fiction maintains this, and Henry cannot change places with her. Henry's greatest wish, from Sotherton on, is to control the show. "Resolved that writing should answer [his] purpose," resolved to "make Mrs. Rushworth Maria Bertram again," he tries his hand at that authorial magic, that happy ability to alter forms and persons by way of memory. But he is not the author; nor is he tantamount to an Anne Elliot or a Fanny Price. All along, Henry has played a very different part: that of the consummate actor. In the end, he is not the master of events and feelings but a mere reflection, and to this extent his role has a tragic cast. To "make Mrs. Rushworth Maria Bertram [once] again" is to cross the line. In clinging to a memory, Henry forgets himself.

Moreover, this is not the only thing that Henry forgets. He loses track of just exactly what he is up to and about. Subject to the rapid "changes" of an all too "human mind," Fanny's form—not "absent long"—makes its silent disappearance. Exchanging a fantasy for the old-hat ruse, Henry forgets to remember what he wished for. It is but the work of a moment.

Crawford's "destiny" is no decision, but a quiet passage of feeling that emphasizes the mind's engagement with the world as something "immediate." His error is not one of failed intentions per se, but it is one of bad timing. Here, Austen triumphs in her preference for a fiction that makes what it will of memory's sublime collision with imagination. Henry's mind automatically chooses a past reality over his present fantasy; in doing so, it severs imagination from memory, and accidentally produces a future out of Humean habit. Intentions are had and then lost, but the lost intention is not what makes Henry's character immoral. In fact, it humanizes him. His error comes from his failure to *remember* those intentions—and even to reflect on them once they have been lost.

Instead, it is the reader who must confront the lost intention, who must mourn its passing. We *feel for* Henry not in the sympathetic sense but in the reparative moral sense of experiencing a judgment or reflection that he does not. And so it is this transient feeling for Henry, for the fiction that might have been, that anticipates the novel's end. In this sense, reading is neither what represents nor what mediates the real. Rather, it is a practice of ephemeral loving, an act of letting go. We enter the book with the intention of escaping our reality, but we return to that reality, having to let go of the fiction that so dangerously enticed us away in the first place. The feeling we get when reading emphasizes the fact that feelings change. They exist in temporal flux, evolution, and exchange. In this manner, reading reclaims the ethics of intention by subjecting feelings to the laws of time. Intentions *are* there, but they often do not line up with our actions; we glimpse them only in retrospect. So often desires are laid to waste, failing to influence our behaviors. However, we feel their presence, their absence, and their loss. We mourn their passing, and in doing so, we pass on to other feelings, other mental states.

In this letting go, the lost intention finds a moral life, albeit an ephemeral one, as we briefly consider what might have been. The plot that could have occurred, the *failed fiction* in Austen's novel, exists in the space of memory. Reflecting on what might have been, we find reckoning in retrospective feeling. This memory of the *fiction's fiction* poses an alternative reading, not a rereading or reiteration, of the text. In its brevity, it quickly gives way to the novel's actual ending, to that moment when we close the book to move on into other worlds of feeling: "On that event they removed to Mansfield, and the parsonage there, which under each of its two former owners, Fanny had never been able to approach but with some painful sensation of restraint or alarm, soon grew as dear to her heart, and as thoroughly perfect in her eyes, as every thing else, within the view and patronage of Mansfield Park, had long been" (321). This end is an "event" described as a "removal," an exit that memorializes our "former" feelings only to emphasize that "sensation" like "every thing else ... [that has] long been" must "grow" and change. The revolving point of view that marks the novel's close places memory, with feeling, on shifting ground. Reading itself, Austen suggests, is a kind of remembering that allows us to survive, and outlive, former feeling.

❖ AFTERTHOUGHTS ❖

Remembering the Archive

> We live in time—it holds us and moulds us—... yet it takes only the smallest pleasure or pain to teach us time's malleability.
> —JULIAN BARNES, *The Sense of an Ending*

When I first entered the business of literary criticism, it was as a research assistant to a Victorianist at Brown University. It was then that I was introduced to the archive. Back then, the digitization of materials had not yet taken flight. Everything was on microfiche or microfilm. I spent long, tedious hours trying to recover dull, fuzzy images in a small, windowless room. I was young, in college, full of dreams and fantasies about professorial research. Maybe it was my time of life, or the length of time spent in searching, but I remember feeling a thrilling hope that I was going to discover something there—a strange sense that somewhere in that pile of forgotten things was a winsome treasure just waiting to be seen (again). I remember thinking that this was how history was made, and I longed to be a part of it.

Perhaps owing to the depths of my own wishful thinking, I did find something that summer in the John Hay Library. But unlike Fanny in her East room, my forgotten things never changed the course of history. Over time, I did become a professor, but one whose interests began to stray far from the archive—into aesthetic theory, cognitive philosophy, form and narratology. Still, fifteen years later, I found myself back again, this time at the British Library, ever so barely touching with my own hands a letter that Jane Austen had once sent to her sister, Cassandra. I felt the same magic wash over me again. It was voyeurism, really, a sense of being on the brink of some prospect—just a little bit closer to the truth of someone else's history.

The lines were immaculate: ink slanting all in one, measured direction, without blots, as if the thoughts were perfectly thought through. Nothing like Laurence Sterne's or Fanny Burney's writing, with their wild cross-outs and nervous, energetic marks. I left London with piles of notes and a rather stiff neck. History was there safe and sound, locked up in little houses, centuries old; occasionally, it was opened to the light. I had changed none of it.

But the memory of the letter remained. It was not what one might assume from a letter between sisters, that is, the vulnerability of fraught feelings and intense, emotional intimacy. Rather, the sentiment was all controlled, always just hidden behind an edifice of irony, that same skillful architecture we so often admire in Austen's novels. The handwriting betrayed nothing but the craft of a great novelist, a supreme teller of stories. It felt partly performative, partly elusive. It imparted nothing, just the stunning stuff of sublime illusion. *Perhaps*, I thought, *this is why Cassandra let this one escape the fire.*

I no longer feel about history as I used to in my college days, though my love for historical novels remains undiminished. In writing this book, I have come to read history as mediated by the powerful forces of memory and its many fictions. According to Julian Barnes, "History is that certainty produced at the point where the imperfections of memory meet the inadequacies of documentation."[1] *The Sense of an Ending* tells a story familiar now to the reader of contemporary fiction. Perfectly aware of memory's errors, Barnes's main character searches through his memories like an archivist grasping for truth. In the end, when memories and documents have been restitched together via threads very unlike what is imagined from the images the novel opens with, the tapestry reveals a horrifying tableau. All along, memory has tampered with history like a fiction that covers up personal responsibility.

The same ethical imperative pervades Ian McEwan's *Atonement* or Kazuo Ishiguro's *The Buried Giant*. Buried beneath the curtains of memory lies humanity's ugliest errors. With the return of the repressed truth, trauma begins anew. In his latest book, *The Buried Giant*, Kazuo Ishiguro figures forgetting as a dense and mythical mist that unwittingly permeates persons and bodies, vast lands and capacious cultures. At the end of the novel the mist lifts, only to reveal Axel standing on the shore alone. His wife is dead;

Saxon war wages again. Although Axel's memories are restored to him, he cannot recuperate the losses of his errors.[2] Similarly, Barnes describes Tony's memory archive as an "accumulation" of "responsibility" that leaves him at life's end with nothing more than the tortures of a "great unrest."[3] As Ian McEwan might say, the archive is a catalogue of errors for which we can only atone: "There was a crime. But there were also the lovers.... If [only] I had the power to conjure them..." Briony laments, "But now I must sleep."[4]

Like their eighteenth-century counterparts, millennial novels know all too well the truth about memory: its fictions, its fuzziness, its errant, wandering ways. But these works fail to embrace memory fiction in the manner of an Uncle Toby or a Fanny Price. Undoubtedly, Mary Carruthers was right about the culture of memory today: such novels were written in a posttraumatic age, in which the power of unconscious memory has become something to be feared.[5]

Similarly, for twenty-first century cognitive psychologists, memory comes with a warning label. What Daniel Kahneman calls "the automatic function of memory" can be rectified in much the same way as Daniel Schacter's seven sins of forgetting: through the strain of time and effort, judgment and consciousness.[6] Memory errs and minds wander, but science today promises us that we can always come full circle. *Conserve, preserve, excavate, appropriate.* We still believe, as it were, in the magic of the memory archive.

Of course, even the history of science and psychology has its aberrations. In the 1980s, the psychologist Shelley Taylor attempted to rectify the association of memory in her field with bias and error by giving personal history a new vocabulary: "*Error* and *bias* imply short-term mistakes and distortions, respectively, that might be caused by careless oversight or other temporary negligences. *Illusion*, in contrast, implies a more general, enduring pattern of error, bias, or both that assumes a particular direction or shape."[7] Taylor draws a distinction between error and illusion that might as easily be applied to the novel form as it was, in her case, to the psychology of real persons. Novels are illusions because they give error a narrative; "short-term mistakes" take "direction or shape" over a more "enduring" pattern and story line. What begins as an error—a bit of playful, mental wandering—turns the corner into an entirely new world. Created so as to delude, illusions may be read, reread, revisited, and absorbed over time.

The slow, temporal nature of narrative illusion-making is a truth equally applied to the fictional forms of both the eighteenth and the twenty-first centuries. But early English novels better manifest the aims of Taylor's psychotherapeutic approach. In 1988, Taylor coined the term "positive illusions" for those long-term memory distortions that promote happiness and facilitate "production and creation." "A chief value of these illusions," Taylor writes, "may be that they can create self-fulfilling prophecies."[8] For Taylor, memories do not simply bury and repress, they create. Scanning the history of memory can reify desire: those "self-fulfilling prophecies," those imagined, would-be realities, when slowly nourished over a long length of time, can come true. I wonder if Dr. Taylor had been reading Jane Austen?

After many hours spent in a dark room with fragile paper and a dizzying desire for truth: an all-too-perfect letter, letters slanting ever so meticulously to the right. Culled from the archive, a secret window into Austen's real world of fiction:

> My dear Cassandra,
>
> Shall you expect to hear from me on Wednesday or not?—I think you will, or I should not write, as the three days and half which have passed since my last letter was sent, have not produced many materials towards filling another sheet of paper.—But like Mrs. Hastings, "I do not despair—" and you perhaps like the faithful Maria may feel still more certain of the happy Event.—I have been here ever since a quarter after three on Thursday last, by the Shrewsbury Clock, which I am fortunately enabled absolutely to ascertain because Mrs. Stent once lived at Shrewsbury, or at least at Tewksbury. I have the pleasure of thinking myself a very welcome guest and the pleasure of spending my time very pleasantly.—(Sunday, November 30, 1800)[9]

Correspondence commences with an admission of nothing to report, intimating at a painful ennui that plagues the writer even as it frustrates her reader. Although days have passed with no information to give, the blank paper begs to be filled, reminding the writer of her audience's demand. Of course, such pains are never explicitly named; we merely intuit them. "Despair" is quickly dashed away with an invocation of Warren Hastings's wife and her companion, Miss Maria. Real-life characters stand ready to occupy the author's mind and revitalize the "faith" of her reader. To write is to remember (and imagine) the feelings of others, and then adopt them as one's own. As borrowed sentiments stand in for the writer's lack thereof, epistolary consciousness proves nothing more than a remembered fiction.

In writing to her sister, Jane Austen accounts for the passage of time through someone else's experience. Moreover, time is perceived, or "ascertained," from an uncertain place. (Is it by the Shrewsbury or the Tewksbury clock that time runs on?) The letter, like the point of view, avows no temporal realism, only the subjective pleasures of a kind of time clocked by conscious feelings. Time pleases because it is spent in thinking of oneself as one wants to be perceived. The writer imagines what others must think of her, deciding they must be pleased with her presence simply because the thought itself is pleasing. And so all goes on pleasantly, as self-consciousness is memorialized into a "positive illusion."[10]

The letter is an "inadequate" historical document, in Barnes's terminology, for it records, it transfers, nothing but its own fictional transcription. But let us consider for a moment the satisfaction the letter creates, and not just for its writer, who benefits from such self-aggrandizing reflections, but for the reader, who likewise delights in the form of the illusion itself— its laughing irony, its inspiring self-awareness, its sneaky repetitiousness, which exchanges the tedium of the clock for the insistent, literary pace of pleasure itself.

When calendrical time "produces [no] material," fiction is there at the ready. It re-members time and feeling, turning dullness and listlessness into shared and self-sustaining pleasures. All is filtered through various shades of subjective and intersubjective experience. Jane's letter to her sister, Cassandra, obliterates the pressures of clocked time as they metamorphose into a new tempo: that is, the pleasing *art* of cognition itself.

There is an emotional infrastructure to consciousness, whether it be of the literal or the literary kind. According to Daniel Kahneman, thinking can sometimes feel like a good stroll in the park: "It is normally easy and actually quite pleasant to walk and think at the same time . . . cognitive work is not always aversive. . . . People who experience flow describe it as 'a state of effortless concentration so deep that they lose their sense of time, of themselves, of their problems.'"[11] In other words, cognitive flow evokes the perfectly aligned rhythms of body and mind when they move along at the same pace but are still absorbed in entirely different activities. For Kahneman, this pace is precise. The pleasures of flow occur at a seventeen-minute mile.

A fourteen-minute mile destroys it all. Most fascinating is the temporal paradox of flow. Although it has a rather precise time of its own, flow is what happens when, by reflecting, we lose track of time and also a sense of personal distress. Although they may differ in length, Kahneman's path along the San Francisco Bay bears an uncanny resemblance to Mary Crawford's furlong.

Imagine: a marvelous simultaneity perfectly syncopated though not at all registered. It looks something like Anne Elliot at her pianoforte: "These were some of the thoughts which occupied Anne, while her fingers were mechanically at work, proceeding for half an hour together, equally without error, and without consciousness" (*Persuasion*, 48). Fingers and minds hover. Floating along in parallel universes, Austen's synecdoches intimate a power that lies beyond our experience of unwanted sensation. In what looks like a plug for materialism or mind-body dualism, the energies of mental occupation set aside the work of the body. But the cadence, the *form* of the narrative structure, lies not in its diction (the apparent binary of minds and "fingers") but in its punctuation, in what synchronizes the sentence and changes our reading of the whole. With a series of commas, the narrative "proceeds," linking minds and bodies "together," much like the "half an hour" memorialized and forgotten through the fiction's flow. Most important, Austen's use of parallelism suggests that "error" and "consciousness" are one and the same, or rather that the lack of the one leads to the absence of the other.

The thoughts that "occupy" Anne while her fingers are "at work" strain to avoid what is for Anne most presently painful. She is at a lavish party and plays piano for the guests, who are all in "high spirits." Among them is her past lover, whom she has longingly remembered every day for seven years. He is flirting with two other women. Herself the forgotten wallflower, she marvels at appearances, meditating on what it must feel like to be the object of "such eager admiration" (48). The mind thinks while the hands play. Heartbreak strikes a chord. She does not miss a beat.

But this is the musical set piece of a moment. Mechanical and brief, avoidance quickly is subsumed back into illusion: if only *Anne* could be the object of "such eager admiration" once again. The impulse is an *error*—a mental wandering that asks the reader, with Anne, imaginatively to remember a past so very different from things as they are now. It quickly gives way to the novel's long-term illusion. Although it seems that perfection inheres in Anne's unconscious fingers, *Persuasion* continues only to expose the wonderfully productive nature of consciousness as error—of how we can revisit and revise our own history by wandering through thought and time, by reading and writing anew.

Seven years of wishing she could alter memory's truth, and Anne has her way. The novel ends with Captain Wentworth's "heart returning to her" (123), but this time, all conspires so that a marriage between the two characters is possible. We are left with nothing but Anne's "high-wrought felicity" (163) as she canters off to sea. And although the language of the eighteenth-century nostalgia disease is there as a satirical backdrop to the whole, Austen's memory illusion is anything but pathological.

A letter between sisters. A woman at her pianoforte. They distract; they forget. They remember, and they also create. Memory's ability to alter history produces nothing but pleasure in the highest degree. It tempers feelings and retempos time, so that Austen's reader, so easily seduced by the music, proves "faithful" to the "happy Event" of what remains. In the summer of 2017, a scholar travels across the Atlantic to visit a famous archive, only "absolutely to ascertain" nothing of truth from a document that transforms times and places, feelings and events. What she finds instead is history in its most fragile form. It is a memory error—the conscious markings of an extraordinary pathway into newly embodied territories. In the palm of the hand, a page that prompts its reader to wander from feeling freely—only to transform the ghostly shadows of what she once sensed she knew.

❖ NOTES ❖

INTRODUCTION

1. See especially my discussions of John Locke and David Hume in this introduction.
2. Engell, *The Creative Imagination*, 6.
3. Coleridge, *Biographia Literaria*, 296–97.
4. Johnson, *The Rambler*, 41, August 7, 1750.
5. Ian Watt's account of the novel is the most famous for thinking about autobiographical modes of storytelling and remembering: *The Rise of the Novel*, 191–93, 100–101, 107, 209, 292, 295. See especially pages 191–92, wherein Watt speaks to the novel's attempt to portray "inner life" as the "ceaseless flow of thought" or the "minute-by-minute content of consciousness." For other psychological and ideological studies, see also McKeon, *The Origins of the English Novel*, and Armstrong, *How Novels Think*. For more mediational accounts of the novel as a social form, see Warner and Siskin, *This Is Enlightenment*; Lynch, *The Economy of Character*; Warner, *Licensing Entertainment*; Vermeule, *Why Do We Care about Literary Characters?*; Zunshine, *Why We Read Fiction*; and Palmer, *Fictional Minds*.
6. Draaisma, *Why Life Speeds Up*, 2; Nalbantian, *Memory in Literature*, 136–37.
7. I'm locating this around the time of Watt's *The Rise of the Novel* (1957), if not before. See note 9.
8. Watt, *The Rise of the Novel*, 13–301; McKeon, *The Origins of the English Novel*, 135–38, 2, 3, 17–18, 167–68, 197–226, 202–49.
9. Watt, *The Rise of the Novel*, 12. According to Watt, the term "realism" that we use for the novel comes to us from the French school of Realists (in painting) in 1835 ("réalisme"). Realism only becomes a literary term in 1856 (*The Rise of the Novel*, 10). For a full account of the origins of realism in literary studies, see Watt, *The Rise of the Novel*, 9–34, 292–301.
10. Armstrong, *How Novels Think*, 3.

11. Lynch, *The Economy of Character*; Warner, *Licensing Entertainment*; Vermeule, *Why Do We Care about Literary Characters?*; Zunshine, *Why We Read Fiction*; Palmer, *Fictional Minds*.
12. Warner and Siskin, *This Is Enlightenment*, 1–36, passim.
13. Catherine Gallagher, "The Rise of Fictionality," 336–63.
14. Ibid., 347.
15. Warner, *Licensing Entertainment*; Siskin, *System*; Bender, *The Ends of Enlightenment*, 38–56, 95–108; Hodgson Anderson, *Eighteenth-Century Authorship and the Play of Fiction*, 1–20.
16. See especially Pasanek, *Metaphors of Mind*; Silver, *The Mind Is a Collection*; Keiser, "Nervous Figures"; Chico, *The Experimental Imagination*.
17. Engell, *The Creative Imagination*, 6.
18. Pasanek, *Metaphors of Mind*. In the field of psychology, see also Draaisma, *Metaphors of Memory*.
19. According to Joseph Addison in his *The Pleasures of the Imagination*, allegory and metaphor activate and please the imagination of the reader (578). Moreover, imagination (or "fancy") "copie[s] after the Understanding, transcribing ideas out of the Intellectual World into the Material" (*The Spectator*, Thursday, July 3, 1712), 577. For the empiricists John Locke and David Hume, memory is the activity of creating associations (forms such as likeness, simile, or metaphor) in the mind. This is true for modern brain studies as well. We now know that memory is actually what happens when neurons form connections, or associations, in the brain.
20. Pasanek, *Metaphors of Mind*, 253.
21. From the Latin "transfer" or the Greek to ferry or "carry across." See Silver, *The Mind Is a Collection*, 27.
22. Palmer, *Fictional Minds*; Zunshine, *Why We Read Fiction*; Vermeule, *Why Do We Care about Literary Characters?*
23. Deidre Lynch helps us to understand character as something legible, not internal, inward, or strictly psychological. It is also something material and circulated in the world. My semiotic approach to reading the outward signs of metaphor as an indexical system for the powers of memory is partially inspired by her work. See Lynch, *The Economy of Character*, 1–79.
24. Carruthers, *The Book of Memory*, 23.
25. Ibid., 23.
26. Doody, "'A Good Memory Is Unpardonable,'" 67.
27. This language is taken from John Locke's "association of ideas" (chap. 23 of *An Essay Concerning Human Understanding*, 394–401) and parodied in Laurence Sterne's *Tristram Shandy*.
28. Silver, *The Mind Is a Collection*, 1.

29. Carruthers, *The Book of Memory*, 1.
30. Dames, *Amnesiac Selves*, 4, 6, 9.
31. Ibid., 4.
32. Doody, "A Good Memory Is Unpardonable," 70.
33. Baier, *Postures of the Mind*, 18.
34. Ibid.
35. Silver, *The Mind Is a Collection*, 3.
36. Dames, *Amnesiac Selves*, 4.
37. Joyce, *Ulysses*, 644.
38. Bender, *The Ends of Enlightenment*, 105.
39. René Descartes, *Discourse on Method and Meditations on the First Philosophy*, 67.
40. Descartes, *Meditations on the First Philosophy*, 67–68 (my emphasis).
41. Locke, *An Essay Concerning Human Understanding*, 156.
42. Descartes, *The Treatise on Man*, 150.
43. Ibid., 68.
44. Most famously, Foucault, "What Is Enlightenment?," 37, 45, 35; Habermas, *The Structural Transformation of the Public Sphere*, 104; Horkheimer and Adorno, *Dialectic of Enlightenment*, 1–34.
45. Spinoza, *Ethics*.
46. These questions speak to various theories of Enlightenment materialism, as well as mechanism and vitalism. Numerous studies of the new science in the long eighteenth century have recently emerged. For further reading on materialist accounts of the period, see Thompson, *Fictional Matter*; Chico, *The Experimental Imagination*; and Goldstein, *Sweet Science*. See also Kramnick, *Paper Minds*, chap. 7.
47. Hume, *A Treatise of Human Nature*, 59; Berkeley, *A Treatise Concerning the Principles of Human Knowledge*; idem, *Three Dialogues between Hylas and Philonous*.
48. Kant, *Critique of Pure Reason*.
49. With increasing frequency, critics consider Locke in the tradition of materialism. For a thorough and original account of Locke's relationship to materialism, see Kramnick, *Action and Objects*, 141–67, 61–98.
50. Locke, *An Essay Concerning Human Understanding*, 98 (my emphasis).
51. Ibid., 152–53, passim (my emphasis).
52. Draaisma, *Why Life Speeds Up*, 1.
53. Locke, *An Essay Concerning Human Understanding*, 151–52, passim (my emphasis).
54. Richardson, "Jane Austen and the Perils of Mental Time Travel," 59; Richardson, "Memory and Imagination in Romantic Fiction," 281.

55. Hobbes, *Leviathan*, 16.
56. Ibid., 16, passim.
57. Hume, *A Treatise of Human Nature*, 59.
58. Ibid., 59, 11.
59. Ibid., 60.
60. Ibid., 60.
61. Stroud, *Hume*, 17.
62. Hume, *A Treatise of Human Nature*, 7.
63. Stroud, *Hume*, 19.
64. Locke, *An Essay Concerning Human Understanding*, 149–50.
65. Ibid., 395.
66. Ibid., 396.
67. Ibid., 150.
68. Ibid., 396.
69. For discussions of Hume's associationism that relate directly to this book, see especially Lynch, *Loving Literature*, 171; and Lee, *Failures of Feeling*, 143–44.
70. Hume, *A Treatise of Human Nature*, 12.
71. Ibid., 14 (my emphasis).
72. Lee, *Failures of Feeling*, 143–44.
73. See the editors' (David Fate Norton's and Mary J. Norton's) annotations on p. 429 of the Oxford Philosophical edition.
74. Hume, *A Treatise of Human Nature*, 409–13, 416.
75. Ibid., 416.
76. Ibid., 417.
77. Kramnick, *Paper Minds*, 57.
78. Garrett, *Hume*, 68–69. Garrett describes how Locke's notion of mimetic ideas as "contained" in the mind emerges from Descartes' more literal, material account.
79. Garrett, *Hume*, 37, 46, 72–74; Stroud, *Hume*, 20, 24 (see especially simple versus complex ideas); Lynch, *Loving Literature*, 171.
80. Garrett, *Hume*, 69.
81. Helen Thompson's materialist reading of Locke seemingly counters my claims about mimetic ideation in this introduction. For Thompson, Lockean ideas are productive because they not only inhabit bodies but shuttle between person and object, exemplifying "matter's retroactively specified power to trigger sensation 'in us' (80)"; see also *Fictional Matter*, 3, 7, 23, 69, 80. Amit Yahav likewise reads Lockean cognition and memory as more mediational than mimetic (*Feeling Time*, 26–28). These arguments aptly underscore the tricky problem for empirical philosophy to account

for the effects of feeling minds in their environments. Although my reading of Locke differs from Thompson's and Yahav's because I identify Lockean memory and thought as imitative, I do agree that Locke's consciousness is in some sense "mediational." Kevis Goodman best describes this kind of media as "the pathways of perception and communication," that to some extent position the objective world at an intellectual remove so that sensation does not "emerge from some kind of immediate contact with the real" (*Georgic Modernity and British Romanticism*, 8).
82. This stance is supported by Locke's discussion of "extension" in chapter 13 of book 2 of the *Essay*, 178–80.
83. Silver, *The Mind Is a Collection*, 29.
84. Ibid., 29–32. I have described here two different manners of reading Locke and Hume in this introduction. Whereas Thompson, Yahav, and Silver resist the notion of mimesis in empirical ideation and memory, Kramnick, Stroud, and Garrett acknowledge the "representational" aspects of ideation in Locke and Hume. For Kramnick, representation "is understood to be a structural relation between acts or entities of the mind and properties or features of the world" (*Paper Minds*, 59). Deidre Lynch synthesizes these two readings in her analysis of Humean structural and emotional thought patterns. For Lynch, Humean association *imitates, mediates,* and *produces*: "Philosophy in this mode repeatedly raises the distinctions between emotions engendered by experience and emotions caused by the fictions that merely simulate experience only to put them aside" (*Loving Literature*, 171). As we have seen from this introduction, Hume still borrows much from Locke in his new account of associationism.
85. In his lyric poem "Memory," William Wordsworth describes empirical versus Romantic models of remembrance. Whereas the former is akin to an inked inscription, the latter is heralded as a "tool" of imagination (l. 13). The pencil becomes the overriding metaphor for Romantic memory in the poem; it both traces and erases, softening even the hardest of images and experiences. Echoing through "channel[s] smooth and deep," memory "creep[s]" like a moving force (ll. 27–28). Its sartorial function is to cut, taper, and color truth so as to satiate and surpass the "heart's demand" (l. 8). In this sense, Wordsworth's creative memory is a powerful panacea—an allayer of personal distress.
86. Freud, "An Infantile Neurosis," 49, my emphasis.
87. Freud, "Screen Memories", 122.
88. "As aptly, also, might be given / A Pencil to her hand; / That, softening objects, sometimes even / Outstrips the heart's demand" (Wordsworth, "Memory," ll. 5–8).

89. Freud, "Screen Memories," 118ff.
90. Kandel, *In Search of Memory*, 388.
91. See especially Schacter, *Searching for Memory*, and idem, *The Seven Sins of Memory*.
92. Schacter, *The Seven Sins of Memory*, 7.
93. Hunt and Chittka, "False Memory Susceptibility," 3.
94. Schooler and Engslter-Schooler, "Verbal Overshadowing of Visual Memories," 36–71, 1.
95. This is called "transactive memory." For an argument about how social media affect the neural networks of the brain, see Wegner, Erber, and Raymond, "Transactive Memory in Close Relationships," 923–29.
96. Loftus, *Memory*. See also Loftus, *Eyewitness Testimony*, and Loftus with Ketcham, *The Myth of Repressed Memory*. *Memory* is Loftus's most comprehensive overview of memory, whereas *Eyewitness Testimony* and *The Myth of Repressed Memory* are important for how they changed cultural and psychological assumptions about memory in the late twentieth century. *Eyewitness Testimony* extends Loftus's findings on memory to the legal system. *The Myth of Repressed Memory* overturns assumptions about trauma and abuse. This last work is key for scholars today, since it undermines the continued use of "repressed memory" theory and the work of Sigmund Freud.
97. "Confabulation denotes the emergence of memories of experiences and events which never took place" (Nahum, Guggisberg, Bourzeda-Wahlen, et al., "Forms of Confabulation," 2524–34; see abstract).
98. For an overview of these types of memory errors, see the collection *Memory Distortion*, edited by Daniel Schacter, and Kandel, *In Search of Memory*. In *The Seven Sins of Memory*, Schacter describes "source misattribution" (sometimes referred to as "source confusion") as when we "misattribute the source of [our] knowledge" or information. Sometimes we attribute something to our own memory and experience when it was in fact derived from someone else's story (93–94). This is just one way in which memory can be mediated by impersonal information.
99. Nalbantian, *Memory in Literature*. See also Nalnantian, Matthews, and McLelland, eds., *The Memory Process*; and Singer, "Austen Agitated," 200–221. Although the following works do not particularly pertain to the crossovers between memory and imagination, they are formative for the study of literature and neuroscience in historical periods: Richardson, *British Romanticism and the Science of the Mind* and *The Neural Sublime*; Spolsky and Richardson, *The Work of Fiction*.

100. Richardson, "Jane Austen and the Perils of Mental Time Travel," *British Romanticism and the Science of the Mind*, 93–113, and *The Neural Sublime*, 79–96; Lau, ed., *Jane Austen and Sciences of the Mind*; Jones, *Jane on the Brain*.
101. Richardson, "Jane Austen and the Perils of Mental Time Travel," 66.
102. Young, "Resilience and Jane Austen," 200–218. Note especially Young's definition of resilience as neuroplasticity (212).
103. Richardson, "Jane Austen and the Perils of Mental Time Travel," 59, and "Memory and Imagination in Romantic Fiction," 281–282.
104. I discuss in chapter 3 these through-line approaches that link theories of mind reading in cognitive psychology to sympathy in Austen's work, citing critics such as Lisa Zunshine, Blakey Vermeule, Beth Lau, and Wendy Jones. However, the same link should not be made between Enlightenment empirical philosophy and neuroscientific models of memory.
105. Moretti, *The Way of the World*, 3–74.
106. Kramnick, *Paper Minds*, 74–77.
107. Caruth, *Unclaimed Experience*, 2.
108. It is important here to distinguish between these kinds of memory sites and classical concepts of the memory loci. As Frances Yates has famously argued, the spaces of memory in the classical tradition draw an analogy between the objective world and the architectural cubbies of the mind, which serve as the foundation for memory's mnemonic arts (*The Art of Memory*, 11). Nor are the memory environments I discuss here akin to Nicholas Dames's concept of chronotopic places of "psychic dislocation" that disconnect subjects from their past (*Amnesiac Selves*, 14). Memory is not a rhetorical craft of retention or inscription or a species of forgetting in my work but a phenomenological force of transformation.
109. Brainerd and Reyna, "Fuzzy Trace Theory and False Memory," 164–69.
110. Definitions 1 and 2a, *Oxford English Dictionary*.

1. ACCOUNTING FOR CRUSOE'S SURVIVAL

1. Novak, "The Cave and Grotto," 120–37.
2. Marshall, "Autobiographical Acts," 916; Lamb, "'Lay Aside My Character,'" 279; Novak, *Realism, Myth and History in Defoe's Fiction*, 45.
3. Lewis, "The Atmospheres of Robinson Crusoe," 33.
4. Seidel, "Robinson Crusoe," 183–84.
5. Starr, *Defoe and Spiritual Autobiography*, and Hunter, *The Reluctant Pilgrim*.
6. Lamb, "'Lay Aside My Character,'" 271–87.

7. Richetti, "Defoe as Narrative Innovator," 127; Houlihan Flynn, *The Body in Swift and Defoe*, 1–2, 7, 154; Novak, *Realism, Myth and History in Defoe's Fiction*, 45; Vickars, *Defoe and the New Sciences*, 105–11.
8. Sherman, *Telling Time*, 229; Starr, *Defoe and Spiritual Autobiography*, 87.
9. Richetti, *Defoe's Narratives*, 125.
10. Lynch, "Money and Character in Defoe's Fiction," 93.
11. Richetti, *Defoe's Narratives*, 9–10, 23, 46.
12. Festa, "Crusoe's Isle of Misfit Things," 444–46.
13. Baier, "Cartesian Persons," in *Postures of the Mind*, 86.
14. Ibid., 88.
15. Baier, "Mixing Memory and Desire," in *Postures of the Mind*, 8.
16. Ibid., 14–16.
17. Damasio, *The Feeling of What Happens*, 195–6.
18. Starr, *Defoe and Spiritual Autobiography*; Hunter, *The Reluctant Pilgrim*; Seidel, "Robinson Crusoe"; Marshall, "Autobiographical Acts in *Robinson Crusoe*."
19. Locke, *An Essay Concerning Human Understanding*, 187, 191.
20. Ibid., 181.
21. Ibid., 182.
22. Yahav, *Feeling Time*, 26.
23. Locke, *An Essay Concerning Human Understanding*, 204.
24. In this chapter, when I use the term "memory" I am signaling the kind of episodic, autobiographical memory that both emerged and departed from empirical prototypes. Another kind of memory that I do not discuss in this chapter but that could easily be applied to theological readings of Defoe is Puritan recollection. As Rachel Trocchio reminds us, Puritan recollection was associated with God's grace and also with activities of composition. Although this type of memory is a craft, it does not resemble the way I wish to speak about memory in this chapter for two reasons. First, it is bound up in Puritan ideals of predeterminism. Second, as Trocchio argues, Puritan recollection directly derives from classical modes of memory formation as mnemonic and rhetorical arts codified in the memory loci ("Memory's Ends," 694, 696, 700, 707–9, 715–16).
25. Catherine Gallagher describes Defoe's use of reference and allegory as a species of truth-telling that causes us to reconceptualize the dimensions of modern realism ("The Rise of Fictionality," 339). See also J. Paul Hunter on association, metaphor, and the meaning of spiritual emblems (*The Reluctant Pilgrim*, 113, 155) and John Richetti on realism and empirical sense perception ("Defoe as Narrative Innovator,"122). Richetti reminds us that the word "realism" is derived from the Latin *res*, "thing," that comes from

the material objects of nature (125). This is similar to John Bender's notion of Defoe's realism wherein the "apparitional quality of the very experience we call the real" in fact demonstrates "the unreality within the real" ("The Novel as Modern Myth," 234).

26. See Richetti's claims about Lockean sense perception in the novel and Crusoe as an "exact" observer of "phenomena" in "Defoe as Narrative Innovator," 122–24.
27. Jayne Lewis describes the novel as a "blur between . . . outside and inside" ("The Atmospheres of Robinson Crusoe," 48) wherein the "true" conditions of Crusoe's environment are only a "state of mind" (51).
28. My argument here complicates Maximillian Novak's early claim that the conditions of the island are not sufficient for survival without removal of things from the wreck (*Economics and the Fiction of Daniel Defoe*, 52). Novak's statement is literally true, but it does not account for the novel's subtle commentary on the role of the mind in situations of distress. His reading of Crusoe as a materialist, venture capitalist led many critics after him to think about Crusoe's survival as thing-oriented instead of mind-oriented.
29. Hunter, *The Reluctant Pilgrim*; Starr, *Defoe and Spiritual Autobiography*.
30. Vickars, *Defoe and the New Sciences*.
31. Starr, *Defoe and Casuistry*.
32. As David Marshall argues, to "reckon" means to "count, estimate, value, and judge, but also to recount, relate, tell, narrate, recite, and utter" ("Autobiographical Acts in *Robinson Crusoe*," 901). Crusoe's calendar is therefore both an autobiographical and an economic account, like the journal itself. Similarly, Deidre Lynch argues, Defoe's protagonists remind readers of the etymology of the verb "to tell"; as tied to the "human activities of narrating and counting," novels "illuminate how telling can be a synonym for counting, counting out, and reckoning up. . . . Defoe's narrators like to tally up and take stock" ("Money and Character in Defoe's Fiction," 84).
33. Paula Backsheider comments on the resemblance of narrative style to financial accounts of credit and debt ("Defoe," 10).
34. Isle Vickars calls Crusoe the quintessential "*Homo faber*," or maker of things (*Defoe and the New Sciences*, 105). However, Vickars sees things as made through the scientific processes of experiment. In this reading, the journal is an allegory for Enlightenment "invention" (105), one that upholds a Baconian approach to experimental science in its tendency to hold "dominion," "mastery," and "empire" over things (111, 103, 105).
35. Although I am not the first to comment on the subjective and metaphorical aspects of Crusoe's dwellings (see Novak, "The Cave and the Grotto,"

120–37), I try to build on Novak's archetypal method of reading to underscore the cognitive pun on "dwelling" in this text as a way of demonstrating a pattern of mind-world dialectics in Defoe's narrative.

36. Richetti, "Defoe as Narrative Innovator," 127.
37. Wall, *The Prose of Things*, 109.
38. Stuart Sherman comments on the obsessive structure of time keeping in the text as necessary to Crusoe's survival (*Telling Time*, 228).
39. Amit Yahav argues for a transition in the narrative from one type of time keeping that tracks time spent to another, related to Crusoe's subjective experience ("Time, Duration, and Defoe's Novels," 2, 37, 39).
40. Locke, *An Essay Concerning Human Understanding*, 193.
41. The corn episode has a long history of critical interpretation. In 1965, G. A. Starr famously read this as a gesture toward Providence wherein Crusoe has a revelatory insight into the "secondary causes" that define a Protestant ethos of providential wonder (*Defoe and Spiritual Autobiography*, 196–97). Since then a variety of readings, secular and religious, have sprung up around the parable of the corn. Robert Folkenflik reads the grain as a semiotic crisis in eighteenth-century modes of discourse, one whose "hallucinatory reality" causes us to trust in the invisible world of Providence ("Robinson Crusoe and the Semiotic Crisis of the Eighteenth Century," 115–17). Isle Vickars reads it as a parable of the natural sciences (*Defoe and the New Sciences*, 127), Kevin Seidel as evidence of a "religious let-down" pattern in Defoe's fiction that casts the story into neither a religious nor a secular discourse ("*Robinson Crusoe* as Defoe's Theory of Fiction," 176). For Seidel, Crusoe is subject to two types of counterbalancing rhetorical modes, one of empirical science, the other of religion (167).
42. Damasio, *The Feeling of What Happens*, 195–96.
43. Kramnick, *Actions and Objects*, 3–4.
44. I embellish on Stuart Sherman's observation that the corn episode causes Crusoe to lose track of time. Sherman argues that conversion is the mechanism that renders time unreliable and no longer calendrical (*Telling Time*, 234).
45. It is also possible to read this episode as an "occasional reflection" in the more religious vein of what Courtney Weiss Smith has described as a meditative or devotional practice of empiricism. For Smith, such occasions signal analogies between the self and world in which we observe God's design in nature through intensive observation (*Empiricist Devotions*, 1–68). The parable may be read as Crusoe finding himself in the nature of God's design as he takes up a new craft of agricultural sowing. This account dovetails more nicely with Puritan concepts of recollection, which Rachel Trocchio

has described as both mnemonic systems of recall (like the marking of Crusoe's calendrical time) and hermeneutics (like Crusoe's interpretation of his newly summoned memory) ("Memory's Ends," 707).
46. Sherman, *Telling Time*, 226; Marshall, "Autobiographical Acts in *Robinson Crusoe*," 899.
47. Jayne Lewis reads the umbrella as a thing that springs from Crusoe's "great Mind" ("The Atmospheres of Robinson Crusoe," 49).
48. I counterclaim that *Robinson Crusoe* shows evidence of a psychological trauma narrative. See Kraft, "The Revaluation of Literary Character," 40, 44, 54. See also Juengel, "The Early Novel and Catastrophe," 443. Although in Defoe's novel, catastrophic events may reveal shifts in temporal order, the use of memory as a survival mechanism poses problems for traumatic readings of the text.
49. Vickars, *Defoe and the New Sciences*, 127; Yahav, "Time, Duration, and Defoe's Novels," 40–41, Folkenflik, "Robinson Crusoe and the Semiotic Crisis of the Eighteenth Century," 111; Festa, "Crusoe's Isle of Misfit Things," 464.
50. See especially Lynn Festa's reading of the footprint as an enduring example of how the imagination works to fill in the gaps between person and thing ("Crusoe's Isle of Misfit Things," 464).
51. Jonathan Lamb considers the "immobile boat" as a "joke" in the novel representative of a rare occasion in which the imagination fails ("Lay Aside My Character," 279). I qualify the imagination's failure as due to its disconnection from memory. This embellishment on Lamb's argument also takes into account critical perspectives on the boat as a representative "memorandum" of narrative events (Seidel, "Robinson Crusoe," 194).

2. RE-MEMBERING THE REAL

1. Moglen, *The Philosophical Irony of Laurence Sterne*, 154; Sagal, "An Hobby-Horse Well Worth Giving a Description Of," 105–33.
2. I am not the first to imply the healing nature of the bowling green. Everett Zimmerman made a similar point in his work on history and narrative representation. My argument takes this suggestion further by emphasizing the role of memory and imagination in Toby's physical recovery ("Tristram Shandy and Narrative Representation," 136).
3. On the side of John Locke, see Cash, "The Lockean Psychology of *Tristram Shandy*," 125–35; Moglen, *The Philosophical Irony of Laurence Sterne*; John Freeman, "Delight in the Disorder of Things," 141–61; Alryyes, "Uncle Toby and the Bullet's Story in Laurence Sterne's *Tristram Shandy*," 1109–34; and Traugott, *Tristram Shandy's World*. Note Traugott explicitly reads the novel as a satire on Locke; Moglen and Alryyes see the novel as

exaggerating Locke's terms. On the side of Hume, see Lamb, *Sterne's Fiction and the Double Principle;* Simpson, "At This Moment in Space," 142–58; and Christina Lupton, "*Tristram Shandy,* David Hume and Epistemological Fiction," 98–115.

4. For readings of the novel as a satire on materialism, see Porter, "Against the Spleen," 91; New, "Sterne and the Modernist Moment," 160–73; Wehrs, "Anarchic Signification and Motions of Grace in Sterne's Novelistic Satire," 77–99; and Nowka, "Talking Coins and Thinking Smoke-Jacks,"195–222. For more representative takes on Sterne's rhetoric of materialism, see Loveridge, "Liberty in *Tristram Shandy,*" 126–27; Hawley, "*Tristram Shandy,* Learned Wit, and Enlightenment Knowledge," 35–36; and Fanning, "Small Particles of Eloquence," 360–92. Juliet McMaster's discontinuous conception of mind and body in this novel warrants a unique place in this list ("Uncrystalized Flesh and Blood,'" 201–5).

5. Judith Hawley unearths a system of medical reference in the novel, but unlike other critical focuses on Sterne's material bodies (Porter, "Against the Spleen," and McMaster, "Uncrystalized Flesh and Blood"), Hawley figures the text as both a "parody" of "literal materialism" and a metaphor for the "perfect medium through which to express the mixed nature of embodied experience" ("The Anatomy of *Tristram Shandy,*" 94).

6. See Jack Lynch on the novel's use of "copia" in his "The Relicks of Learning," 1–17. Melvyn New also uses this term to describe Sterne's style ("Sterne, Warburton, and the Burden of Exuberant Wit," 271).

7. John Traugott sees minds as impermeable in the novel, which he reads as a commentary on Locke (*Tristram Shandy's World,* 8–10). Juliet McMaster has argued that metaphors in the novel are what make the mind capable of apprehension by way of the body ("Uncrystalized Flesh and Blood," 206).

8. Hawley, "*Tristram Shandy,* Learned Wit, and Enlightenment Knowledge" 46.

9. Caruth, *Unclaimed Experience,* 2.

10. Sagal, "An Hobby-Horse Well Worth Giving a Description Of," 105–7, 111–12.

11. Caruth, *Unclaimed Experience,* 2.

12. Moglen, *The Philosophical Irony of Laurence Sterne,* 154. For a counterargument, see Cash, "The Sermon in *Tristram Shandy,*" 401. Cash argues that Sterne denies the possibility of an unconscious and is anti-Freudian in his psychology.

13. Caruth, *Unclaimed Experience,* 1–6.

14. Ibid., 3.

15. Lamb, *Sterne's Fiction and the Double Principle,* 59, 62.

16. Freud, *Beyond the Pleasure Principle,* 19.

17. Freud, "From the History of an Infantile Neurosis," 123–24.

18. Freud, "Screen Memories," 124.
19. Moglen, *The Philosophical Irony of Laurence Sterne*, 119.
20. Bloom and Bloom, "'This Fragment of Life,'" 58.
21. Ibid., 61.
22. New, "Sterne, Warburton, and the Burden of Exuberant Wit," 258.
23. Hawley, "The Anatomy of *Tristram Shandy*," 84; Sagal, "An Hobby-Horse Well Worth Giving a Description Of," 105.
24. Christopher Fanning argues for the "interactive" nature of the text as a "point of contact" between reader and author and insists that the materiality of the text is vital to its proper reception ("Sterne and Print Culture," 125). See also Dale, "Dolly's Inch of Red Seal Wax," 133–51; and Chibka, "Every Jerkin Has a Quicksilver Lining," 121–32. Both authors comment on the narrative's capacity to shuttle back and forth between minds. Dale sees this as a process of authorial transmission wherein Tristram imprints the reader's mind with his own impressions ("Dolly's Inch of Red Seal Wax," 133).
25. William Warner was among the first to take up the novel as an object of cultural production that serves as a mode of "entertainment" or a "reprieve" from real life (*Licensing Entertainment*, 1–44, 46).
26. Simpson, "At This Moment in Space," 149, 155; Freeman, "Delight in the Disorder of Things," 141. See also Hunter, "Clocks, Calendars, and Names," 175–76. James Swearingen argues that the novel pushes back against the linear temporality of empiricism (*Reflexivity in Tristram Shand*, 59).
27. Swearingen sees memory as the replacement for linear time (*Reflexivity in Tristram Shandy*, 70) whereas Jeffrey Williams posits an implied linear chronology to the novel ("Narrative of Narratives," 1043). Another critical trend reads the tragedy of the birth as a paradox that underscores time's tyrannical system (Keymer, *Sterne, the Moderns, and the Novel*, 383).
28. Lupton, "*Tristram Shandy*, David Hume and Epistemological Fication"; Lamb, *Sterne's Fiction and the Double Principle*; Moglen, *The Philosophical Irony of Laurence Sterne*.
29. Alryyes, "Uncle Toby and the Bullet's Story in Laurence Sterne's *Tristram Shandy*"; Traugott, *Tristram Shandy's World*.
30. Nowka, "Talking Coins and Thinking Smoke-Jacks."
31. Porter, "Against the Spleen," 93; New, "Sterne and the Modernist Moment," 168–69; Traugott, *Tristram Shandy's World*, 47.
32. Moglen, *The Philosophical Irony of Laurence Sterne*; Sagal, "An Hobby-Horse Well Worth Giving a Description Of."
33. Carol Houlihan Flynn argues that the medical genesis of the hobbyhorse is derived from a machine invented by George Cheyne that was designed

to move matter and thereby heal humoral imbalance ("Running Out of Matter," 147–85).

34. New, *Laurence Sterne as Satirist*, 76–79, 145; Chibka, "The Hobby-Horse's Epitaph," 125–51.
35. Cash, "The Lockean Psychology of *Tristram Shandy*."
36. Alryyes, "Uncle Toby and the Bullet's Story in Laurence Sterne's *Tristram Shandy*."
37. For Sterne's relationship to Augustan modes of satire: New, *Laurence Sterne as Satirist*. For his relationship, more specifically, to the Scribblerian mode of Menippean satire, see Fanning, "Small Particles of Eloquence."
38. Although the healing capacity of the hobbyhorse is not the dominant focus of critical attention, both Helene Moglen and Jonathan Lamb briefly note this aspect of the definition (Moglen, *The Philosophical Irony of Laurence Sterne*, 87, and Lamb, *Sterne's Fiction and the Double Principle*, 40).
39. Flynn, "Running Out of Matter," 148.
40. Porter "Against the Spleen," 85; Loveridge, "Liberty in *Tristram Shandy*," 127–28; Hawley, "The Anatomy of *Tristram Shandy*," 37–38; Hunter, "Clocks, Calendars, and Names," 182; Freeman, "Delight in the Disorder of Things," 142–44, 150–58; Alryyes, "Uncle Toby and the Bullet's Story in Laurence Sterne's *Tristram Shandy*," 1110, 1119.
41. Judith Hawley notes the pun on "fortification" in the text as both a physical structure and a psychological "defense mechanism" (Hawley, "*Tristram Shandy*, Learned Wit, and Enlightenment Knowledge," 37).
42. Yates, *The Art of Memory*, xi.
43. The *Oxford English Dictionary* definitions 1a and 1b align with the notion that history is a record of factual, public events in time. Definition 1b presumes that history is "truthful." Definition 2a, on the other hand, predominated in the eighteenth century and simply implied a "record of past events." Presumably, these could be either personal or public, and as either part of a truthful or fictional account. See also Definition II. 7a and b for a similar meaning; definition II 8 accounts for the assimilation of the term "history" in the origins of the novel, for here it connoted a voyage or journey that was popularly mocked in satires of the romance narrative.
44. Porter, "Against the Spleen," 93; New, "Sterne and the Modernist Moment," 16–69; Traugott, *Tristram Shandy's World*, 47.
45. Noë, *Out of Our Heads*, 4.
46. James Swearingen's phenomenological reading of the text supports my argument. In that reading, Swearingen's ecstatic view of time allows us to transcend the limits of the material world and form new possibilities (*Reflexivity in Tristram Shandy*, 119, 250, 252).

47. Sedgwick, *Between Men*.
48. See Harries, "Words, Sex, and Gender in Sterne's Novel," 111–24. Harries delivers an account of sexual innuendo's role in the novel's "double function" of "objects" (111).
49. Lamb, *Sterne's Fiction and the Double Principle*, 50.
50. Chibka, "The Hobby-Horse's Epitaph."
51. Addison, *Spectator Papers*, nos. 411–21 (1712).
52. On how the artillery mirrors Swift's diminutive satire, see New, *Laurence Sterne as Satirist*, 69.
53. Moglen, *The Philosophical Irony of Laurence Sterne*, 59, 84; New, *Laurence Sterne as Satirist*, 164–67, 204. Alryyes's historical investigation into the science of the bullet presents a fresh take on the phrase "war games" ("Uncle Toby and the Bullet's Story in Laurence Sterne's *Tristram Shandy*," 1109).
54. Moglen characterizes the amours as an "anti-romance" narrative (*The Philosophical Irony of Laurence Sterne*, 118–19). New sees the affair as akin to Toby's "mock battles" on the bowling green, since he views both as "imitations of the real thing" (*Laurence Sterne as Satirist*, 204).
55. Lamb, *Sterne's Fiction and the Double Principle*, 69.
56. Flynn, "Running Out of Matter," 147–49. If we take Flynn's definition of the hobbyhorse into account, then Toby's need to return to the bowling green is a medical and physiological imperative.
57. Lupton, "*Tristram Shandy*, David Hume and Epistemological Fiction," 98–99.
58. Lamb, *Sterne's Fiction and the Double Principle*, 118; Flynn, "Running Out of Matter," 173; Lupton, "*Tristram Shandy*, David Hume and Epistemological Fiction," 101.
59. Zimmerman, "*Tristram Shandy* and Narrative Representation," 136.

3. EVELINA AND THE VIRTUES OF MEMORY

1. Brown, *Ends of Empire*, 86, 89.
2. Ferguson, "Rape and the Rise of the Novel," 91.
3. Moretti, *The Way of the World*, 16.
4. Ibid., 22–23.
5. Ibid., 68.
6. Ibid., 69.
7. Ibid., 35.
8. Bakhtin, "The *Bildungsroman* and Its Significance in the History of Realism," 23.
9. For a longer account of this divide, see the introduction to this book.
10. Armstrong, *How Novels Think*; McKeon, *The Origins of the English Novel*; Watt, *The Rise of the Novel*.

11. In this, I join Amit Yahav, whose recent study provides us with an alternative reading of the novel's rise that focuses on time's "qualities," "intensities," and "variations" (*Feeling Time*, 3).
12. Kramnick, *Actions and Objects*, 25.
13. Ibid., 3, 5.
14. Ibid., 6–8, passim.
15. See, e.g., Lamb, Lynch, Park, and Wall.
16. Kramnick, *Actions and Objects*, 25.
17. Ibid., 3.
18. This notion of consciousness as linked to agency and memory echoes what Antonio Damasio would later call "extended consciousness." The concept of "extended consciousness" in neuropsychology is notably different from early empiricist concepts of mind. The phrase "extended consciousness" presumes that extension can be a property of time, not merely matter or substance (unlike time in John Locke's *Essay*). Neuropsychological understandings of the mind in time consider the possibility of a type of human consciousness that can occupy multiple temporalities at once, thereby exceeding the limits of chronological, or successive, duration illustrated in Locke's *Essay*: "Extended consciousness goes beyond the here and now . . . both backward and forward. The here and now is still there, but it is flanked by the past . . . and, just as importantly, it is flanked by the anticipated future. . . . Extended consciousness . . . may span the entire life of an individual, from the cradle to the future, and it can place the world beside it" (*The Feeling of What Happens*, 195–96). My claims regarding various types of self-consciousness and their relationship to time in the early novel reveal the genre's innovative contributions to theories of mind-body relations long before the work of popular neuroscientists such as Damasio.
19. Moretti, *The Way of the World*, 16.
20. For works that consider complexities that arise from philosophical and novelistic accounts of sympathy in the eighteenth century, see Mullan, *Sentiment and Sociability*, Marshall, *The Surprising Effects of Sympathy*; David Fairer, "Sentimental Translation in Mackenzie and Sterne," 161–80; Csengei, *Sympathy, Sensibility, and the Literature of Feeling in the Eighteenth Century*; Nazar, *Enlightened Sentiments*.
21. Lamb, *The Things Things Say*, 69.
22. Smith, *The Theory of Moral Sentiments*, 11–12.
23. Hume, *A Treatise of Human Nature*, 2.2.9, 245–46.
24. Kramnick, *Actions and Objects*, 8.
25. Pino, "Burney's Evelina and Aesthetics in Action," 275–78, 269.

26. According to Gabrielle Starr, the novel's engagement with taste brings about a problematic portrayal of women as both subjects and objects ("Burney, Ovid, and the Value of the Beautiful," 84). For Park, this status of women as objects has more to do with the fashion industry and a cultural fetishization of mechanical objects (*The Self and It*, 38, 145).
27. Lynch, *Economy of Character*, 165, 166, 178.
28. Zunshine, *Why We Read Fiction*, 6.
29. Vermeule, *Why Do We Care about Literary Characters?*, 34.
30. When Palmer extends theory of mind to our reading of fictional thought processes, he considers how literature mediates text and world, and how minds read and operate through their engagement with textual signs (*Fictional Minds*, 1–27).
31. Park defines female automatism as follows: The growing absorption in what it means to be a machine produced a mechanics of affect. Burney indicates the cultural evolution of the automaton in the eighteenth century when, in . . . *Evelina* (1778), venues such as Cox's Mechanical Museum featured as stopping points in the heroine's fashionable London excursions. . . . In Burney's world, the uncertainty of existing on social and psychic borderlines threatens to produce the self as an abject spectacle of automated being, divided form her individual and rational self" (*The Self and It*, xxvii). Lynch associates automatism with motion: "Seeming to work by themselves, but not working for their selves, automatons emblemized the ambiguities built into that new insistence on conjoining identity and activity" (*The Economy of Character*, 192).
32. Park equates the shame experienced by Burney's heroines with the etymology of "mortification," emphasizing how this type of self-consciousness renders subjects into objects: "These frequent moments of 'mortification' . . . render them as much little corpses as little dolls shaped by both propriety and fashion" (*The Self and It*, 132).
33. Yahav, *Feeling Time*, 10.
34. Smith, *The Theory of Moral Sentiments*, 11.
35. Patricia Meyer Spacks argues that "autonomy" for Burney is always less desirable than "sympathy" (*Imagining a Self*, 45).
36. The rhetoric of inconsistent "action" that I use here should not be confused with the "inconsistent" subjectivity or "identity" that Leanne Maunu discusses in *Women Writing the Nation*. Maunu expresses an anxiety about the status of "mutability" in this novel: "Identities should be fixed, should be stable," she argues, and yet this complicates the parameters of novelistic *Bildung* (53). Gabrielle Starr's reading of the novel's relationship to

"mutability" as the "hallmark of aesthetics" is more in line with my rhetoric ("Burney, Ovid, and the Value of the Beautiful," 78). Starr also considers the dangers of mutability in her reading, linking this to the metamorphic properties of sensibility and the passions (97, 99).

37. I counter the assumption that writing in the sentimental novel is necessarily an authentic expression of selfhood or agency (Straub, *Divided Fictions*, 153, 157, 170). The shift in Evelina's narrative style over the course of the novel reveals that writing by itself should not necessarily be confounded with authority or self-agency. Evelina writes long before she attains autonomy.
38. For a counterargument to my own about the novel's resolution, see: Newton, "*Evelina*," 79.
39. My argument counters Park's claim that Evelina's "complete and triumphant metamorphosis is questionable" since her marriage "leave[s] [her], in circular fashion, with [a] husband" who simply supplants the "paternal mentor figure" (*The Self and It*, 132).
40. In reading Evelina as a subject who attains psychological enlightenment by the end of the novel, I depart from Lynch's and Park's ultimate argument about the woman as automaton. Park especially sees Evelina as inevitably bound to a status of objecthood as she is obliged to follow the conditions of patriarchy (*The Self and It*, 148).
41. Laura Brown reads the monkey as implicitly representative of the "violent" potential of the heterosexual "marriage prospect"; the monkey defies the novel's ideals of "companionate marriage" and feminine "conduct" (*Homeless Dogs and Melancholy Apes*, 91–111).
42. Park argues that fashion dissolves the boundaries between person and thing (*The Self and It*, 38). Lynch also discusses the risks of fashion on personhood; however, she sees fashion as a possible venue for self-construction in its dependence on decision-making (*The Economy of Character*, 185). Lynch poses an interesting dialectical problem that complicates Park's notion of the relationship between the self and consumerism. However, I would argue that the kind of self-making in Lynch's description is transient, offering a fleeting form of self-recognition that never attains the form of self-consciousness I demonstrate in Evelina's reflections at the end of the novel.
43. Park, *The Self and It*, 135.
44. Fashionable people function like automata, Park argues, in that they are always "signs and referents of something else" (*The Self and It*, 145).
45. Park, *The Self and It*, 23.
46. I am not the first to suggest that the theatrical portions of the text provide a contrast to Burney's new project for the novel. See Michals, "'Like a Spoiled Actress off the Stage,'" 191; Nachumi, *Acting Like a Lady*, 124, 125, 128.

47. Park considers the eighteenth-century novel as an empirical form that by "mediating human subjectivity through an object" of the text renders the reader a common thing (*The Self and It*, xxi).
48. I echo here the manner in which Lynch reads eighteenth-century character, not "as our fellow traveler through time and the expressive analogue to ourselves" (*The Economy of Character*, 2) but as a semiotic system of cultural referents.

4. STRANGE CONCUSSIONS OF NATURE

1. Pinch, *Strange Fits of Passion*, 161.
2. Ibid., 162–63, passim.
3. Ibid., 162.
4. Curran, "Charlotte Smith," 179.
5. Pinch, *Strange Fits of Passion*, 63.
6. See Bloom, *The Anxiety of Influence*.
7. Andrews, "Herself . . . Fills the Foreground," 15–18; Behrendt, "Charlotte Smith, Women Poets, and the Culture of Celebrity," 202.
8. Pinch, *Strange Fits of Passion*, 66.
9. Sandy, *Romanticism, Memory, and Mourning*, 64, 63.
10. Duckling, "Tell my Name to Distant Ages," 204.
11. Andrews, "Herself . . . Fills the Foreground," 15–18.
12. See especially Labbe, "Introduction," in *Charlotte Smith in British Romanticism*, 2.
13. Porter, "From Nosegay to Specimen Cabinet," 44.
14. From Coleridge, "Frost at Midnight," 120.
15. Brewer, "Charlotte Smith's Celestina and the Rousseauvian Moral Self," 240–45; Astbury, "Charlotte Smith's The Banished Man in French Translation," 131; Garnai, "The Alien Act and Negative Cosmopolitanism," 101–12.
16. Amy Garnai compares Smith's *The Letters of a Solitary Wanderer* with Rousseau's *Reveries of the Solitary Walker* ("The Alien Act and Negative Cosmopolitanism," 109). William Brewer compares Celestina with Rousseau's Julie ("Charlotte Smith's Celestina and the Rousseauvian Moral Self," 231).
17. For an account of the issue of the "hard problem" as it relates to mind and matter in eighteenth-century literature, see Kramnick, *Actions and Objects*, 1–60.
18. I am not the first to note Charlotte Smith's self-conscious allusion to the pleasures of poetic posterity: see Curran, "Charlotte Smith," 179; and Behrendt, "Charlotte Smith, Women Poets, and the Culture of Celebrity," 201.

19. Pinch, *Strange Fits of Passion*, 53–58.
20. Particularly, I have in mind Wordsworth's poem, "A slumber did my spirit seal," in Wordsworth, *The Major Works*, 147.
21. Suzie Park applies the term "compulsory narration" to Smith's sensibility novels. She characterizes Smith's descriptions of feeling in *Emmeline* as a technology that "challenges demands for 'more' persuasive representations of depth" ("Compulsory Narration, Sentimental Interface," 180). Similarly, Smith's description of memory leaves something to be desired at this moment, but it does so in a manner that challenges eighteenth-century concepts of memory as an association machine.
22. See, for example, Jonathan Swift's "The Lady's Dressing Room," wherein radical fancy leads to widespread misassociation (*The Writings of Jonathan Swift*, 535).
23. See chapter 5 for a full discussion of eighteenth-century nostalgia. This relates to Smith's treatment of nostalgia in *Celestina*.
24. See Douglas Murray's analysis of this pattern in Jane Austen's later novel, *Mansfield Park* ("Spectatorship in Mansfield Park," 1–26).
25. Lorraine Fletcher attributes these citations to James Thomson, and perhaps Robert Colvill; however, the latter reference remains unclear. See footnotes 3 and 4 on page 291 of the Broadview edition of the text.
26. All citations of James Thomson's *The Seasons* are taken from *The Seasons*, ed. James Sambrook (Oxford: Oxford University Press, 1981).
27. Lorraine Fletcher identifies the quotation's source in footnotes 1 and 2 on page 308 of the Broadview edition. However, as with the quotation from Thomson above, I flesh out the lines in full, looking at their connection to the larger verse paragraphs as they appear within Thomson's poem so as to catch the purpose of Smith's reference.
28. For fuller accounts of the reviews of both of Smith's contemporaries, see: Duckling, "Tell my Name to Distant Ages," 208, and Markley, "Charlotte Smith, The Godwin Circle, and the Proliferation of Speakers in *The Young Philosopher*," 93.
29. Even here, Celestina's reading seems referential. The author could be alluding to Tobias Smollett or Laurence Sterne.
30. I borrow this phrase "turning away" from Jonathan Culler's famous work on apostrophe in the Romantic lyric to emphasize the shared structure between Celestina's only lyric and the novel's momentary departure from a mind-body dialectic. With her choice of literary form, Smith seems to imply the dangers of self-enclosed consciousness. In turning away from nature, Celestina also "turns away" from her listener, or audience, into a kind of radical interiority (Culler, *The Pursuit of Signs*, 138).

31. See, in particular, Brewer, "Charlotte Smith's *Celestina* and the Rousseauvian Moral Self," 241, and Garnai, "The Alien Act and Negative Cosmopolitanism in *The Letters of a Solitary Wanderer*," 108.

5. WISTFUL THINKING

1. Kelly, "Austen and Enclosure," 1–14; François, *Open Secrets*, 256, 257. These readings, along with my own, defy what Janet Todd has said about the novel: "In fact hedgerows play little part in *Mansfield Park*" (*The Cambridge Introduction to Jane Austen*, 81).
2. Although there is much critical work on the role of prospects in Austen's *Mansfield Park*, most notable is Nicholas Williams's essay, for it touches on the relationship between prospects and memory in the novel ("Literally or Figuratively?," 317–23), specially p. 318.
3. "Confabulation denotes the emergence of memories of experiences and events which never took place": Nahum, Guggisberg, Bouzerda-Wahlen, et al., "Forms of Confabulation," 2524–34 (see abstract).
4. Of course, I am not the first to investigate the overlap between memory and imagination in Austen's works. In his essay "Jane Austen and the Perils of Mental Time Travel," Alan Richardson discusses the relationship between memory and imagination in Austen's novels as related to recent theories of neuroplasticity in cognitive science. Like Richardson, I stage various scenes in *Mansfield Park* in which memory becomes infiltrated by imaginative desire. However, my reading of transactive memory in Austen's novel leads me to a different conclusion from Richardson in his account of this novel. Richardson reads Fanny's imaginative memories as productive of "peril." On the other hand, I show how they reconstruct reality so as to heal psychological distress, produce pleasure, and reify desire (Richardson, "Jane Austen and the Perils of Mental Time Travel," 66). To use Kay Young's term for Austenian neuroplasticity, I read *Mansfield Park* as in an early novelistic tradition of cognitive "resilience" (Young, "Resilience and Jane Austen," 212.)
5. Dames, *Amnesiac Selves*, 74.
6. Ibid., 23.
7. Ibid., 16.
8. Lynch, *The Economy of Character*, 213–20, 238–39; Zunshine, "Why Jane Austen Was Different, and Why We May Need Cognitive Science to See It," 275–98; Pinch, *Strange Fits of Passion*, 137–63.
9. Freud, "Screen Memories," 124.
10. Goodman, "Romantic Poetry and the Science of Nostalgia," 195–215, and "'Uncertain Disease,'" 197–227; Dames, *Amnesiac Selves*, 23–34. See also Dames, "Nostalgia," 413–21.

11. Goodman, "Romantic Poetry and the Science of Nostalgia, 196; "Uncertain Disease," 199, 201, 208.
12. Goodman, "Uncertain Disease," 204 (my emphasis).
13. Ibid., 208.
14. Dames, "Nostalgia," 417, and *Amnesiac Selves*, 20-75.
15. See, for example, Nina Auerbach's reading of nostalgia and immobility in the novel (*Romantic Imprisonment*, 22-37). Lionel Trilling also claims that the novel privileges "rest over motion" (*The Opposing Self*, 185, 186-88). Lorraine Clark's work on reflection in *Mansfield Park* is an exception to this trend in Austen criticism ("Remembering Nature," 353-79).
16. Doody, "A Good Memory Is Unpardonable," 67-94. See also Greenfield, "The Absent-Minded Heroine," 347.
17. Lamont, "Jane Austen and the Old," 669.
18. For unflattering portrayals of Austen's heroine, see Auerbach, *Romantic Imprisonment*; Trilling, *The Opposing Self*, and Tanner, *Jane Austen*, 142-75.
19. Galperin, *The Historical Austen*, 4, 61, 69, 73, 130; Hofkosh, "The Illusionist," 101-11.
20. Galperin's and Hofkosh's work can be read as a pushback against Alistair Duckworth's claim that the imagination is a site of limitation in Austen's novels (*Improvement of the Estate*, 33-34).
21. Hofkosh, "The Illusiuonist," 110
22. Baier, *Postures of Mind*, 19.
23. Sherman, *Telling Time*. Additionally, in his reading of this episode, Colin Jager notes that "by the late seventeenth century London produced more watches and clocks than any other European city, and historians have noted the link between the rationalization of time and the increase in watch production. . . . By 1700, the minute hand had made its appearance, and it is to this that Edmund appeals" (*The Book of God*, 149).
24. Lynn Voskuil's reading differs from my own but acknowledges the distinctive ways that both characters read time and space ("Sotherton and the Geography of Empire," 601). See also Anne-Lise François's reading, which emphasizes the characters' differing modes of speech as literal versus figural (*Open Secrets*, 246).
25. Banfield, "The Moral Landscape of Mansfield Park," 3-7, and "The Influence of Place," 28-48; Skinner, "Exploring Space," 126-48; Valihora, "Impartial Spectatorship," 89-114; Clark, "Remembering Nature," 360; Park, "What the Eye Cannot See," 169-81; Wall, "The Impress of the Invisible," 996; Rohrbach, "Austen's Later Subjects," 738; Auerbach, *Romantic Imprisonment*, 5, 7, 21.

26. This dichotomy seems to have a critical origin in Alastair Duckworth's claims about the evils of improvement in the novel (*The Improvement of the Estate*, ix, 39, 54). See also Clark, "Remembering Nature," 365; and Auerbach, *Romantic Imprisonment*, 24, 35, 36. Notably, Douglas Murray disrupts this trend in Austen criticism by claiming that all characters in the novel are improvers ("Spectatorship in Mansfield Park," 3–5). Important to my own reading is the manner in which he links the notion of spatial "overlooking" to fictionalized, or "retouched," memories in *Mansfield Park* ("Spectatorship in Mansfield Park," 11). Most recently, Alan Richardson strategically unites these two distinct temporal perspectives in Austen studies when he claims: "What critics have failed to note as of yet concerns the intimate linkage found throughout Austen's fictional works between imagination and memory, interrelated mental faculties that can function—or malfunction—together for good or ill" ("Jane Austen and the Perils of Mental Time Travel, 58).
27. Most critics read the episode as charged with sexual innuendo and as an allegory that foreshadows the novel's forthcoming events: Stevenson, "Slipping into the Ha-Ha," 309–39; Banfield, "The Moral Landscape of Mansfield Park," 10–11; Skinner, "Exploring Space," 147; Duckworth, *The Improvement of the Estate*, 25; Todd, *The Cambridge Introduction to Jane Austen*, 87–88. Although her reading of the ha-ha counters my own, Julie Park relates the ha-ha to perspectival forms of consciousness ("What the Eye Cannot See," 177).
28. Sun Lee, "Austen's Scale-Making," 173.
29. See especially Margaret Anne Doody's work on the use of hyperbole, personification and allegory in *Mansfield Park* ("Turns of Speech and Figures of Mind," 165–84). Her claim regarding how "geographical locations" as metaphors help to "draw physical reality into fantasy" is especially key to my reading of metaphor and illusion in the novel (178).
30. François, *Open Secrets*, 245.
31. I use distraction not in a negative sense here but as referring to a type of simultaneous and multidirectional concentration. This is what Natalie Phillips has called the "multifocal" model of distraction in eighteenth-century literature (*Distraction*, 7). She characterizes Austen as a masterful illustrator and promoter of this style of attention (*Distraction*, 28, 174–211).
32. Hofkosh, "The Illusionist," 102.
33. Most especially Stevenson, "Slipping into the Ha-Ha," 309–39.
34. See Daniel O'Quinn's analysis of Rushworth's memory, which he explores in relation to the *Lovers Vows* performance scenes ("Jane Austen and Performance," 381–82).

35. To some extent, I push back against Colin Jager's claims about the autonomous nature of feeling in the novel (*The Book of God*, 124, 134). The strange way that consciousness crosses the boundary between interiority and externality also complicates what Deidre Lynch has argued about the legibility of character and consciousness (*The Economy of Character*, 215–16).
36. This is similar to what cognitive science calls "source misattribution," in that the source of the information is misattributed to a personal memory or experience (Schacter, *The Seven Sins of Memory*, 88–111).
37. David Marshall introduces the various implications of the verb "to act" in the novel when he considers the difference between actors and roles (*The Frame of Art*, 76, 78).
38. Valihora, "Impartial Spectator Meets Picturesque Toursit," 111; Doody, "Turns of Speech and Figures of Mind," 177; Johnson, *Jane Austen*, 116; Festa, "The Noise in Mansfield Park," 453.
39. McGrail, "Fanny Price's 'Customary' Subjectivity," 57–70 (see especially p. 66).
40. I am not the first to associate Fanny's consciousness with styles of acting. As Joseph Litvak notes, the theater survives throughout *Mansfield Park* in a "less conspicuous form" (*Caught in the Act*, 3). For Litvak, acting in everyday life is also part and parcel of the novel's "leitmotif" of "boundary-confusion" (*Caught in the Act*, 8). Insofar as this definition of theatricality bears on the line between mind and world, fiction and reality, my argument about fiction in this chapter is indebted to his work. Emily Hodgson Anderson's work on theater as a conduit for expressing "individual desires" (14) also makes a noteworthy connection between fiction and fact, private consciousness and performativity. Her "epilogue" speaks to this fusion in *Mansfield Park* (*Eighteenth-Century Authorship and the Play of Fiction*, 133–39). Likewise, Misty Anderson notes that the theater in *Mansfield Park* is a space for realizing "fantasy" and acting out desire ("Different Sorts of Friendship," 174). By considering the theater as a space of real feeling, critics such as Hodgson Anderson and Anderson conflate theatricality with true consciousness itself. See also Nachumi, *Acting Like a Lady*, 166–69.
41. Wood, "Time and Her Aunt," 199.
42. Lionel Trilling writes of Austen's irony that it is "only secondarily a matter of tone. . . . It perceives the world through an awareness of its contradictions, paradoxes, and anomalies" (*The Opposing Self*, 181). Likewise, D. A. Miller underscores the "numerous binaries that burrow through *any* Austen sentence, and open this unit of Style to the additional closure of matched-up opposites" (*Jane Austen, or the Secret of Style*, 84).

43. Dames, "Nostalgia," 420.
44. Miller, *Jane Austen, or the Secret of Style*, 84.
45. Dames, *Amnesiac Selves*, 58.
46. I read "charm" antithetically to Nina Auerbach (*Romantic Imprisonment*, 22, 24, 35).
47. Arendt, *The Human Condition*, 52 (my emphasis).
48. Abrams, *The Mirror and the Lamp*, i–vii.
49. On architectural metaphors for mind in the novel, see Rohrbach, "Austen's Later Subjects," 738, 740.
50. This is M. H. Abrams's phrase in *The Correspondent Breeze*.
51. My argument counters Barbara Benedict's claims about the role of things in Austen's novels ("The Trouble with Things," 346).
52. My reading of the legibility of objects and allegory expands on Alistair Duckworth's concept of the estate in Jane Austen's novels (*The Improvement of the Estate*, 38, 40).
53. On Derrida's idea of the gift in this novel, see: Elliot, "Gifts Always Come with Strings Attached," 50–59, and McGrail, "Fanny Price's 'Customary' Subjectivity," 67. Claudia Johnson also notes, with Fanny, "Austen explores the sinister aspects of benevolence and the burden of gratitude it places on a recipient" (*Jane Austen*, 107). Here I borrow Johnson's phrase "revolution of mind," which she deploys to characterize the many vicissitudes of Fanny's consciousness in the novel (120).
54. Valihora, "Impartial Spectatorship Meets Picturesque Tourist," 95; Auerbach, *Romantic Imprisonment*, 24, 35–36.
55. Pinch, *Strange Fits of Passion*, 137–63.
56. Greenfield, "The Absent-Minded Heroine," 338.
57. Kramnick, *Actions and Objects*, 25.
58. Juliet McMaster characterizes this mode of reading in Austen's novel as a type of symptom checking (*Jane Austen, the Novelist*, 122).
59. Again, I draw an implicit connection here in my reading of *Mansfield Park* to Adela Pinch's reading of *Persuasion* in *Strange Fits of Passion* (137–63).
60. Nina Auerbach comments that the "action" of the novel "happens as [Fanny] wills. . . . In its essence, the world of *Mansfield Park* is terrifyingly malleable" (*Romantic Imprisonment*, 36).
61. François, *Open Secrets*, 224.
62. Galperin, "The Missed Opportunities of Mansfield Park," 123.
63. Dames, "Nostalgia," 416.
64. Sonia Hofkosh remarks on how these lines rupture the illusory nature of Austen's text ("The Illusionist," 107–8).
65. Galperin, "Missed Opportunities," 127–9.

66. Warner, *Licensing Entertainment*, 1–44.
67. Lupton, "Contingency, Codex, and the Eighteenth-Century Novel," 1183.

AFTERTHOUGHTS

1. Barnes, *The Sense of an Ending*, 18.
2. Ishiguro, *The Buried Giant*, 317.
3. Barnes, *The Sense of an Ending*, 163.
4. McEwan, *Atonement*, 349–51.
5. Carruthers, *The Book of Memory*, 1.
6. Kahneman, *Thinking Fast and Slow*, 46.
7. Taylor and Brown, "Illusion and Wellbeing," 193–210, 194.
8. Ibid., 198, 199.
9. I transcribe the letter here according to my own findings. However, a reprinted version (with some slight variations) can be found in *Jane Austen's Letters*, 4th ed., edited by Deidre Le Faye (Oxford: Oxford University Press, 2011), 66.
10. Taylor and Brown, "Illusion and Wellbeing," 194.
11. Kahneman, *Thinking Fast and Slow*, 39–40.

❖ BIBLIOGRAPHY ❖

Abrams, M. H. *The Correspondent Breeze: Essays on English Romanticism.* New York: W. W. Norton, 1984.

———. *The Mirror and the Lamp: Romantic Theory and the Critical Tradition.* Oxford: Oxford University Press, 1953.

Addison, Joseph, and Richard Steele. *The Spectator.* Edited by Donald F. Bond. 5 vols. Oxford: Clarendon Press, 1987.

Alryyes, Ala. "Uncle Toby and the Bullet's Story in Laurence Sterne's *Tristram Shandy.*" ELH 82, no. 4 (2015): 1109–34.

Anderson, Misty. "The Different Sorts of Friendship: Desire in Mansfield Park." In *Jane Austen and Discourses of Feminism,* edited by Devoney Looser, 167–84. New York: St. Martin's Press, 1995.

Andrews, Kerri. "'Herself . . . Fills the Foreground': Negotiating Autobiography in *The Elegiac Sonnets* and *The Emigrants.*" In *Charlotte Smith in British Romanticism,* edited by Jacqueline Labbe, 13–28. London: Pickering and Chatto, 2008.

Arendt, Hannah. *The Human Condition.* Chicago: University of Chicago Press, 1958.

Armstrong, Nancy. *How Novels Think: The Limits of Individualism from 1719–1900.* New York: Columbia University Press, 2005.

Astbury, Katherine. "Charlotte Smith's The Banished Man in French Translation; or The Politics of Novel-Writing during the French Revolution." In *Charlotte Smith in British Romanticism,* edited by Jacqueline Labbe, 129–43. London: Pickering and Chatto, 2008.

Auerbach, Nina. *Romantic Imprisonment: Women and Other Glorified Outcasts.* New York: Columbia University Press, 1985.

Austen, Jane. *Jane Austen's Letters.* Edited by Deidre Le Faye. 4th ed. Oxford: Oxford University Press, 2011.

———. *Mansfield Park*. Edited by Claudia L. Johnson. New York: W. W. Norton, 1998.

———. *Pride and Prejudice*. Edited by Donald Gray. New York and London: W. W. Norton, 2001.

Backsheider, Paula. "Defoe: The Man and the Works." In *The Cambridge Companion to Daniel Defoe*, edited by John Richetti, 5–24. Cambridge: Cambridge University Press, 2008.

Baier, Annette. "Cartesian Persons." In *Postures of the Mind: Essays on Mind and Morals*. Minneapolis: University of Minnesota Press, 1985.

———. "Mixing Memory and Desire." In *Postures of the Mind: Essays on Mind and Morals*. Minneapolis: University of Minnesota Press, 1985.

Bakhtin, Mikhail. "The *Bildungsroman* and Its Significance in the History of Realism (Toward a Historical Typology of the Novel)." In *Speech Genres and Other Late Essays*. Translated by Vern W. McGee, edited by Caryl Emerson and Michael Holquist. Austin: University of Texas Press, 1986.

Banfield, Ann. "The Influence of Place: Jane Austen and the Novel of Social Consciousness." In *Jane Austen in a Social Context*, edited by David Monaghan, 28–48. Totowa, NJ: Barnes and Noble, 1981.

———. "The Moral Landscape of Mansfield Park." *Nineteenth-Century Fiction* 26, no. 1 (1971): 1–24.

Barnes, Julian. *The Sense of an Ending*. New York: Vintage Books, 2011.

Behrendt, Stephen. "Charlotte Smith, Women Poets, and the Culture of Celebrity." In *Charlotte Smith in British Romanticism*, edited by Jacqueline Labbe, 189–202. London: Pickering and Chatto, 2008.

Bender, John. *The Ends of Enlightenment*. Stanford, CA: Stanford University Press, 2012.

———. "The Novel as Modern Myth." In *Defoe's Footprints: Essays in Honor of Maximillian E. Novak*, edited by Robert M. Maniquis and Carl Fisher, 223–38. Toronto: University of Toronto Press, 2009.

Benedict, Barbara. "The Trouble with Things: Objects and Commodification of Sociability." In *A Companion to Jane Austen*, edited by Claudia Johnson and Clara Tuite, 343–54. Chichester: Blackwell, 2009.

Berkeley, George. *A Treatise Concerning the Principles of Human Knowledge*. Edited by Kenneth Winkler. Indianapolis: Hackett, 1994.

———. *Three Dialogues between Hylas and Philonous*. Edited by Robert Adams. Indianapolis: Hackett, 1979.

Bloom, Edward A., and Lillian D. Bloom, "'This Fragment of Life': From Process to Mortality." In *Laurence Sterne: Riddles and Mysteries*," edited by Valerie Grosvenor Myer. London: Vision Press, 1984.

Bloom, Harold. *The Anxiety of Influence: A Theory of Poetry*. 2nd ed. Oxford: Oxford University Press, 1997.
Brainerd, C. J., and V. F. Reyna, "Fuzzy Trace Theory and False Memory." *Current Directions in Psychological Science* 11, no. 5 (2002): 164–69.
Brewer, William. "Charlotte Smith's Celestina and the Rousseauvian Moral Self." *Eighteenth-Century Novel* 8 (2011): 240–45.
Brown, Laura. *Ends of Empire: Women and Ideology in Early Eighteenth-Century Literature*. Ithaca, NY: Cornell University Press, 1993.
———. *Homeless Dogs and Melancholy Apes: Humans and Other Animals in the Modern Literary Imagination*. Ithaca, NY: Cornell University Press, 2010.
Burney, Frances. *Evelina: Or the History of a Young Lady's Entrance into the World*. Edited by Vivien Jones and Edward Bloom. London: Oxford University Press, 2008.
Carruthers, Mary. *The Book of Memory: A Study of Memory in Medieval Culture*. 2nd ed. Cambridge: Cambridge University Press, 2008.
Caruth, Cathy. *Unclaimed Experience: Trauma, Narrative and History*. Baltimore, MD: Johns Hopkins University Press, 1996.
Cash, Arthur H. "The Lockean Psychology of *Tristram Shandy*." *ELH* 22, no. 2 (1955): 125–35.
———. "The Sermon in Tristram Shandy," *ELH* 31, no. 4 (1964): 401.
Chibka, Robert. "Every Jerkin Has a Quicksilver Lining: Tristram's Rumpled Dualisms." In *Sterne, Tristram, Yorick: Tercentenary Essays on Laurence Sterne*, edited by Melvyn New, Peter de Voogd, and Judith Hawley, 121–32. Newark: University of Delaware Press, 2016.
———. "The Hobby-Horse's Epitaph: Tristram Shandy, Hamlet, and the Vehicles of Memory." *Eighteenth-Century Fiction* 3, no. 2 (1991): 125–51.
Chico, Tita. *The Experimental Imagination: Literary Knowledge and Science in the British Enlightenment*. Stanford, CA: Stanford University Press, 2018.
Clark, Lorraine. "Remembering Nature: Soliloquy as Aesthetic Form in *Mansfield Park*." *Eighteenth-Century Fiction* 24, no. 2 (2011–12): 353–79.
Coleridge, Samuel Taylor. *Biographia Literaria*. Edited by James Engell and W. Jackson Bate. Princeton, NJ: Princeton University Press, 1983.
———. "Frost at Midnight." In *Coleridge's Poetry and Prose*. Edited by Nicholas Halmi, Paul Magnuson, and Raimonda Modiano, 120. New York: W. W. Norton, 2004.
Csengei, Ildiko. *Sympathy, Sensibility, and the Literature of Feeling in the Eighteenth Century*. Hampshire: Palgrave Macmillan, 2011.
Culler, Jonathan. *The Pursuit of Signs: Semiotics, Literature, Deconstruction*. Ithaca, NY: Cornell University Press, 2002.

Curran, Stuart. "Charlotte Smith: Intertextualities." In *Charlotte Smith in British Romanticism,* edited by Jacqueline Labbe, 175–88. London: Pickering and Chatto, 2008.

Dale, Amelia. "Dolly's Inch of Red Seal Wax, or, Impressing the Reader in *Tristram Shandy.*" In *Sterne, Tristram, Yorick: Tercentenary Essays on Laurence Sterne,* edited by Melvyn New, Peter de Voogd, and Judith Hawley, 133–51. Newark: University of Delaware Press, 2016.

Dames, Nicholas. *Amnesiac Selves: Nostalgia, Forgetting, and British Fiction: 1810–70.* Oxford: Oxford University Press, 2003.

———. "Nostalgia." In *A Companion to Jane Austen,* edited by Claudia Johnson and Clara Tuite, 413–21. Chichester: Blackwell, 2009.

Damasio, Antonio. *The Feeling of What Happens: Body and Emotion in the Making of Consciousness.* New York: Harcourt Brace, 1999.

Defoe, Daniel. *Robinson Crusoe.* Edited by Michael Shinagel. New York: W. W. Norton, 1994.

Descartes, René. *Discourse on Method and Meditations on the First Philosophy.* 4th ed. Translated by Donald Cress. Indianapolis: Hackett, 1998.

———. *The Treatise on Man.* In *The World and Other Writings,* edited by Stephen Gaukroger. Cambridge: Cambridge University Press, 1998.

Doody, Margaret Anne. "'A Good Memory Is Unpardonable': Self, Love, and the Irrational Irritation of Memory." *Eighteenth-Century Fiction* 14, no. 1 (2001): 67–94.

———. "Turns of Speech and Figures of Mind." In *A Companion to Jane Austen,* edited by Claudia Johnson and Clara Tuite, 165–84. Chichester: Blackwell, 2009.

Draaisma, Douwe. *Metaphors of Memory: A History of Ideas about the Mind.* Cambridge: Cambridge University Press, 2001.

———. *Why Life Speeds Up as You Get Older: How Memory Shapes Our Past.* Cambridge: Cambridge University Press, 2001.

Duckling, Louise. "'Tell my Name to Distant Ages': The Literary Fate of Charlotte Smith." In *Charlotte Smith in British Romanticism,* edited by Jacqueline Labbe, 203–18. London: Pickering and Chatto, 2008.

Duckworth, Alastair. *The Improvement of the Estate: A Study of Jane Austen's Novels.* Baltimore, MD: Johns Hopkins University Press, 1971.

Elliot, Dorice Williams. "Gifts Always Come with Strings Attached: Teaching *Mansfield Park* in the Context of Gift Theory." In *Approaches to Teaching Austen's Mansfield Park,* edited by Marcia McClintock Folsom and John Wiltshire, 50–59. New York: Modern Language Association of America, 2014.

Engell, James, *The Creative Imagination: Enlightenment to Romanticism*. Cambridge, MA: Harvard University Press, 1981.

Fairer, David. "Sentimental Translation in Mackenzie and Sterne." In *Translating Life: Studies in Transpositional Aesthetics*, edited by Shirley Chew and Alistair Stead, 161-80. Liverpool: Liverpool University Press, 1999.

Fanning, Christopher. "Small Particles of Eloquence: Sterne and the Scribblerian Text." *Modern Philology* 100, no. 3 (2003): 360-92.

———. "Sterne and Print Culture." In *A Cambridge Companion to Laurence Sterne*, edited by Thomas Keymer, 125-41. Cambridge: Cambridge University Press, 2009.

Ferguson, Frances. "Rape and the Rise of the Novel." *Representations* 20 (1987): 88-112.

Festa, Lynn. "Crusoe's Isle of Misfit Things." *Eighteenth Century* 52, no. 3-4 (2011): 443-71.

———. "The Noise in Mansfield Park." *Persuasions* 36 (2014): 151-64.

Folkenflik, Robert. "Robinson Crusoe and the Semiotic Crisis of the Eighteenth Century." In *Defoe's Footprints: Essays in Honor of Maximillian E. Novak*, edited by Robert M. Maniquis and Carl Fisher, 98-125. Toronto: University of Toronto Press, 2009.

Foucault, Michel. "What Is Enlightenment?" In *The Foucault Reader*, edited by Paul Rabinow. New York: Pantheon Books, 1984.

François, Anne-Lise. *Open Secrets: The Literature of Uncounted Experience*. Stanford, CA: Stanford University Press, 2008.

Freeman, John. "Delight in the Disorder of Things: *Tristram Shandy* and the Dynamics of Genre." *Studies in the Novel* 34, no. 2 (2002): 141-61.

Freud, Sigmund. *Beyond the Pleasure Principle*. Edited by James Strachey, introduction by Peter Gay. New York: W. W. Norton, 1961.

———. *A Child Is Being Beaten*. Edited by Ethel Spector Person. New Haven, CT: Yale University Press, 1997.

———. "From the History of an Infantile Neurosis" (1914). In *An Infantile Neurosis and Other Works*, vol. 17 of *The Complete Psychological Works of Sigmund Freud*. Edited by James Strachey with Anna Freud. London: Hogarth Press, 1917-19.

———. "Screen Memories" (1899). In vol. 3 of *The Complete Psychological Works of Sigmund Freud*. Edited by James Strachey with Anna Freud. London: Hogarth Press, 1917-19.

Gallagher, Catherine. "The Rise of Fictionality." In *The Novel*, edited by Franco Moretti, 2 vols., 1:336-63. Princeton, NJ: Princeton University Press, 2006.

Galperin, William. *The Historical Austen*. Philadelphia: University of Pennsylvania Press, 2003.

———. "The Missed Opportunities of Mansfield Park." In *A Companion to Jane Austen*, edited by Claudia Johnson and Clara Tuite, 123–32. Chichester: Blackwell, 2009.

Garnai, Amy. "The Alien Act and Negative Cosmopolitanism in *The Letters of a Solitary Wanderer*." In *Charlotte Smith in British Romanticism*, edited by Jacqueline Labbe, 101–12. London: Pickering and Chatto, 2008.

Garrett, Don. *Hume*. London: Routledge, 2015.

Gaskell, G. D., D. B Wright, and C. A. O'Muircheartaigh. "Telescoping of Landmark Events: Implications for Survey Research." *Public Opinion Quarterly*, 64, no. 1 (2000): 77–89.

Goldstein, Amanda Jo. *Sweet Science: Romantic Materialism and the Logics of New Life*. Chicago: University of Chicago Press, 2017.

Goodman, Kevis. *Georgic Modernity and British Romanticism: Poetry and the Mediation of History*. Cambridge: Cambridge University Press, 2004.

———. "Romantic Poetry and the Science of Nostalgia." In *The Cambridge Companion to British Romantic Poetry*. Edited by James Chandler and Maureen N. McLane, 195–215. Cambridge: Cambridge University Press, 2008.

———. "Uncertain Disease: Nostalgia, Pathologies of Motion, Practices of Reading." *Studies in Romanticism* 49, no. 2 (2010): 197–227.

Greenfield, Susan. "The Absent-Minded Heroine or, Elizabeth Bennet Has a Thought. *Eighteenth-Century Studies* 39, no. 3 (2006): 337–50.

Habermas, Jürgen. *The Structural Transformation of the Public Sphere: An Inquiry into a Category of Bourgeois Society*. Translated by Thomas Burger. Cambridge, MA: MIT Press, 1991.

Harries, Elizabeth. "Words, Sex, and Gender in Sterne's Novel." In *A Cambridge Companion to Laurence Sterne*, edited by Thomas Keymer, 111–24. Cambridge: Cambridge University Press, 2009.

Hawley, Judith. "The Anatomy of *Tristram Shandy*." In *Literature and Medicine during the Eighteenth Century*, edited by Marie Mulvey Roberts and Roy Porter, 84–100. New York: Routledge, 1993.

———. "*Tristram Shandy*, Learned Wit, and Enlightenment Knowledge." In *A Cambridge Companion to Laurence Sterne*, edited by Thomas Keymer, 34–48. Cambridge: Cambridge University Press, 2009.

Hobbes, Thomas. *Leviathan*. Edited by Richard Tuck. Cambridge: Cambridge University Press, 1996.

Hodgson Anderson, Emily. *Eighteenth-Century Authorship and the Play of Fiction: Novels and the Theater: Haywood to Austen*. New York: Routledge, 2009.

Hofkosh, Sonia. "The Illusionist: *Northanger Abbey* and Austen's Uses of Enchantment." In *A Companion to Jane Austen*, edited by Claudia Johnson and Clara Tuite, 101–11. Chichester: Blackwell, 2009.

Horkheimer, Max, and Theodor W. Adorno. *Dialectic of Enlightenment: Philosophical Fragments*. Edited by Gunzelin Schmid Noerr, translated by Edmund Jephcott. Stanford: Stanford University Press, 2002.

Houlihan Flynn, Carolyn. *The Body in Swift and Defoe*. Cambridge: Cambridge University Press, 2005.

———. "Running Out of Matter: The Body Exercised in Eighteenth-Century Fiction." In *The Languages of Psyche: Mind and Body in Enlightenment Thought*, edited by G.S Rousseau, 147–85. Berkeley: University of California Press, 1990.

Hume, David. *A Treatise of Human Nature*. Edited by David Norton and Mary Norton. Oxford: Oxford University Press, 2000.

Hunt, Kathryn, and Lars Chittka. "False Memory Susceptibility Is Correlated with Categorisation Ability in Humans." October 16, 2014. F1000Research.com.

Hunter, J. Paul. "Clocks, Calendars, and Names: The Troubles of Tristram and the Aesthetics of Uncertainty." In *Rhetorics of Order / Ordering Rhetorics in English Neoclassical Literature*, edited by Douglas Canfield and J. Paul Hunter, 173–205. Newark: University of Delaware Press, 1989.

———. *The Reluctant Pilgrim: Defoe's Emblematic Method and the Quest for Form in Robinson Crusoe*. Baltimore, MD: Johns Hopkins University Press, 1966.

Ishiguro, Kazuo. *The Buried Giant*. New York: Vintage Books, 2015.

Jager, Colin. *The Book of God: Secularization and Design in the Romantic Era*. Philadelphia: University of Pennsylvania Press, 2007.

Johnson, Claudia. *Jane Austen: Women, Politics, and the Novel*. Chicago: University of Chicago Press, 1988.

Johnson, Samuel. *The Rambler*, 41, August 7, 1750.

Jones, Wendy. *Jane on the Brain: Exploring the Science of Social Intelligence with Jane Austen*. New York: Pegasus Books, 2017.

Joyce, James. *Ulysses: The Corrected Text*. Edited by Hans Walter Gabler and Wolfhard Steppe. New York: Random House, 1986.

Juengel, Scott. "The Early Novel and Catastrophe." *Novel: A Forum on Fiction* 3 (2009): 443–50.

Kahneman, Daniel. *Thinking Fast and Slow*. New York: Farrer, Straus and Giroux, 2011.

Kandel, Eric R. *In Search of Memory: The Emergence of a New Science of Mind*. New York: W. W. Norton, 2006.

Kant, Immanuel. *Critique of Pure Reason.* Translated and edited by Paul Guyer and Alan Wood. Cambridge: Cambridge University Press, 1998.

Keiser, Jess. "Nervous Figures: Enlightenment Neurology and the Personified Mind" *ELH* 82 (2015): 1073–108.

Kelly, Helena. "Austen and Enclosure." *Persuasions* 30, no. 2 (2010): 1–14.

Keymer, Thomas. *Sterne, the Moderns, and the Novel.* Oxford: Oxford University Press, 2002.

Kraft, Elizabeth. "The Revaluation of Literary Character: The Case of Crusoe." *South Atlantic Review* 74, no. 2 (2008): 37–58.

Kramnick, Jonathan. *Actions and Objects from Hobbes to Richardson.* Stanford, CA: Stanford University Press, 2010.

———. *Paper Minds: Literature and the Ecology of Consciousness.* Chicago: University of Chicago Press, 2018.

Labbe, Jacqueline. "Introduction." In *Charlotte Smith in British Romanticism*, edited by Jacqueline Labbe, 1–12. London: Pickering and Chatto, 2008.

Lamb, Jonathan. "'Lay Aside My Character': The Personate Novel and Beyond." *Eighteenth Century* 52, no. 3–4 (2011): 271–87.

———. *Sterne's Fiction and the Double Principle.* Cambridge: Cambridge University Press, 1989.

———. *The Things Things Say.* Princeton, NJ: Princeton University Press, 2011.

Lamont, Claire. "Jane Austen and the Old." *Review of English Studies* 54, no. 217 (2003): 661–74.

Lau, Beth, ed. *Jane Austen and Sciences of the Mind.* New York: Routledge, 2018.

Lee, Wendy. *Failures of Feeling: Insensibility and the Novel.* Stanford, CA: Stanford University Press, 2018.

Lewis, Jayne. "The Atmospheres of Robinson Crusoe." In *Defoe's Footprints: Essays in Honor of Maximillian E. Novak,* edited by Robert M. Maniquis and Carl Fisher, 32–54. Toronto: University of Toronto Press, 2009.

Litvak, Joseph. *Caught in the Act: Theatricality in the Nineteenth-Century English Novel.* Berkeley: University of California Press, 1992.

Locke, John. *An Essay Concerning Human Understanding.* Edited by Peter H. Nidditch. Oxford: Oxford University Press, 1975.

Loftus, Elizabeth. *Eyewitness Testimony: With a New Preface.* Cambridge, MA: Harvard University Press, 1996.

———. *Memory.* New York: Rowman and Littlefield, 1988.

Loftus, Elizabeth, with Katherine Ketcham, *The Myth of Repressed Memory: False Memories and Allegations of Sexual Abuse.* New York: St. Martin's Griffin, 1994.

Loveridge, Mark. "Liberty in *Tristram Shandy.*" In *Laurence Sterne: Riddles and Mysteries,* edited by Valerie Grosvenor Myer, 126–41. London: Vision Press, 1984.

Lupton, Christina. "Contingency, Codex, and the Eighteenth-Century Novel." *ELH* 81, no. 4 (2014): 1183.
———. "*Tristram Shandy*, David Hume and Epistemological Fiction." *Philosophy and Literature* 27, no. 1 (2003): 98–115.
Lynch, Deidre. *The Economy of Character: Novels, Market Culture, and the Business of Inner Meaning.* Chicago: University of Chicago Press, 1998.
———. *Loving Literature: A Cultural History.* Chicago: University of Chicago Press, 2015.
———. "Money and Character in Defoe's Fiction." In *The Cambridge Companion to Daniel Defoe*, edited by John Richetti, 84–101. Cambridge: Cambridge University Press, 2008.
Lynch, Jack. "The Relicks of Learning: Sterne amongst the Renaissance Encyclopedists." *Eighteenth-Century Fiction* 13, no. 1 (2000): 1–17.
Macpherson, Sandra. *Harm's Way: Tragic Responsibility and the Novel Form.* Baltimore, MD: Johns Hopkins University Press, 2009.
Markley, A. A. "Charlotte Smith, the Godwin Circle, and the Proliferation of Speakers in *The Young Philosopher*." In *Charlotte Smith in British Romanticism*, edited by Jacqueline Labbe, 87–100. London: Pickering and Chatto, 2008.
Marshall, David. "Autobiographical Acts in *Robinson Crusoe*." *ELH* 71 (2004): 899–920.
———. *The Frame of Art: Fictions of Aesthetic Experience, 1750–1815.* Baltimore, MD: Johns Hopkins University Press, 2005.
———. *The Surprising Effects of Sympathy: Marivaux, Diderot, Rousseau, and Mary Shelley.* Chicago: University of Chicago Press, 1988.
Maunu, Leanne. *Women Writing the Nation: National Identity, Female Community, and the British-French Connection, 1770–1820.* Lewisburg, PA: Bucknell University Press, 2007.
McEwan, Ian. *Atonement.* New York: Anchor Books, 2001.
McGrail, Anne B. "Fanny Price's 'Customary' Subjectivity: Rereading the Individual in Mansfield Park." In *A Companion to Jane Austen Studies*, edited by Laura C. Lambdin and Robert T. Lambdin, 57–70. London: Greenwood Press, 2000.
McKeon, Michael. *The Origins of the English Novel, 1600–1740.* Baltimore, MD: Johns Hopkins University Press, 2002.
McMaster, Juliet. *Jane Austen, the Novelist: Essays Past and Present.* New York: Palgrave Macmillan, 1996.
———. "'Uncrystalized Flesh and Blood': The Body in Tristram Shandy." *Eighteenth-Century Fiction* 2, no. 3 (1990): 197–214.
Meyer Spacks, Patricia. *Imagining a Self: Autobiography and Novel in Eighteenth-Century England.* Cambridge, MA: Harvard University Press, 1976.

Michals, Teresa. "'Like a Spoiled Actress off the Stage': Anti-Theatricality, Nature, and the Novel." *Studies in Eighteenth-Century Culture* 39 (2010): 191–214.

Miller, D. A. *Jane Austen, or the Secret of Style*. Princeton, NJ: Princeton University Press, 2003.

Moglen, Helene. *The Philosophical Irony of Laurence Sterne*. Gainesville: University Presses of Florida, 1975.

Moretti, Franco. *The Way of the World: The Bildungsroman in European Culture*. London: Verso, 2000.

Mullan, John. *Sentiment and Sociability: The Language of Feeling in the Eighteenth Century*. Oxford: Clarendon Press, 1990.

Murray, Douglas. "Spectatorship in Mansfield Park: Looking and Overlooking." *Nineteenth-Century Literature*. 52, no. 1 (1997): 1–26.

Nachumi, Nora. *Acting Like a Lady: British Women Novelists and the Eighteenth-Century Theater*. New York: AMS, 2008.

Nahum, Louis, Adrian G. Guggisberg, Aurélie Bouzerda-Wahlen, et al. "Forms of Confabulation: Disassociations and Associations." *Neuropsychologia* 50, no. 10 (2012): 2524–34.

Nalbantian, Suzanne. *Memory in Literature: From Rousseau to Neuroscience*. New York: Palgrave MacMillan, 2003.

Nalbantian, Suzanne, Paul Matthews, and James L. McClelland, eds. *The Memory Process: Neuroscientific and Humanistic Perspectives*. Cambridge, MA: MIT Press, 2011.

Nazar, Hina. *Enlightened Sentiments*. Bronx, NY: Fordham University Press, 2012.

New, Melvyn. *Laurence Sterne as Satirist: A Reading of Tristram Shandy*. Gainesville: University Presses of Florida, 1969.

———. "Sterne and the Modernist Moment." In *A Cambridge Companion to Laurence Sterne*. Edited by Thomas Keymer, 160–73. Cambridge: Cambridge University Press, 2009.

———. "Sterne, Warburton, and the Burden of Exuberant Wit." *Eighteenth-Century Studies* 15, no. 3 (1982): 245–74.

Newton, Judith Lowder. "*Evelina*: A Chronicle of Assault." In *Evelina*, edited by Harold Bloom, 59–83. New York: Chelsea House, 1988.

Noë, Alva. *Out of Our Heads: Why You Are Not Your Brain, and Other Lessons from the Biology of Consciousness*. New York: Hill and Wang, 2010.

Novak, Maximillian. "The Cave and Grotto: Realist Form and Robinson Crusoe's Imagined Interiors." *Eighteenth-Century Life* 32, no. 2 (2002): 120–37.

———. *Economics and the Fiction of Daniel Defoe*. Berkeley: University of California Press, 1962.

———. *Realism, Myth and History in Defoe's Fiction.* Lincoln: University of Nebraska Press, 1983.

Nowka, Scott. "Talking Coins and Thinking Smoke-Jacks: Satirizing Materialism in Gildon and Sterne." *Eighteenth-Century Fiction* 22, no. 2 (2009-10): 195-222.

O'Quinn, Daniel. "Jane Austen and Performance: Theatre, Memory, and Enculturation." In *A Companion to Jane Austen*, edited by Claudia Johnson and Clara Tuite, 377-88. Chichester: Blackwell, 2009.

Palmer, Alan. *Fictional Minds.* Lincoln: University of Nebraska Press, 2004.

Park, Julie. *The Self and It: Novel Objects in Eighteenth-Century England.* Stanford, CA: Stanford University Press, 2010.

———. "What the Eye Cannot See: Interior Landscapes in Mansfield Park," *Eighteenth-Century Theory and Interpretation* 54, no. 2 (2013): 169-81.

Park, Suzie. "Compulsory Narration, Sentimental Interface: Going through the Motions of Emotion." *Eighteenth Century: Theory and Interpretation* 50, no. 2-3 (2009): 165-83.

Pasanek, Brad. *Metaphors of Mind: An Eighteenth-Century Dictionary.* Baltimore, MD: Johns Hopkins University Press, 2015.

Phillips, Natalie. *Distraction: Problems of Attention in Eighteenth-Century Literature.* Baltimore, MD: Johns Hopkins University Press, 2016.

Pinch, Adela. *Strange Fits of Passion: Epistemologies of Emotion, Hume to Austen.* Stanford, CA: Stanford University Press, 1996.

Pino, Melissa. "Burney's Evelina and Aesthetics in Action." *Modern Philology: Critical and Historical Studies in Literature, Medieval through Contemporary* 108, no. 2 (2010): 263-303.

Porter, Dahlia. "From Nosegay to Specimen Cabinet: Charlotte Smith and the Labour of Collecting." In *Charlotte Smith in British Romanticism*, edited by Jacqueline Labbe, 29-44. London: Pickering and Chatto, 2008.

Porter, Roy. "Against the Spleen." In *Laurence Sterne: Riddles and Mysteries*, edited by Valerie Grosvenor Myer, 84-98. London: Vision Press, 1984.

Richardson, Alan. *British Romanticism and the Science of the Mind.* Cambridge: Cambridge University Press, 2001.

———. "Jane Austen and the Perils of Mental Time Travel." In *Jane Austen and Sciences of the Mind*, edited by Beth Lau, 58-74. New York: Routledge, 2018.

———. "Memory and Imagination in Romantic Fiction." In *The Memory Process: Neuroscientific and Humanistic Perspectives,* edited by Suzanne Nalbantian, Paul Matthews, and James L. McLelland, 277-296, Cambridge, MA: MIT Press, 2011).

———. *The Neural Sublime: Cognitive Theories and Romantic Texts.* Baltimore, MD: John Hopkins University Press, 2010.

———. "Studies in Literature and Cognition: A Field Map." In *The Work of Fiction: Cognition, Culture and Complexity,* edited by Ellen Spolsky and Alan Richardson, 1–29. New York: Routledge, 2016.

Richetti, John. "Defoe as Narrative Innovator." In *The Cambridge Companion to Daniel Defoe,* edited by John Richetti, 121–38. Cambridge: Cambridge University Press, 2008.

———. *Defoe's Narratives: Situations and Structures.* Oxford: Clarendon Press, 1975.

Rohrbach, Emily. "Austen's Later Subjects." *SEL: Studies in English Literature, 1500–1900* 44, no. 4 (2004): 737–52.

Sagal, Anna K. "An Hobby-Horse Well Worth Giving a Description Of: Disability, Trauma, and Language in *Tristram Shandy.*" In *The Idea of Disability in the Eighteenth Century,* edited by Chris Mounsey, 105–28. Lewisburg, PA: Bucknell University Press, 2014.

Sandy, Mark. *Romanticism, Memory, and Mourning.* Farnham: Ashgate, 2013.

Schacter, Daniel L. *Searching for Memory: The Brain, the Mind, and the Past.* New York: Basic Books, 1996.

———. *The Seven Sins of Memory: How the Mind Forgets and Remembers.* New York: Houghton Mifflin, 2001.

Schacter, Daniel L., ed. *Memory Distortion: How Minds, Brains, and Societies Construct the Past.* Cambridge, MA: Harvard University Press, 1995.

Schooler, J. W., and T. Y. Engslter-Schooler. "Verbal Overshadowing of Visual Memories: Some Things Are Better Left Unsaid." *Cognitive Psychology* 22, no. 1 (1990): 36–71.

Sedgwick, Eve Kosofsky. *Between Men: English Literature and Male Homosocial Desire.* New York: Columbia University Press, 1985.

Seidel, Kevin. "*Robinson Crusoe* as Defoe's Theory of Fiction." *Novel* 44, no. 2 (2011): 165–85.

Seidel, Michael. "*Robinson Crusoe*: Varieties of Fictional Experience." In *The Cambridge Companion to Daniel Defoe,* edited by John Richetti, 182–99. Cambridge: Cambridge University Press, 2008.

Sherman, Stuart. *Telling Time: Clocks, Diaries, and English Diurnal Form, 1660–1785.* Chicago: University of Chicago Press, 1996.

Silver, Sean. *The Mind Is a Collection: Case Studies in Eighteenth-Century Thought.* Philadelphia: University of Pennsylvania Press, 2015.

Simpson, K. G. "At This Moment in Space: Time, Space, and Values in *Tristram Shandy.*" In *Laurence Sterne: Riddles and Mysteries,* edited by Valerie Grosvenor Myer, 142–58. London: Vision Press, 1984.

Singer, Kate. "Austen Agitated: Feeling Emotions in Mixed Media." In *Jane Austen and the Sciences of the Mind*, edited by Beth Lau, 96–114. New York: Routledge, 2018.

Siskin, Clifford. *System: The Shaping of Modern Knowledge*. Cambridge, MA: MIT Press, 2016.

Skinner, John. "Exploring Space: The Constellations of *Mansfield Park*." *Eighteenth-Century Fiction* 4, no. 2 (1992): 126–148.

Smith, Adam. *The Theory of Moral Sentiments*. Edited by Knud Haakonssen. Cambridge: Cambridge University Press, 2002.

Smith, Charlotte. *Celestina*. Edited by Loraine Fletcher. Toronto: Broadview Press, 2004.

Spinoza, Benedict de. *Ethics: Proved in Geometrical Order*. Edited by Matthew J. Kisner, translated by Michael Silverthorne. Cambridge: Cambridge University Press, 2018.

Spolsky, Ellen, and Alan Richardson, eds. *The Work of Fiction: Cognition, Culture and Complexity*. New York: Routledge, 2016.

Starr, G. A. *Defoe and Casuistry*. Princeton, NJ: Princeton University Press, 1971.

———. *Defoe and Spiritual Autobiography*. Princeton, NJ: Princeton University Press, 1965.

Starr, Gabrielle. "Burney, Ovid, and the Value of the Beautiful." *Eighteenth-Century Fiction* 24, no. 1 (Fall 2011): 77–104.

Sterne, Laurence. *The Life and Opinions of Tristram Shandy, Gentleman*. Edited by Ian Campbell Ross. Oxford: Oxford University Press, 2009.

Stevenson, Jill Heydt. "Slipping into the Ha-Ha: Bawdy Humor and Body Politics in Jane Austen's Novels." *Nineteenth-Century Literature* 55, no. 3 (200): 309–39.

Straub, Kristina. *Divided Fictions: Fanny Burney and Feminine Strategy*. Lexington: University Press of Kentucky, 1987.

Stroud, Barry. *Hume*. London: Routledge, 1977.

Sun Lee, Yoon. "Austen's Scale-Making." *Studies in Romanticism* 52, no. 2 (2003): 171–95.

Swearingen, James. *Reflexivity in Tristram Shandy: An Essay in Phenomenological Criticism*. New Haven, CT: Yale University Press, 1977.

Swift, Jonathan. *The Writings of Jonathan Swift*. Edited by Robert Greenberg and William Piper. New York: W. W. Norton, 1973.

Tanner, Tony. *Jane Austen*. Cambridge, MA: Harvard University Press, 1986.

Taylor, Shelley E., and Jonathan Brown. "Illusion and Wellbeing: A Social Psychological Perspective on Mental Health." *Psychological Bulletin* 103 (1988): 193–210.

Thompson, Helen. *Fictional Matter: Empiricism, Corpuscles, and the Novel.* Philadelphia: University of Pennsylvania Press, 2017.

Thomson, James. *The Seasons.* Edited by James Sambrook. Oxford: Oxford University Press, 1981.

Todd, Janet. *The Cambridge Introduction to Jane Austen.* Cambridge: Cambridge University Press, 2006.

Traugott, John. *Tristram Shandy's World: Sterne's Philosophical Rhetoric.* Berkeley: University of California Press, 1954.

Trilling, Lionel. *The Opposing Self: Nine Essays in Criticism.* New York: Harcourt Brace, 1955.

Trocchio, Rachel. "Memory's Ends: Thinking as Grace in Thomas Hooker's New England." *American Literature* 90, no. 4 (2018): 693–722.

Valihora, Karen. "Impartial Spectatorship Meets Picturesque Tourist: The Framing of *Mansfield Park*." *Eighteenth-Century Fiction* 20, no. 1 (2007): 89–114.

Vermeule, Blakey. *Why Do We Care about Literary Characters?* Baltimore, MD: Johns Hopkins University Press, 2010.

Vickars, Isle. *Defoe and the New Sciences.* Cambridge: Cambridge University Press, 2006.

Voskuil, Lynn. "Sotherton and the Geography of Empire: The Landscapes of Mansfield Park." *Studies in Romanticism* 53, no. 4 (2014): 591–615.

Wall, Cynthia. "The Impress of the Invisible: Lodges and Cottages" *ELH* 79, no. 4 (2012): 989–1012.

———. *The Prose of Things: Transformations of Description in the Eighteenth Century.* Chicago: University of Chicago Press, 2006.

Warner, William. *Licensing Entertainment: The Elevation of Novel Reading in Britain, 1684–1750.* Los Angeles: University of California Press, 1998.

Warner, William, and Clifford Siskin. *This Is Enlightenment: An Invitation to the Form of an Argument.* Chicago: University of Chicago Press, 2010.

Watt, Ian. *The Rise of the Novel: Studies in Defoe, Richardson, and Fielding.* London: Random House, 1957.

Wegner, D. M., R. Erber, and P. Raymond. "Transactive Memory in Close Relationships." *Journal of Personality and Social Psychology* 61, no. 6 (1991): 923–29.

Wehrs, Donald R. "Anarchic Signification and Motions of Grace in Sterne's Novelistic Satire." In *Sterne, Tristram, Yorick: Tercentenary Essays on Laurence Sterne.* Edited by Melvyn New, Peter de Voogd, and Judith Hawley, 77–99. Newark: University of Delaware Press, 2016.

Weiss Smith, Courtney. *Empiricist Devotions: Science, Religion, and Poetry in Eighteenth-Century England.* Charlottesville: University of Virginia Press, 2016.

Williams, Jeffrey. "Narrative of Narratives." *Modern Language Notes* 105, no. 5 (1990): 1032–45.
Williams, Nicholas. "Literally or Figuratively? Embodied Perception and Figurative Prospect in *Mansfield Park*." *European Romantic Review* 24, no. 3 (2013): 317–23.
Wood, Michael. "Time and Her Aunt." In *A Companion to Jane Austen*, edited by Claudia Johnson and Clara Tuite, 195–205. Chichester: Blackwell, 2009.
Wordsworth, William. "Memory," "Lines Composed a Few Miles above Tintern Abbey." In *The Major Works*. Edited by Stephen Gill. Oxford: Oxford University Press, 1984.
Yahav, Amit. *Feeling Time: Duration, the Novel, and Eighteenth-Century Sensibility*. Philadelphia: University of Pennsylvania Press, 2018.
———. "Time, Duration, and Defoe's Novels." *Partial Answers* 6, no. 1 (2008): 33–56.
Yates, Frances. *The Art of Memory*. Chicago: University of Chicago Press, 1966.
Young, Kay. "Resilience and Jane Austen." In *Jane Austen and the Sciences of the Mind*, edited by Beth Lau, 200–221. New York: Routledge, 2018.
Zimmerman, Everett. "Tristram Shandy and Narrative Representation." *Eighteenth Century Theory and Interpretation* 28, no. 2 (1987): 127–47.
Zunshine, Lisa. "Why Jane Austen Was Different, and Why We May Need Cognitive Science to See It." *Style* 41, no. 3 (2007): 275–98.
———. *Why We Read Fiction: Theory of Mind and the Novel*. Columbus: Ohio State University Press, 2006.

❖ INDEX ❖

Abrams, M. H., 194–95
Addison, Joseph: *The Pleasures of the Imagination*, 218n19
aesthetics, 2, 61, 72, 93, 97, 183, 209; eighteenth-century, 117; judgments of, 117–18, 121; modes of taste in, 137–38; mutability and, 233n36; pleasure in, 96, 117; of unboundedness, 177. See also philosophy
agency: autonomous, 115, 120, 139; and memory, 115, 232n18; mind losing its grip on, 164; notion of, 141; and self-consciousness, 117; of women, 112–13, 123–25, 129, 131, 135–37
allegory, 139, 160, 165, 182–83, 189–90; of the hedgerow, 180; legibility of objects and, 241n52; literary device of, 183; of memory, 151; and metaphor, 218n19; poetic, 173; reference and, 224n25; self-conscious, 177; of solitude, 163; of time, 183
Andrews, Kerri, 144
aposiopesis, 76, 81; elusive, 108
archetype: biblical, 58; of empiricism, 52; Enlightenment, 52, 57; of exploration, 41; of helplessness, 44; of memory, 2, 30–31, 36, 160–61, 189; of mind, 99; novelistic, 110
archive: empiricism as an, 111; of the mind, 22; remembering the, 209–15. See also memory

Arendt, Hannah, 194
art: and life, 168; and nature, 146, 152, 163–64, 169; work of, 164, 174
associationism, 20–25; empirical, 70, 218n19; Enlightenment, 29; of Hume, 220n69, 221n84; mechanistic system of, 79, 102, 236n21; operations of, 78
Astbury, Katherine, 147
Auerbach, Nina, 196, 238n15, 241n60
Augustans, 78; modes of satire of the, 230n37
Austen, Jane, 5, 8, 41, 131; concept of fiction of, 183; *Mansfield Park*, 3, 28–32, 155, 172, 176–208, 237n2, 239n26, 240n40; *Persuasion*, 142–44, 196, 202, 214–15; *Pride and Prejudice*, 1, 120; *Sense and Sensibility*, 110; symbolism of, 177
(auto)biography, 191; as fiction, 5; novel and, 217n5; of pain, 158
automatism: definition of female, 233n31; movement in terms of, 121, 233n31; sentiment of, 198; thinking in terms of, 31, 113. See also automaton; mechanism
automaton: cultural evolution of the, 233n31; figure of the, 121; woman as, 114, 123, 234n40. See also automatism

Baier, Annette, 10; "Cartesian Persons," 35; "Mixing Memory and Desire," 35–36, 180–81
Bakhtin, Mikhail, 112

Barbauld, Anna Laetitia, 167
Barnes, Julian: *The Sense of an Ending*, 209–11
Behrendt, Stephen, 144
Bender, John, 12, 225n25
Bildung, 29–30, 111–12, 115, 140; as autonomy, 123; novelistic, 140, 233n36; as self-awareness, 117
Bildungsroman, 29–30, 108, 110–12; classical, 110–11; early, 110, 112. *See also* novel
body: desensitized, 151; materialism of the, 79; memory and, 71; mind and, 15, 51, 60, 67–69, 76, 81, 88, 95, 105, 111, 147–49, 158–61, 170, 179, 228n4; natural, 96; pleasures of the, 105; and society, 138. *See also* materialism
Brewer, William, 147, 235n16
Burke, Edmund, 160–61
Burney, Frances, 210; *Evelina*, 3, 30–32, 108–41, 233n31

Carruthers, Mary, 8–9, 211
Caruth, Cathy, 69
causation, 102, 114, 144; agent of, 206; Humean, 201; mental, 114; origins of, 114
Chibka, Robert, 91
Chittka, Kathryn, 26
Cleland, John: *Fanny Hill*, 89, 110
cognitive literary studies, 25–29, 209. *See also* theory of mind
cognitive processes: mechanistic, 76; of memory, 30; pleasing art of, 213; of reasoning, 35; and self-consciousness, 132. *See also* cognitive science
cognitive science, 26, 237n4, 240n36; memory in, 19. *See also* science
Coleridge, Samuel Taylor, 23, 27, 112; *Biographia Literaria*, 3–4
colonization, 34
comedy: Restoration, 140; and satire, 78; sentiment and, 140; and tragedy, 96. *See also* satire

confabulation, 28, 178, 222n97, 237n3
consciousness: abstract forces of, 39; aesthetic complications of, 140; animal, 36; boundless version of, 187; character, 160; dangers of self-enclosed, 236n30; defining feature of, 86; development of, 115; early novelistic representations of, 183; eighteenth-century theories of, 114–15; and emotion, 167, 213; enlightened, 131; epistolary, 213; as error, 215; extended, 232n18; fictional, 183; hard problem of, 149, 235n17; human, 36, 53, 64; landscape and, 160; lawlessness of feminine, 183; Locke on, 57, 221n81; memory and, 5, 8, 115, 117, 177, 232n18; metaphor for, 52, 57; minute-by-minute content of, 217n5; operations of, 138; plagued, 192; reflective, 199; regretful, 185; representational model of, 24; role of, 35, 70; Romantic, 182; rudimentary form of, 130; social, 94; stream of, 187, 197; and sympathy, 116; and time, 37–38, 113–14; transition of, 205; virtual, 205. *See also* mind; self-consciousness
craft: of memory, 20, 223n108, 224n24; of the novel, 210
creativity, 58; of memory, 29, 32, 66, 112, 175, 212; of reflective consciousness, 199
Curran, Stuart, 144

Dames, Nicholas, 10, 31, 178–79, 203; *Amnesiac Selves*, 178, 223n108
death: the "enviable rest" of, 151; and extinction, 165; imagining of, 16; pleasures of, 151; wish for, 150–51
Defoe, Daniel: *Robinson Crusoe*, 3, 5, 30, 33–66, 108, 163, 227n48
Derrida, Jacques, 241n53
Descartes, René, 6, 37; materialism of, 220n78; *Meditations*, 15; *Treatise on Man*, 14, 22; wax of, 12–20

desire: actualization of, 183, 199; environment of, 199; imagination and, 120, 237n4; indifference over, 198; innermost, 200; for insensibility, 175; memory and, 125, 152, 205; obligation and, 126; resolution and, 125; secret, 202; unfulfilled, 154, 186; waste of, 207. *See also* emotion; love
Diderot, Denis, 199
distress, 145–47, 154, 156, 162–63, 169; agents of, 198; emotional, 175; mental, 203; physical, 175; scene of, 192; situations of, 225n28; soothing of, 202; and trauma, 178. *See also* emotion
Donne, John: *Meditations,* 33
Doody, Margaret, 8–10, 179, 239n29
Draaisma, Douwe, 5; *Why Life Speeds Up as You Get Older,* 15–16
dualism: mind-body, 214; reading the novel through a, 183
Duckling, Louise, 145
Duckworth, Alistair, 238n20, 239n26, 241n52

eighteenth-century novel, 2–7, 11, 25–26, 29, 72; literary realism of the, 6; mind and matter in the, 20; personhood in the, 111; rape in the, 110; studies of the, 15, 29; womanhood in the, 111. *See also* history of the novel; literary history
emotion: awareness of, 129; comparative technology of, 167; consciousness and, 167; of distress, 145–47, 154, 156, 162–63, 169; duty and, 130, 133–34; feminine, 150; of grief, 158; history of, 149; intersubjective nature of, 154; intimacy of, 210; of melancholy, 156, 158, 174; memory and, 2, 48, 134, 161, 168, 192; and motion, 149; painful, 196; paradoxical, 156; passionate, 125–26, 135; pleasure in, 173; and the problem of affective property, 152; reading and, 72; recompensing transactions of, 147–48; recurrent, 116; relative nature of, 168, 175; self-conscious, 133; sentimental, 168, 206; of serenity, 158; shades of, 198; sympathetic, 132; that one is forgotten, 167; transient, 207. *See also* desire; distress; love; nostalgia; sympathy
empiricism, 2, 5–12, 28–29, 36, 83, 91, 111, 113, 143, 182; archetype of, 52; associative mechanisms of, 70, 79, 102, 154; challenge to, 13, 25; of Defoe, 39–40, 45–49, 61; devotional practice of, 226n45; Enlightenment philosophies of, 115; of Hobbes, 17; of Hume, 18, 22, 68; of Locke, 15, 20, 49, 68; materialism and, 76; meditative practice of, 226n45; parody of, 183; on recollection, 178; sensationalism of, 79; "storehouse" of memory as a concept of, 177; student of, 101; and temporality, 50
Engell, James, 3–4
England, 161
Enlightenment: and autonomy, 115; epistemology in the, 146; as an era of doubt, 15; gendered concept of, 135; literary scholarship of the, 7; memory in the, 8, 146; paradox of the, 111; philosophy of the, 4, 6, 9, 15, 25, 28; science in the, 114; social, 136; theories of mind in the, 19
epiphenomenalism, 114. *See also* causation
epistemology: dubious, 150; historical, 29; memory and, 146, 203–4; sentimental, 77. *See also* philosophy
ethics: curious, 205; of duty, 196; of self-sacrifice, 196. *See also* philosophy
etiology, 150
experience: absorptive, 172; of feeling, 147; fiction and, 150, 156; history of, 45, 116; logic of, 41; memory and, 65, 139, 181–82, 197, 222n98; personal, 161; of reading, 143; redefining of, 151;

experience (*continued*)
reflection on, 130, 135; registers of, 49, 181; repetition of, 41; revision of, 183; Romantic, 184; self-conscious, 140; sensory, 117, 133, 171, 178, 185; subjectivization of, 183; tactile nature of, 142; time as, 185; transacted, 178; of unwanted sensation, 214

feeling. *See* emotion
feminism, 118, 136. *See also* women
Ferguson, Frances, 109
Festa, Lynn: "Crusoe's Isle of Misfit Things," 35, 227n50
fiction: autobiography as, 5; commentary on, 106; delusions of, 97; in the Enlightenment, 2, 6–7, 10; and experience, 150; fact and, 146, 152, 167, 178; failed, 207; gift of, 200; historical memory of, 137; language of, 104; lost, 158; making of, 31, 33, 70–75, 91, 168, 179, 191, 202; mechanism of, 90; memory and, 172, 182, 186, 197, 211; as an object of mediation, 205; pleasure of, 92; poetic composition and, 171; poetry as a restylized, 152; power of, 85, 102; projected mental, 157; reading of, 199; and reality, 146–47, 161, 169–72, 204–5; remembering of, 199, 203, 213; space of, 102; and time, 175; truth and, 107–8, 202; women of, 110. *See also* fictionality studies; imagination; novel
fictionality studies, 6–7. *See also* fiction
Flynn, Carol Houlihan, 78–79, 229n33, 231n56
forgetting, 9–11, 16, 76, 121, 189–90, 198, 206–7, 210; act of, 52–53, 76, 84, 178; blissful nature of, 178; pain and, 178; seven sins of, 211; of time, 46. *See also* memory
French Revolution, 147
Freud, Sigmund, 22, 26, 69–71, 105, 222n96; *Beyond the Pleasure Principle*, 70; "A Child Is Being Beaten," 26; "An Infantile Neurosis," 26, 71; "Screen Memories," 71; "The Wolf Man," 71

Gallagher, Catherine, 6–7, 224n25
Galperin, William, 180, 203, 205, 238n20
Garnai, Amy, 147, 235n16
Garrett, Don, 24, 220n78
Garrick, David, 117
gender: and Enlightenment, 135; and mind, 123; stereotypes of, 136
God, 13, 37, 40; faith in, 54; nature of the design of, 226n45
Goodman, Kevis, 24, 179, 221n81

Hawley, Judith, 69, 228n5, 230n41
Haywood, Eliza: *Love in Excess*, 110
history: alteration of, 183–84; of archetypal signs, 195; collective, 67; colonial, 34; definition of the term, 230n43; of emotion, 149; of empiricism, 10; of epistemology, 29; of experience, 45, 51, 102; of female subjection, 139; fictional, 85, 104–5; fragile form of, 215; of ideas, 25; intellectual, 112; lesson in, 182; making of, 84, 88, 91; of mediation, 6; of memory, 8–9, 29, 194, 212, 222n96; of mind, 13, 35, 89, 195; narrative, 106; and narrative representation, 227n2; naval, 195; of the nostalgia disease, 195; personal, 2, 5, 30–31, 68, 80, 88, 91, 108, 112, 160; potential meanings of, 85; of rape, 30, 139, 141; rational, 128; reconstruction of, 28; of Romanticism, 194; socially networked model of, 91; somatic, 179; theoretical, 6; truth of, 210; war, 30, 88. *See also* history of the novel; literary history
history of the novel, 3, 5–6, 12, 25, 29–30. *See also* eighteenth-century novel; literary history
Hobbes, Thomas, 9; *Leviathan*, 16–17
Hofkosh, Sonia, 180, 238n20, 241n64

Hume, David, 17–18, 41, 49, 119, 171, 204; associationism of, 220n69, 221n84; definition of sympathy of, 116; epistemology of, 77; logic of causation of, 201; model of cyclical memory of, 167; skepticism of, 17, 102; system of recollection of, 97; theory of causal mind of, 149; theory of ideas of, 22–24; *A Treatise of Human Nature*, 18–20, 22–24
Hunt, Lars, 27
Hunter, J. Paul, 36, 224n25

imagination: activity of, 65, 87, 116; Addison on, 218n19; Coleridge on, 27, 29; compound, 17; confines of, 199; and desire, 120, 237n4; fiction and, 38; as a force, 4, 20; Hume on, 22–25, 29, 32; impossibility of, 190; judgment and, 7, 14; lawlessness of feminine, 201; memory and, 7–19, 47, 55–69, 74, 87–94, 100, 108, 111, 116, 132, 146, 149, 154–58, 163, 168, 172–73, 180–83, 187–90, 200, 203–7, 222n99, 227n2, 237n4; and pain, 149; and perception, 41; powers of the, 170; and reading, 84, 168, 186; and reality, 174; and reason, 127; Romantic, 3–4, 11, 33, 178, 191; sexual transgression and, 188; as a site of limitation in Austen's novels, 238n20; in thinking, 183; unleash the, 200; work of the, 119; of the writer, 73. *See also* fiction
individualism, 33, 113
intention(s): affirmation as an, 12; attribution of, 36; declaration by lovers of, 184; formation of, 183; gifting of, 200; importance of, 139; lost, 207; memory and, 36, 190, 197, 199, 205, 207; in retrospect, 207; sleeping, 198; willful, 202. *See also* intentionality
intentionality, 136; in thinking, 183. *See also* intention(s)
inventio (seeking, finding out), 8–9

invention: genius as, 9; as performance, 138
irony, 138, 170, 181, 185; of Austen, 240n42; edifice of, 210; laughing, 213; and parataxis, 193
Ishiguro, Kazuo: *The Buried Giant*, 210–11
Italy, 161

Jager, Colin, 238n23, 240n35
Johnson, Samuel, 4, 25–26
Jones, Wendy, 28
Joyce, James: *Ulysses*, 11–12
judgment: of aesthetics, 117–18, 121; and imagination, 7, 14

Kahneman, Daniel, 211, 213–14
Kandel, Erik, 26
knowledge: absence of, 132; and memory, 4, 8, 10, 15, 45, 125, 181–82, 191, 203; notion of, 181; of pleasures lost, 167; of the reader, 167; reading and, 84; rise of, 123; of the self, 140; sensation and, 8, 13; systems of, 9; theory of, 204; and time, 127
Kramnick, Jonathan, 24, 53, 221n84; *Actions and Objects*, 113–15, 117

Lamb, Jonathan, 70, 91, 227n51, 230n38; *The Things Things Say*, 116
Lamont Claire: "Jane Austen and the Old," 180
Lau, Beth, 28
Lee, Wendy, 22–23
Lee, Yoon Sun, 184
Lewis, Jayne, 33
Lewis, Matthew Gregory: *The Monk*, 110
literary history, 5, 9, 115; experience of, 163; intertextuality in, 144; of the mind, 11; of the novel, 11, 16; poetic, 165; of the sonnet, 144. *See also* history of the novel
Locke, John, 6, 9–10, 21–25, 34–38, 81, 85, 98, 227n3; *An Essay Concerning*

Locke, John (*continued*)
    Human Understanding, 4, 16, 21–22, 37–38, 52, 218n27, 232n18; materialism of, 24, 219n49; sensationalism of, 15; theory of ideas of, 21–25, 37, 75, 218n27, 220n68, 220n81; theory of knowledge of, 45, 204; theory of language of, 91; theory of recollection of, 149
Loftus, Elizabeth, 27, 222n96
London, 112, 117–18, 155; watches and clocks in, 238n23
love: dangerous, 110; and desire, 200; hope and, 120; and war, 96–106. *See also* desire; emotion
Lupton, Cristina, 102
Lynch, Deidre, 114, 118, 121, 178, 218n23, 221n84, 225n32, 233n31, 234n42, 235n48

Macpherson, Sandra: *Harm's Way*, 114
madness, 77, 86, 199–200
making: of fiction, 31, 33, 70–75, 91; of history, 84, 88, 91
Marshall, David, 36, 225n32, 240n37
masculinity, 90
materialism, 24, 29, 65, 78–79, 101, 105, 114, 151, 198, 214; concepts of the mind in, 181; and empiricism, 76; Enlightenment, 219n46; of Locke, 24, 219n49, 220n81; in mind-body relations, 68, 85, 101; parody of, 77, 228n5; rhetoric of, 42, 228n4; satire on, 228n4; sympathetic, 100; triumph of, 68. *See also* body; science
matter: energies of conscious, 168; force behind, 168; mind and, 69, 72–74, 81, 88, 94, 100, 106, 146, 149–52, 166–68, 174
McEwan, Ian: *Atonement*, 210–11
McKeon, Michael: *The Origins of the English Novel*, 6
McMaster, Juliet, 228n4, 228n7, 241n58

mechanism, 121, 123, 134, 219n46; associative, 79, 102; of Lockean cognition, 21. *See also* automatism
medical discourses, 61, 107, 179, 193, 228n5. *See also* science
memory: abstractions of, 154–55, 168; agency and, 115, 232n18; alteration of, 14; alternative type of, 199; anguish of, 149; archetype of, 2, 30–31, 36, 160–61, 189; associative, 75, 77, 160, 236n21; autobiographical, 5, 35–36, 57, 136, 224n24; as a book, 8–9, 12; classical art of, 82; in cognitive science, 19; as a collection, 2, 11, 145; composite nature of, 46; and consciousness, 5, 8, 115, 117, 177, 232n18; constructivist model of, 26; craft of, 20, 223n108, 224n24; creative powers of, 29, 32, 66, 112, 175, 212, 221n85; culture of, 211; cyclical, 167; definition of, 38; Defoe on, 56, 62; and desire, 125, 152, 205; dissociative, 171; distractive, 171; and emotion, 2, 48, 134, 161, 168, 192; empirical, 30, 38; and epistemology, 146; errors of, 193, 210–11, 215, 222n98; evolution of, 112; and experience, 65, 139, 181–82, 197, 222n98; faculties of, 54, 156; fallibility of, 52–53, 204; false, 27–28; fantasies of, 151, 171, 186; and feeling, 48, 56, 71; fictionalization of, 4–5, 12, 89, 151, 156, 172, 202–3; as a force, 3–4, 7, 20, 25–26, 32, 39, 60–61, 183; forgetfulness over, 198; and form, 162; Freud on, 71; history of, 8–9, 29, 194, 212, 222n96; Hume on, 21, 25, 49, 167, 218n19; ideal, 85; idealism in, 204; ideological, 32; imagination and, 7–19, 47, 55–69, 74, 87–94, 100, 108, 111, 116, 132, 146, 149, 154–58, 163, 172–73, 180–83, 187–90, 200, 203–7, 222n99, 227n2, 237n4; inaccuracies of, 191; inequalities of, 197; and intention, 36,

190, 197, 199, 205, 207; intersubjective nature of, 90; Johnson on, 4; knowledge and, 4, 8, 10, 15, 45, 125, 181–82, 191, 203; landscape and, 160; lapse of, 10–11; Locke on, 21, 25, 56–58, 183, 218n19; long-term, 198; and matter, 102; mediational, 7, 27–28, 169, 220n81; meditation on, 177; memorization and, 181–82; mental work of, 201; metaphor and, 8, 36, 92, 195; mimetic, 4, 31, 80, 220n81; moralizing, 1; narrative, 2; painful, 92, 134; parameters of, 188; as pathological, 71; personal, 2, 98, 153–54, 240n36; of pleasures, 155–56; poetry and, 142, 152, 156, 162; powers of, 45, 47, 134, 155, 177, 194, 218n23; quotation and, 144–46; and reading, 196; real, 5–12; and reflection, 202; reiterative nature of, 21; as repetition, 83; repositories of, 196; representational, 80; repressed, 222n96; retentive, 2; Romantic, 221n85; and self-consciousness, 140; and sensation, 4, 18, 29, 31, 49, 97, 121; short-term, 198; social nature of, 2, 28, 32, 70, 108, 112, 136, 141; space of, 207; as spatial retention, 183; as a storehouse, 5–6, 9, 16, 21, 56–58, 143, 154, 177, 191; sublime experience of, 182–83; and survival, 33–67, 131, 227n48; teleological account of, 111–12; and time, 37, 45, 50–51, 54–56, 59, 120–22, 128, 131, 134, 140, 181, 229n27; truth of, 215; unconscious, 211; untruths of, 178; vague, 198. *See also* archive; forgetting; history; mind; nostalgia; quotation; recollection; reconstructive memory; transactive memory; trauma

metaphor, 7–8, 42, 66, 74, 81, 228n7; allegory and, 218n19; and allusion, 239n29; beautiful, 19; the conduit as, 177; as an indexical system, 218n23; in the management of mind, 44, 95; and memory, 8, 36, 92; of the mind, 34, 43, 69, 99, 173, 195; parallelism of, 107–8; power of, 90; psychological, 44; for Romantic memory, 221n85; signs of, 218n23; time as a, 44

Miller, D. A., 193, 240n42

mind: associative aspects of the, 191; and body, 15, 51, 60, 67–69, 76, 81, 88, 95, 105, 111, 147–49, 158–61, 170, 179, 228n4; and brain, 168; clarity of, 202; as a collection/container, 15, 43, 57; creative powers of the, 58–59, 61–62; empiricist accounts of, 47–48, 67; evolution of, 174; forces of the, 196; gendered concepts of the, 123; history of, 13, 35, 89, 195; impermeable, 228n7; independence of, 115; as a library, 24, 76; materialist concepts of the, 181; and matter, 69, 72–74, 81, 88, 94, 100, 106, 146, 149–52, 166–68, 174, 202, 235n17; metaphor of the, 34, 43, 69, 99, 173, 195; nature and, 159–60; pain as a state of, 167; and perception, 190; phenomenology of the, 52, 140; philosophies of, 7, 15; and physical processes, 147; pleasure in the, 170–71; powers of the, 68, 79, 154, 168, 201; protective mechanism of the, 159; representation and, 119, 154; revolution of, 196; Romantic notions of, 50; sovereign image of the, 171; thinking of the, 142; transactions of the, 151; vital energies of the, 166; and world, 63, 68, 101–2, 114–15, 117, 143, 147–48, 158, 163, 175–79, 204. *See also* cognitive processes; cognitive science; consciousness; memory; mind reading; self-consciousness; subjectivity

mind reading, 106–8, 119–20, 135, 223n104; moment of, 131; and perception, 119; and survival, 119; and sympathetic exchange, 134. *See also* mind

modern/modernity, 6, 8; concept of, 113; culture of, 112; early, 13; readers of, 30; rise of, 139
modernism, 10, 28
Moglen, Helene, 69, 230n38, 231n54
moral feeling, 122, 198
Moretti, Franco, 110–11
music, 214–15

Nalbantian, Suzanne, 5, 28
nationalism, 46
nature: art and, 146, 152, 163–64, 169; as the derivative for writing, 152; force counter to, 165; idealization of, 157; "infinite," 4; materiality of, 166; and memory, 32, 148, 157; and mind, 159–60; pastoral forms of, 169; readings of, 171; recursive cycles of, 167; refuge in, 159; Romantic, 33, 175; strange concussion of, 160; sublime forms of, 169; and survival, 35; time and, 151; type of association in, 21; violent reformations of, 168
Neoplatonic/Neoplatonism, 152, 171
neuropsychology, 5, 25–29; the concept of "extended consciousness" in, 232n18. *See also* psychology
neuroscience, 9, 11, 119, 223n104; "confabulation" in, 178; contemporary psychology and, 16; fuzzy trace theory in, 32; literature and, 222n99
New, Melvyn, 73, 228n6
Noë, Alva, 86
nostalgia, 29–30, 175, 178–79; contemporary notion of, 190; cure for, 195; disease of, 195, 215; Enlightenment pathology of, 179; etymological shift of, 203; and immobility, 238n15; medical, 179–80, 185; medical theories of, 203; pains of, 31, 190, 201; pathological, 191, 194; in reading, 173; rhetoric of, 192; "sober sadness" of, 202; study of, 179; theory of, 166; treatment of, 236n23. *See also* emotion; memory

novel: and autobiography, 217n5; and contemplation, 140; craft of the, 210; end of the, 106; Enlightenment, 10; Gothic, 52; historical, 210; as imitator of consciousness, 6; linear chronology to the, 229n27; millennial, 211; as an object of cultural production, 229n25; origins of the, 12, 29; poetry in the, 142–75; readings of the, 183; sensibility, 236n21; sentimental, 234n37; studies of the, 5–6, 15, 29, 119; theater and the, 240n40. *See also Bildungsroman*; eighteenth-century novel; fiction; history of the novel; poetry; writing

Otway, Thomas: *The Orphan*, 109
Oxford English Dictionary, 230n43

pain: and associationism, 24; autobiography of, 158; distinction between emotional and sensational, 149; diversion from, 79; enduring, 198; and forgetting, 178; imagination and, 149; insensibility to, 168; malingering, 175; of memory, 9–10, 166; and mind, 16, 67; of nostalgia, 31, 190, 201; overriding of, 91; pathological, 26; physical, 69, 93; and pleasure, 70, 73–74, 82, 93, 97, 105, 144, 150, 167–68, 174, 194; recurrent, 197; self-indulgent, 167; sensation of, 154; sensory, 62; as a state of mind, 167; temporal duration of, 80. *See also* trauma
Park, Julie, 114, 121, 138, 233n26, 233nn31–32, 234n39, 234n42, 235n47, 236n21
Pasanek, Brad: *Metaphors of Mind*, 7
patriarchy, 125–29, 132, 134–35; marital conventions of, 135; readings and, 110
perception, 13–14; failure of, 53; feeling and, 117; filters of mental, 178; Hume on, 20; imagination and, 41; laws of, 95; memories of sense, 71; mind

INDEX   267

and, 14, 190; and natural forms, 163; powers of, 41; reliance on, 44; of self, 139. See also sensation
performance/performativity: invention as, 138; of memories, 32, 96; of a musician, 22
personhood, 111, 114; and character, 118. See also history; memory
philosophy: of aesthetic feeling, 173; cognitive, 209; empirical, 220n81; Enlightenment, 4–6, 9, 15, 25, 28, 68, 115, 223n104; medieval, 9; of memory, 188, 203; of memory error, 193; of mind, 149, 178, 180; of nature, 33; Socratic, 193. See also aesthetics; epistemology; ethics
Pinch, Adela, 143–45, 178, 196, 241n59
Pino, Melissa, 117
pleasure: aesthetic, 96, 117; contemplative, 128; of death, 151; disorienting, 100; emotional, 173; of fantasy, 199; healing, 91; insensibility and, 84; libertine, 136; literary pace of, 213; melancholy, 156; memory of, 155–56; in the mind, 170; and pain, 70, 73–74, 82, 93, 97, 105, 144, 150, 167–68, 174, 194; of reading, 92; of regret, 158; searching for, 169; and sensation, 97, 142; subjective, 213; temptation of immediate, 206
poetry: canon of English, 144; and memory, 142, 152, 156, 162; in the novel, 142–75; passionate fondness for, 152; rereading of, 146; as a restylized fiction, 152; Romantic lyric, 169, 175–77, 195, 203, 221n85, 236n30; rural, 150; sensibility, 161; of the sonnet, 150–52, 156–58, 162–66; of Swift, 157; talent for, 169–70; tradition of graveyard, 150–53, 175. See also novel; writing
Pope, Alexander: Dunciad, 78
Porter, Dahlia, 145–46
Protestantism, 44, 226n41

psychology, 26–27, 114–15; anti-Freudian, 228n12; and literature, 69; of trauma, 69–70. See also neuropsychology

quotation: avowed use of, 152; context of, 146; lack of, 173; and memory, 142–46; metonymic function of, 146; and personal experience, 161; recollection as an operation of, 146; and self-authorized production, 145, 165–66; slippery play of meaning in, 165. See also memory; recollection

Radcliffe, Ann, 160; The Mysteries of Udolpho, 110
rape, 31, 109–10, 137; avoidance of, 110; history of, 30, 139, 141. See also violence; women
rationalism, 13; of Locke, 77
reading: absorptive style of, 169; alternative, 208; as collecting quotations, 143; and conversation, 180; deconstructive, 172, 200; distraction of, 198; existential, 150; experience of, 143; fiction, 91; hermeneutic, 172; and imagination, 84; interpretative, 200; and knowledge, 84; mediational accounts of, 6, 27–28; memory and, 196; metaphorical, 184; nostalgia in, 173; of the parable of the corn, 226n41; phenomenological, 230n46; of poetry in the novel, 142–75; practices of, 143, 148, 194, 207; as remembering, 152–53, 208; remembrance, imagination, and, 168; and rereading, 146, 200; and writing, 215
realism: French school of, 217n9; literary, 6, 72, 74, 217n9; memory and, 80, 82; as mimesis, 168; in painting, 2, 217n9; physics of, 83; principles of, 180; temporal, 213
reality/the real: escaping of, 207; fiction and, 146–47, 161, 169–72, 205; Hume on, 204; imagination and, 174; representation and, 164, 205. See also truth

recollection: art of, 8; conscious, 45, 154; empirical theories of, 30, 67, 111, 178; epistemic accounts of, 3; of a feeling, 56; four descriptive terms for, 29; imagination and, 29; Locke's theory of, 149; of memory, 79; as an operation of quotation, 146; powers of, 56, 153–54; Puritan, 224n24, 226n45; of reading sonnets, 150; representational accounts of, 70; sensation and, 37; "sensitive," 154; social, 167; system of, 97. *See also* memory; quotation
reconstructive memory, 11, 70–71, 86, 92, 105, 178. *See also* memory
reference, system of, 105, 174
representation: in literary form, 173; memory and, 15, 153–54; mimetic, 205; and mind, 119, 154; and nature, 143; powers of, 195–96; and reality, 164, 205; recollection and, 70; static scene of, 166; of subjectivity, 113. *See also* sign
Richardson, Alan, 28–29; "Jane Austen and the Perils of Mental Time Travel," 28, 237n4, 239n26
Richardson, Samuel: *Clarissa*, 25, 110, 114; *Pamela*, 110
Richetti, John, 224n25, 225n26; *Defoe's Narratives*, 35
Romanticism, 3, 11, 28, 33, 147, 154; discourse of inspiration of, 195; imagination in, 3–4, 11, 33, 178; plot of, 196; stereotype of, 157

Sagal, Anna, 69
Sandy, Mark, 145
satire, 68–80, 85–86, 94, 101, 118, 136–39, 181; Augustan modes of, 230n37; comedy and, 78; debate and, 182; exposure of, 139; figures of, 137; gentle, 170; on materialism, 228n4; on objectification and materialism, 99–100; pathos and, 193; referential system of, 88; and reform, 75; Restoration tradition of, 140; Scribblerian mode of Menippean, 230n37; social, 140; of Swift, 231n52. *See also* comedy
Schacter, Daniel: *The Seven Sins of Memory*, 26, 211
Schooler, Jonathan, 27
science: Baconian approach to, 225n34; as collecting as a mode of empirical inquiry, 145; eighteenth-century, 68, 114, 219n46; embodied minds in, 179; history of, 211; memory, 74; parody of, 79; and psychology, 211. *See also* cognitive science; materialism; medical discourses
Seidel, Michael, 33, 36, 226n41
self-consciousness, 111, 121–22, 127–32, 137, 213; agency and, 117, 141; catharsis and, 134; definitions of, 117; development of, 113, 119–24, 130, 136–39; as embarrassment, 125, 127, 129; feminine, 136; higher-level order of, 120, 135; memory and, 140; operations of, 135; paradigms of, 113; rudimentary form of, 120; as self-awareness, 123, 132; self-recognition and, 234n42; as sensation, 123; sympathetic, 116, 119; in thinking, 119, 135; and time, 132, 140, 232n18; understanding of, 140; various types of, 232n18. *See also* mind
sensation: emotion and, 147, 155; empiricism and, 143; experience of unwanted, 214; fluidity of, 14; heightened, 201; and knowledge, 4, 8, 13; memory and, 4, 18, 29, 31, 49, 97, 121; mental, 175; of pain, 154, 208; physical, 147, 173, 175; pleasure and, 97, 142; reduction of, 175; shift in, 82, 84; of touch, 100. *See also* perception
sentimentalism: and comedy, 140; and epistemology, 77; perverse, 157
sexuality: allusions of, 88, 108; innuendos of, 97, 231n48, 239n27
Shaftesbury, Earl of (Anthony Ashley Cooper): *The Characteristics*, 73; *Letter concerning Enthusiasm*, 73

INDEX   269

Sherman, Stuart, 36, 226n38, 226n44
she-tragedy, 110, 113; eighteenth-century archetype of the, 137; silent commentary on the importance of intentions of, 139. *See also* tragedy; women
sign, 81, 89, 194; archetypal, 195; character as, 140; engagement with the textual, 233n30; inference of meaning from, 171; invisible, 40; legibility of the, 170; metaphor as a, 8, 218n23; as natural ephemera, 153; object as, 68–69; and readership, 140; reading of the, 154. *See also* representation
Silver, Sean: *The Mind Is a Collection*, 9, 11, 24
Singer, Kate, 28
Siskin, Clifford, 6
skepticism: of Descartes, 13–14; of Hume, 17, 102
Smith, Adam, 80, 116, 119, 121, 124; *The Theory of Moral Sentiments*, 116
Smith, Charlotte: attitude toward cosmopolitanism, 170; *Beachy Head*, 145; *Celestina*, 30–31, 110, 142–75; *Conversation*, 145; *Elegiac Sonnets*, 144–45, 158; self-conscious allusion to the pleasures of poetic posterity, 235n18
Smith, Courtney Weiss, 226n45
sonnet. *See* poetry
source misattribution, 28, 222n98, 240n36
space, 63, 164, 179; finite perception of, 183; of memory, 207; mental, 143, 146; parameters of, 185; time and, 183–84. *See also* time
Starr, G. A., 36, 226n41
Starr, Gabrielle, 233n26, 233n36
Sterne, Laurence, 5, 210; parody in, 218n27; *Tristram Shandy*, 3, 21, 29–30, 67–108, 218n27
Stroud, Barry, 20–21
subjectivity: disavowal of, 138; independent, 132; novelistic, 113; representation of, 113; at risk, 119; threat to, 136. *See also* mind

survival: agency and, 131; memory and, 33–67, 131, 227n48; mind reading and, 119; nature and, 35; and perseverance, 165; as a state of mind, 54–60; time and, 51, 63
Swift, Jonathan, 157; satire of, 231n52
sympathy: abundance of, 168; autonomy and, 233n35; consciousness and, 116; developmental stages of, 121; enthusiasm or, 133; excessive, 128, 140; late eighteenth-century cult of, 145; and mind reading, 119; philosophical and novelistic accounts of, 232n20; seduction and, 133; self-consciousness and, 116; social system of, 144; virtuous sensibility of, 122; writing and, 150. *See also* emotion

Taylor, Shelley, 211–12
theory of mind: associationism in empiricist, 218n19; causal, 149; and reading of fictional thought processes, 233n30; temporal, 5, 36. *See also* cognitive literary studies
Thompson, Helen, 24, 220n81
Thomson, James: *The Seasons*, 161–66, 236n27
time: accounts of, 43, 49; allegory of, 183; calendrical, 43, 49–50, 213, 227n45; consciousness and, 37–38, 113–14; conversion and, 226n44; Defoe on, 66; dual nature of, 56; durational, 49; ecstatic view of, 230n46; eighteenth-century concept of, 182; empirical logics of, 186; ethical decisions in, 124; as experience, 185; as fate, 192; fictional, 194; fiction and, 175; forgetting of, 46, 190; knowledge and, 127; laws of, 207; as a material entity, 49; memory and, 37, 45, 50–51, 54–56, 59, 120–22, 128, 131, 134, 140, 181, 229n27; narrative mind in, 111; and nature, 151; notion of the self in, 117, 130–32; observation of, 54; passing of, 144, 153, 162, 192;

time (*continued*)
  perception of, 213; post-Enlightenment concept of, 183; power of, 154; protracted, 184; psychological notion of, 75; rationalization of, 238n23; and reflection, 130; scales of, 198; seasonal, 49; and self-consciousness, 132, 140, 232n18; and situation, 201; and space, 63, 164, 179, 183–84; and survival, 51; thought and, 149, 215; transposition of, 3. *See also* space
tragedy, 111, 206, 229n27; comedy and, 96; forgetfulness and, 76; lamentation of, 76; rape and, 109; of reality, 60. *See also* she-tragedy
transactive memory, 128, 178, 222n95, 237n4. *See also* memory
trauma, 10, 22–31, 193; etymological shift of, 70; Freudian, 77, 80, 85, 104; nostalgia disease and, 191; physiological, 80, 103; psychological narrative of, 227n48; psychological structures of, 67–77; social, 141; theory of, 25, 27–28. *See also* memory; pain
Trilling, Lionel, 238n15, 240n42
Trocchio, Rachel, 224n24, 226n45
truth: desire for, 106; the Enlightenment as the age of, 15; of experience, 17; fiction and, 107–8, 202; of history, 210; masking of, 107; of memory, 215; pain of, 71; recasting of, 91; of remembered sensation, 29; trespass against, 85. *See also* reality/the real

Valihora, Karen, 196
Vermeule, Blakey, 119
Vickars, Ilse, 41, 225n34, 226n41
Victorian era, 10; studies of the, 28
violence, 104. *See also* rape
vitalism, 151, 159, 219n46; rhetoric of, 168

Wall, Cynthia, 48
Warner, William, 6, 205, 229n25
Watt, Ian: *The Rise of the Novel*, 6–7, 217n5
Wegner, Daniel, 27
Wollstonecraft, Mary, 167
women: accountability of, 132; agency of, 112–13, 123–25, 129, 131, 135–37; as automaton, 114, 126, 234n40; bodies of, 141; fictional, 110; independent thinking of, 126–28, 135–36; and marriage, 110, 134, 136; mental development of, 136, 139–40; misogynistic attack on, 118; and patriarchy, 125–29, 132, 134–35; problematic portrayal of, 233n26; in the public sphere, 111–12, 118; and systematic impulses of commodification, 110; virtue of, 112. *See also* feminism; she-tragedy
Wood, Michael: "Time and Her Aunt," 192
Woolf, Virginia, 57
Wordsworth, William, 3, 26, 151; creative memory of, 221n85; "Lines Written a Few Miles above Tintern Abbey," 176–77, 186–87, 195; "Memory," 221n85
writing: catharsis of, 73; consolation of, 150; fiction, 190; and memory, 152, 212–13; method for, 93; nature as the derivative for, 152; of poetry, 150–52; as a practice of wish fulfillment, 180; process of, 152; and purpose, 206; reading and, 215; in the sentimental novel, 234n37; suffering and, 167; unfeeling practice of, 150–51, 157; use of quotation in, 161; and wandering, 146, 148, 152, 169. *See also* novel; poetry

Yahav, Amit, 24, 37, 124, 220n81, 226n39, 232n11
Yates, Frances, 82, 223n108
Young, Kay, 28, 237n4

Zimmerman, Everett, 104, 227n2
Zunshine, Lisa, 119, 178

www.ingramcontent.com/pod-product-compliance
Lightning Source LLC
Chambersburg PA
CBHW020911020526
44114CB00039B/269